Ginger for Pluck

THE LIFE AND TIMES OF MISS GEORGINA KING

JENNIFER M.T. CARTER AND ROGER CROSS

Wakefield Press

Wakefield Press
1 The Parade West
Kent Town
South Australia 5067
www.wakefieldpress.com.au

First published 2013

Cover designed by Stacey Zass
Text designed and typeset by Wakefield Press
Printed and bound by Five Star Print, Adelaide

National Library of Australia Cataloguing-in-Publication entry

Author:	Carter, Jennifer M.T., 1943– .
Title:	Ginger for pluck: the life and times of Miss Georgina King / Jennifer M.T. Carter and Roger Cross.
ISBN:	978 1 74305 171 9 (pbk.).
Notes:	Includes bibliographical references.
Subjects:	King, Georgina, 1845–1932.
	Women anthropologists – Australia – Biography.
	Women geologists – Australia – Biography.
	Geology – Australia.
	Natural history – Australia – Collectors and collecting.
Other Authors/ Contributors:	Cross, Roger.
Dewey Number:	301.092

Wakefield Press

Ginger for Pluck

Jennifer M.T. Carter grew up in the United Kingdom and took an honours degree in French language, literature and civilization at Aberdeen University in Scotland. She is an independent researcher and writer, and the author of *Painting the Islands Vermilion: Archibald Watson and the brig Carl*, *Eyes to the Future: Sketches of Australia and her neighbours in the 1870s*, and *Burra 1845–1851: A Directory of Early Folk*. Research for her historical novels (written as Mary Talbot Cross) has taken her to England, India and France. As well as travel, she lists among her interests gardening and the pursuit of the eccentric.

Roger Cross and his wife Jennifer moved to the mid north of South Australia on his retirement from the University of Melbourne. As a senior lecturer he was involved in the science education programmes at the University. His research interest into the nature and social aspects of science led to the publication of the highly successful book *Fallout: Hedley Marston and the British Atomic Bomb Tests in Australia* (published by Wakefield Press, 2001) which was used as the basis of the Film Australia documentary *Silent Storm*. Apart from numerous educational publications, he is a co-author (with Avon Hudson) of *Beyond Belief: The British Bomb Tests: Australia's veterans speak out.*

To our mothers

Mabel Carter MSc
Winifred Cross

Both of whom suffered the 'slings and arrows of outrageous fortune' in their desire for knowledge and recognition of their intellectual worth.

Contents

Part Three: Ginger for Pluck

Who's Who

The King family

George King (1813–1899), minister of religion, born in County Tyrone, Ulster.

Jane née Mathewson (1813–1900), also born in County Tyrone. Widow of Alexander Stewart.

Children of George and Jane King

Rebecca May King, born 1841, married Francis ('Frank') Rogers in 1868.

William Selwyn King (1843–1877).

Georgina King (1845–1932), whose experiences form the basis of *Ginger for Pluck*.

Martha West King (1847–1878), married Layman Harrison in 1872.

Rosetta Jane King (1850–1871).

Helena Annie King (1852–1877), married Frederick Humphery in 1875. Mother of Esca Morris Humphery.

George Eccles Kelso King (1853–1943), knighted in 1929, known as Sir Kelso King.

Isabella Alexander Stewart, born 1835, daughter of Jane King's first marriage to Alexander Stewart in 1834. (He died in 1835.)

The Kings' sons-in-law

Frederick Thomas Humphery (1841–1908), merchant, financier and politician. Father of Esca Morris Humphery.

Francis ('Frank') Rogers (1841–1925), lawyer, later judge.

Churchmen, colleagues of Reverend George King

(1) In Western Australia

John Ramsden Wollaston (1791–1856), first Anglican archdeacon in the colony of Western Australia (arrived 1841).

(2) In New South Wales

William Grant Broughton (1788–1853), Anglican Bishop of Sydney and Metropolitan of Australia.

Frederic Barker (1808–1882), successor to Broughton (1854).

William Woolls (1814–1893), Anglican churchman and schoolmaster best known for his promotion of Australian botany.

Georgina King's scientific mentors

(1) In Sydney

George Bennett (1804–1893), former naval surgeon-naturalist. Medical practitioner, physician to the King family.

William Branwhite Clarke (1798–1878), Anglican clergyman and amateur geologist. Colleague and friend of George King.

(2) In Melbourne

Sir Frederick McCoy (1817–1899), geologist. Professor of natural science, University of Melbourne, and first director of 'The Museum of Natural and Applied Sciences' of Victoria. Knighted in 1886.

Baron Sir Ferdinand von Mueller (1825–1896), botanist. Government botanist of Victoria, first director of the Botanic Gardens, Melbourne, 1857–1873.

Members of the Royal Society of New South Wales

Tannatt William Edgeworth David (1858–1932), geologist. Professor of geology, University of Sydney, from 1891. Knighted in 1920 since when known as Sir Edgeworth David. With Archibald Liversidge (below), the main focus of Georgina's spleen.

Robert Etheridge, junior (1846–1920), palaeontologist. Curator of the Australian Museum, Sydney, from 1895.

Carl ('Charles') Adolph Leibius (1833–1893), chemist and public servant. Arrived in Sydney from Germany in 1859; senior assayer at the branch Mint from 1870. Joint honorary secretary to the Society 1875–1886, a vice-president 1886–1887 and 1891–1892, president in 1890–1891.

Archibald Liversidge (1846–1893), chemist. Professor of geology and mineralogy, University of Sydney, 1874–1907, Dean of the Faculty of Science 1879–1907, joint honorary secretary of the Society (with C.A. Leibius) 1874–1884. The motivating force behind the creation in 1888 of the Australasian Association for the Advancement of Science (AAAS).

Joseph Henry Maiden (1859–1925), economic botanist and public servant. Curator of the Technological Museum, Sydney, and active in the movement to protect native forests. He accepted many fossil and plant specimens from Georgina King on behalf of the museum.

Edward Fisher Pittman (1849–1932), geologist and administrator. Appointed New South Wales government geologist in 1891 after the death of C.S. Wilkinson (below), and under-secretary at the Department of Mines in 1902.

Edward Ramsey (1842–1916), ornithologist and zoologist. Curator of the Australian Museum 1874–1894.

Henry Chamberlain Russell (1836–1907), government astronomer. Fellow of the Royal Astronomical Society (1871) and three times president of the local Royal Society.

Thomas Peter Anderson Stuart (1856–1920), professor of physiology and indefatigable medical administrator. A supporter of the acceptance of women into medicine; knighted in 1914. Georgina, whom he treated kindly, gives his family name as 'Anderson Stuart'.

William Henry Warren (1852–1926), engineer and educationist. 'The acknowledged leader of his profession, with a reputation extending beyond Australia' (*ADB*). President of the local Royal Society 1892–1893.

Charles Smith Wilkinson (1843–1891), geologist. Geological surveyor in charge at the New South Wales Department of Mines from 1875, he was joined by T.W.E. David in 1882.

Other scientific men of note

Robert Logan Jack (1845–1951), Queensland government geologist. President of the Geology Section of the first (1888) meeting of the Australasian Association for the Advancement of Science (AAAS) attended by Georgina.

William Sharp Macleay (1792–1865), scholar and gentleman-naturalist. Son of Alexander McCleay (sic), colonial secretary of New South Wales 1825–1836 and builder of Elizabeth Bay House; his house at Elizabeth Bay was a meeting place for scientific enthusiasts, a tradition inherited from his father. A Fellow of the Royal Society (London), he was keenly interested in the Australian Museum.

William John Macleay (1820–1891), pastoralist, politician and patron of science. Nephew of Alexander McCleay and cousin of William Sharp Macleay and Sir George Macleay (from whom he leased Elizabeth Bay House after the death of W.S. Macleay in 1865). First president of the Linnean Society of New South Wales (formed in 1874); knighted in 1889.

Friends of Georgina King

William Wyatt Gill (1828–1896), South Seas missionary and author related to the Kings by marriage.

Harriet Scott (1830–1907) and Helena Scott (1832–1910), naturalists and commercial artists, cousins of Rose Scott (below).

Rose Scott (1847–1925), feminist and Sydney celebrity. Founding member of the Women's Literary Society (1889) and of the Womanhood Suffrage League of New South Wales (1891).

Daisy May Bates (1863–1951), welfare worker among Aborigines and controversial anthropologist.

Others

Caroline ('Cara') Martha David née Mallett (1856–1951), wife of T.W.E. David.

Charles Moore (1820–1895), merchant, auctioneer, alderman and Mayor of Sydney 1867–1869. Neighbour of Georgina during her Springwood years.

Alexander Stuart (1824–1886), merchant and politician. Chairman and proprietor of the Coal Cliff Coal Company from the late 1870s. Colonial treasurer of New South Wales 1876–1877, premier and colonial secretary 1883–1885; knighted in 1885.

William Tom (1823–1904), farmer at 'Sunset' near Orange, New South Wales. Co-discoverer with E.H. Hargraves of payable gold at Ophir.

Recognition will come – after we are with our loved ones – & I am content, though at the same time I shall always use my pen against wrong, from whatever source that wrong comes. We both have that fighting spirit, though you & I are personally so different. You staid, dignified, quiet, earnest, sincere – & myself the incarnation of impulsiveness – but there is one thing we can hug ourselves over – they may ignore, or belittle our work – but they can't question its accuracy – & by & by when that accuracy will be established & recognised – the petty little pinpricks will be seen in their true light. Posterity will deal rightly with us.

Daisy Bates to Georgina King, 16 June 1927

Preface

Georgina King was born in Fremantle, Western Australia, in 1845. She was the second daughter of the Reverend George King, a significant figure in the early history of the Anglican Church in Australia. The King family arrived in Sydney in 1849, and it was there that Georgina died at the age of eighty-seven. In some respects Georgina King was no different to many other middle-class females of her day. She was educated at home, did not marry, and lived with her ageing parents until they died in the late 1890s. Her lot as an 'old maid' was by no means unusual; it was her determined bid to be a recognised member of the world of scientific research that was to set her apart from other women in her situation.

As a child in Sydney, Georgina met the two men who influenced her studies from a tender age. By then, the clergyman William Branwhite Clarke had given up his forays as a pioneering geologist into the New South Wales hinterland and was based in the North Shore parish of St Leonard's. It was there that Georgina was introduced to the wonders of geology and Clarke's amazing collection of fossils. Clarke was not alone in noticing the bright intellect of his colleague's daughter. Dr George Bennett, naturalist *par excellence* and former ship's surgeon, had settled in Sydney in 1834 where he established himself as a force in local science. Charismatic and learned, and despite his continuing interest in the natural world, he continued to practise medicine and was the King family's doctor. Like Clarke, he fostered Georgina's interest in scientific research and remained her mentor until he died in 1893.

From childhood Georgina King experienced the best of Australian natural science; in her middle years she encountered the worst. She had been brought up to value integrity and honesty – she saw her own father battle on points of principle with his bishop at great personal cost – and it was her tragedy to have her expectations blighted. When she set about her research in earnest in 1892 and attempted to break into the scientific circles of Sydney, the mood in colonial science was changing. Science in New South Wales had been elitist for years but where once it was the province of gentlemen and gentlemen-collectors, it had become the domain of the paid professional – be they public servant or academic. With the emphasis increasingly focused on performance and results, Georgina found herself confronted with what the French term *mauvaise foi*. Dishonesty, insincerity, unfairness, plagiarism, academic theft . . . according to Georgina King she fell victim to the lot. Not that she was the first 'scientific handmaiden' to be cynically exploited by men who should have known better – and very probably did.

Georgina's life is a study in courage and determination, and what sets her apart (in our opinion) is the extent to which she stood by her convictions and refused absolutely to be deterred, no matter the personal hurt. Before her death in 1932, Miss King prepared a memoir in the form of two volumes of autobiography. These she lodged in the Mitchell Library, Sydney, along with papers relevant to her scientific research and letters sent her by some of Australia's 'great and good' – all of which she intended to be read by posterity in order to vindicate her claims against the scientific community. (This material was later joined by family documents gifted by Georgina's niece, the late historian Dr Hazel King.) Taken together, the papers create a compelling portrait. Georgina's correspondence with Melbourne University's flamboyant professor of natural history, Sir Frederick McCoy, for example, reveals the vulnerable side of a woman who in public must often have appeared unsubtle and insensitive in her defiance.

Georgina's long life began when Australian science was in its infancy and paralleled its coming of age and steps towards international recognition. The collected papers illuminate this 'Brave New World' in unexpected ways. If Georgina's mentor Parson Clarke was the 'Father of Australian Geology', then T.W.E. David was its most ardent promoter. The man who is best known as Sir Edgeworth David was adept at self-promotion too, but Georgina's criticisms of him went much further than that. Her protracted campaign against the eminent geologist and those she termed 'the scientific clique' became increasingly strident, libellous and embittered as her life wore on.

While Miss King proved an implacable enemy, she was also a loyal friend. In return, she attracted a coterie of staunch supporters among Sydney's independent women. Rose Scott the feminist reformer needs no introduction, nor does Helena Forde (nee Scott) the botanical artist who for a time earned her living by her art. Daisy M. Bates, the indomitable 'Queen of the Never Never', spoke out on Georgina's behalf. The feisty Olive King, fresh from her adventures in the 'Great War to end all Wars' (where she drove an ambulance in the Serbian Army) typed out letters of protest and complaint on behalf of her ageing Aunt Georgie.

Georgina King's obituary in the *Sydney Morning Herald* (11 June 1932) noted:

> *She was interested in scientific affairs, chiefly geology and anthropology, and was the author of several pamphlets, including 'The Mineral Wealth of New South Wales', 'The Discovery of Gold, and How it was Found', 'Two Stone Ages, Australia', and 'The Antiquity of the Australian Aborigines'. Most of the papers have appeared in 'The Sydney Morning Herald' at various times. Miss King was also helpful to patriotic and charitable institutions in whose welfare she was interested.*

A harmless old lady then, if a little eccentric in her chosen pursuits … Such were public perceptions at the moment of her death, and no one had taken her seriously for years.

Nothing much has changed over the past eight decades. The interested reader will have to dig deep for any sympathetic reference to Miss Georgina King. The *Australian Dictionary of Biography* (volume 9, 1891–1939, published in 1983) allows her two sentences as an appendage to her influential brother, Sir George Eccles Kelso King – sentences that allude to her 'long and bitter campaign for recognition'. In the later 'Supplement, 1580–1980' (published in 2005), Georgina King fares a little better. The summary of her life is comprehensive, but the judgment of its authors – that her ideas on geology were 'grand, romantic, and wrong' – is made with the benefit of hindsight and shows little appreciation of the historical context.

As we have said, geology in 1880s' and 1890s' Australia was a relatively young science; science as an institution was undergoing change. The dominant members of the Royal Society of New South Wales were, more often than not, university academics or government employees. Some – like T.W.E. David, whose university qualifications were in classics, not in science – might be considered unlikely 'keepers of the flame'. The Society was a forum for the airing of new ideas and theories, not necessarily 'romantic' as were Georgina's, but often equally 'wrong'. For what *was* right and what *was* wrong in nineteenth-century Australian geology?

The biography we have written is not intended as a validation of the theories and exploration undertaken by Georgina (set out in the Appendix) – although in context, it must be said that these seem as worthy as many others in that scientific period. Rather, it is an account of a courageous and principled woman; an account of how life changed her from a generous-hearted human being to one who saw persecution where, possibly, it did not always exist. Our account shows how great expectations in science were dashed by circumstances against which a woman such as Georgina had little control. Just as her aspirations were thwarted in her lifetime, we believe that she has been consciously ignored by serious historians of science ever since. We might have called this biography *For the Sake of all Women* – Georgina King certainly fought her battles for members of her sex as well as for herself. But given that she possessed all the pugnaciousness of her Irish forbears and the vivid colouring associated with the Celtic race, we have called her poignant story *Ginger for Pluck*, the nickname given her as a little girl.

Part One

The Beginning of Wisdom

[illegible] their own [illegible] would have [illegible] them.

[illegible] hemisphere [illegible] still does [illegible] – the most [illegible] whether [illegible] taken [illegible] the term 'trans[illegible] entered the English language when [illegible] as forced labour to West Indian [illegible]

CHAPTER ONE

Bread upon the Waters

Georgina King was born at Fremantle on 6 June 1845, the third child of George and Jane King, emigrants from County Tyrone in the north of Ireland (or Ulster, as it was known). The couple had been in the Swan River colony for almost four years and Georgina's father was known as an energetic (if not universally respected) parson.

George King came from Fintona, a town at Ulster's heart, where his father was a linen merchant, one of many in a district also concerned with the manufacture of coarse woollens, earthenware, whisky and soap. As the merchant's second son, George was destined for holy orders rather than commerce. When he graduated from Trinity College, Dublin, in 1836, he was created a deacon in the Episcopal Church of Ireland by Bishop Mant of Down and Connor, and was ordained the following year. In June 1840 he married the widowed Jane Stewart, also from County Tyrone. They were both twenty-seven. By then George was minister of Holywood near Belfast, a secure living in the personal gift of Bishop Mant,[1] yet within a year the Kings were on their way to Western Australia. Little Isabella Stewart, the only child of Jane's first marriage, and their own two-week-old baby daughter, Rebecca May, went with them.[2]

Discounting death, emigration to the southern hemisphere represented – and arguably still does represent – the most drastic disruption to human existence whether willingly taken, or unwillingly in the form of transportation. The term 'transportation', meaning 'deportation', entered the English language when felons were first sent as forced labour to West Indian and North American plantations, sometime around 1669. Irreconcilable differences with its transatlantic subjects a century later forced the British Crown to look elsewhere, and from 1788 New South Wales and then Tasmania (via Norfolk Island) took over from Barbados and the Americas as legal depositories for criminal undesirables. Thus, when the King family left London in May 1841, voyages to Australia had been a phenomenon in the British Isles for several generations.

After the failure of the second Jacobite uprising in 1746, absentee landlords introduced sheep in their thousands to the Scottish Highlands – part of an inexorable process of land and human degradation that made emigration to Australia an almost happy option for the crofters thus dispossessed. Hunger drove starving labourers from rural England and Ireland, too; and political troublemakers were expelled. Religious dissenters left of their own volition to find heaven on earth elsewhere, as did those who burned with missionary zeal rather than a sense of persecution. Ambitious younger sons left home to make a fortune overseas; family embarrassments were shipped out to shut them up for good.

None of these reasons, however, applied to the Reverend King, so why did he choose to uproot his family as he did? Ulster was a predominantly Catholic part of Ireland where Protestantism uneasily held sway. George King enjoyed the patronage of his superior – 'The Bishop preached frequently, & took part in the Communion Services'[3] – and, with a fair share of luck thrown in, he could have expected to rise within the Church of Ireland. Yet the Ulsterman turned his back on a comfortable living and transplanted his family to a continent half a world away.

When Georgina's interest turned to anthropology in her later years, she claimed that interest in the Australian Aborigines had attracted her father to missionary service.[4] George himself wrote that his wife had asked him 'to seek employment in Australia' as she was anxious to leave Ireland on account of the cold climate affecting 'her lungs asthmatically'.[5] The second reason seems more likely than the first: the Emerald Isle is undoubtedly beautiful and its misty mountains a source of poetic inspiration, but it owes its verdant reputation to generous amounts of rain. The island is damp with large areas of bog, and for any nineteenth-century Irish resident afflicted with lung disease the place held all the appeal of an imminent sentence of death.

On the other hand, a letter George King wrote to his pregnant wife dated 4 December 1840 hints at a worldlier motive:

> *With regard to Australia I can say nothing decisive, but as you seem to think favourably of it, I begin to think it might not be a bad speculation: if you could put yourself in possession of any information regarding the proper channel through which to apply, it might be well but don't put yourself to the slightest inconvenience. I could apply myself to Lord John Russel [sic], who is secretary to the Colonies, but of that more hereafter.*[6]

A single letter is little enough to go on, but the use of the word 'speculation', linked as it is with the idea of risk and gain, may be significant. At this time the Swan River colony of Western Australia was attracting a great deal of interest in Britain. Lord John Russell's brief stint as colonial secretary (1839–1841) coincided with the formation of the Western Australian Company, an enterprise pledged to follow the colonising ideals of Edward Gibbon Wakefield. What appeared to be working in South Australia was surely worth a try elsewhere, so the company made plans to create a settlement called 'Australind', on the Leschenault Inlet 90 miles south of Perth.

This scheme may have been the 'speculation' to which George King refers in his letter. What if the state of the family fortunes had something to do with the Kings' decision to emigrate? – the population of Ireland was shrinking and the minister's stipend was quite possibly dwindling with it. There were few clergymen in Western Australia, and no reason (he may have thought) why an enterprising man of the cloth should not prosper along with the rest.

Whatever the reason or reasons, and it does seem the couple weighed up their prospects dispassionately before they decided to leave, George King was duly interviewed and appointed a missionary for the Society for the Propagation of the Gospel in Foreign Parts. The Kings sailed for the Swan River colony in May 1841, with Bishop Mant's reluctant blessing on their heads.[7]

By this time, the Australind settlers, who were led by Marshall Clifton, a former public servant and a relation of Wakefield by marriage, had already reached journey's end. In March 1841, Clifton's daughter, Lucy, recorded her dismal first impressions of her new home.[8] So did John Ramsden Wollaston, a clergyman who travelled with the party.[9] Later in the year, when spring came to the Leschenault Inlet and the Collie River, the shrubs and plants would strike Wollaston as 'curious and beautiful; the flowers brilliant, & characterised generally by great delicacy of texture',[10] but in the topsy-turvy world of Australia, March meant it was early autumn, not spring. Although Marshall Clifton and his party had been told that the site of Australind was 'lovely' and 'beautifully laid out',[11] their 'rural' 100-acre allotments proved to be uncompromising, uncleared virgin bush with the outlandish and 'ugly' desiccated-looking banksia the dominant tree.[12]

This was no South Australia with a ready source of immigrant workers. Genteel settlers were forced to abandon their ideas of living on quarter-acre blocks in town while others laboured for them, out of sight and in the bush. In Australind they had to be their own workforce, do their own digging, raise their own crops – unless they chose to starve.[13]

When George King had his first sight of land off Fremantle after a voyage lasting six months, he was no less disappointed than the Reverend Wollaston before him. 'The appearance of the coast of Western Australia as you approach f[ro]m the Sea is most uninviting', Wollaston wrote in his journal.

> *It consists entirely of white sand, wherever rocks do not make their appearance. The Sand Hills, wh[ich] rise gradually in the background are very little varied in form & height, & are for the most part covered with stunted trees & the scrub peculiar to the Climate.*[14]

In old age King recalled the 'majestic oaks' of Ireland's Mountjoy Forest, 'their lofty wide-spreading branches so closely interlaced' that a boy might 'crawl on from one tree to another, for miles along, without touching the ground'.[15] Stepping safely onto the Australian continent in October 1841, the trees King saw were evergreen, 'of the most sombre uniform hue imaginable', and lacked what Wollaston termed 'freshness'.[16]

There was much worse to come. Led to believe by his employers that his ministry would centre on York, the oldest inland settlement founded in 1831, George soon learned that he had arrived too late: the district had newly been entrusted to William Mears, a former Royal Navy chaplain. King was quick to inform his superiors that Mears was hardly suitable. His recent retirement from the Service was (King told them) due to 'a nervous impediment which embarrassed almost to suffocation, when he arose to address a large, or mixed congregation'.[17] It made no difference: for Mears it was a case of 'being in the right place at the right time'. With his salary guaranteed by the good folk of York, the interloper refused to budge and King was forced to seek a position elsewhere.

The colony on which George King had pinned his hopes had been established in 1829 on the site of present-day Perth and owed its origins to a set of misconceptions. When Captain James Stirling, RN – afterwards the colony's first governor – visited the area in 1827, he was totally misled by the apparent fertility of the land and the unseasonal mildness of the summer weather (although that would have been small consolation to the equally misled Parson King). Stirling returned to England convinced of the district's suitability for colonisation. After a prolonged publicity campaign, 4000 settlers left for the Swan River in February 1829. Generally speaking, settlers found the eastern colonies of Australia more attractive and, once in Western Australia, only 1500 elected to remain. Given the 'patchy' nature of the soil away from the fertile regions, speculators who bought up vast acreages were soon bankrupted.[18] The estate of one of them provided the setting for Australind, that romantic notion of Australia and India linked through trade and fraternal ties.

It was an inauspicious beginning, and spiritual affairs proceeded along equally shaky lines. For the first few months of the settlement Captain Irwin of the 63rd Regiment was responsible for divine service. Then relief *pro tem* was provided by the Reverend Thomas Hobbes Scott, former Archdeacon of New South Wales, whose landfall through shipwreck while on his way back to England might be called an 'Act of God' in the true sense of the expression. For a year or so Scott worked alongside the Reverend John Burdett Wittenoom, appointed colonial chaplain from January 1830, and whose chief enthusiasms proved to be 'schoolteaching and farming', plus an affection for the 'cello.[19] Once Scott left, the ministry in Western Australia relied to a great extent on a group of diligent laymen, with Wittenoom the only professional clergyman until 1836. As a pastor he was adequate if not enterprising, but perhaps it did not matter: the choice alluvial land alongside inlets and estuaries was quickly snapped up for agriculture, but, generally speaking, the colony proved more suitable for four-legged animals than two.

John Wollaston, whose early impressions of Western Australia are recorded above, arrived from Cambridgeshire in eastern England. Restlessness, a need to spread God's word in pastures new, and other more worldly motives influenced him – as apparently they had the Reverend King. In Wollaston's case he had a large and maturing family, and the Antipodes offered splendid opportunities for an adventurous father of seven. He was initially promised the post of resident chaplain to the community at Australind, but before sailing he learned that such an arrangement was not forthcoming. Even so, he joined the group, trusting in the Lord to smile upon his aspirations. His faith proved justified, and he made a good job of settling in.[20] Eighteen months after his arrival, when the Kings first met him, he had built his own church at Picton near Bunbury and was harvesting his own provisions from his ample, if not particularly fertile, acres. He was the Anglican rector of Picton, and later, in 1849, he became Western Australia's first archdeacon.

George King knew nothing of the difficulties at Australind or those awaiting him at his own destination of Fremantle. Even when he arrived, and found a stammering ex-matelot superseding him at York, he still viewed the colony as promising terrain. Deprived of his rightful place in the Avon Valley, King staked his claim to the 'ten establishments consisting of fifty souls' on the Murray River and the four communities on the Canning. Such a widespread parish meant travelling through areas of great isolation, or, as he put it, 'one thick, unbroken forest, usually called "the Bush"' in which there was 'not a single habitation, nor a drop of water to be seen except during the four rainy months'.[21]

He also turned his attention to Fremantle, a spiritual rather than an actual desert. For over seven years it had been subject to great neglect; no communion service had been conducted there or in the surrounding area during that time (although the same, of course, could be said for many other places). The port town harboured transient sailors and inhabitants 'chiefly of the lower class' and was the site of the colony's gaol. As well, there was 'a dissenting methodist chapel in the course of being finished'. (The Anglicans had to make do with 'divine service in the court house'.)

King proved equal to the challenge set him by the Nonconformists.[22] He might not have the honour of building the first church in the settlement (Wollaston's church at Picton preceded the one at Fremantle) but he immediately got down to business. On 13 November 1841, a mere month after his arrival in the colony, he called for tenders from local tradesmen to build his own church.[23]

CHAPTER TWO

Feed my Lambs

The first meeting between John Wollaston and George King took place the following January when Wollaston visited the Kings' home half a mile outside Fremantle. They were 'broad Irish', he noted, while Mrs King was 'amiable' and her health apparently no longer a problem. Wollaston was immediately struck by King's suitability to his task: he was 'a pleasant, single-hearted young Man' and the Society for the Propagation of the Gospel in Foreign Parts 'could not have chosen a fitter person'.[1]

A year later he began to have serious misgivings about his colleague. First, there was King's tendency towards self-aggrandisement: 'Been reading S.P.G. [Society for the Propagation of the Gospel] Papers – there is a little mistake in Mr. King's account', Wollaston wrote as early as February 1842, '. . . he has nothing to do with Perth'.[2] Exaggeration in letters home to his superiors was one thing; King's overbearing disposition was another. Unlike Wollaston, the younger man bothered to cultivate neither the land nor his fellow clerics, and by 1843 was revealing a more unpleasant side to his nature.

In contrast to Wollaston's little wooden church at Picton – the result of sixteen months' hard labour by Wollaston and his sons at the clergyman's expense[3] – King's church at Fremantle was the result of public subscription and built splendidly of stone. Wollaston later criticised the heavy debt incurred (the flagstones and communion rails, for example, were sent out especially from England). Nor did the design meet with Wollaston's approval: the building stood 'more N. & S. than E. & W. The *style*, I suppose, must be called *Western Australian*'. 'However', he went on, 'it is a *House of God* – And thank God for it'.[4]

Whatever its architectural idiosyncrasies, the consecration of the Church of St John on Wednesday, 26 July 1843, should have been a joyous occasion. Flags were up and bunting out, yet inner tensions soon spilled into the open, and the day proved memorable more for friction and discontent. The governor and his entourage travelled to Fremantle for the opening service, as did the Reverend Wittenoom, the colonial chaplain. The Reverend William Mitchell came from Guildford, a straggling little village on the middle Swan, although poor stuttering William Mears did not manage to make it from York. When John Wollaston arrived in his turn, he found that King – due to 'inexperience & disinclination' – had failed to consult with his brother clergy 'lest he sh[oul]d not have the lead'. King, he noted afterwards, was 'very tenacious & jealous'.[5]

Inside the vestry Wollaston watched in horror as two-fifths of the colony's clergy squared up to one another over the right to preach the first sermon to the assembled faithful – King standing on his dignity as incumbent, and Wittenoom, as colonial chaplain, equally unyielding. Containing such a display of muscular Christianity required all Wollaston's diplomacy, but eventually 'everything went off well & solemnly . . . & universal satisfaction was expressed'. With, that is, the probable exception of Chaplain Wittenoom, for George King had delivered the vital sermon in triumph.

Wollaston found the 'great elevated Pulpit at the back of the Altar' – and possibly the occupant's behaviour – 'very offensive'.[6] King's manner was finding him very few friends, for while there was much to admire about his zeal there was little laudable about his style. Enthusiasm was no substitute for tact, and King's very considerable efforts to further his ministry took a serious toll on himself and everyone around him, including Jane, his loyal wife.

The struggle to maintain standards was a hard one, in surroundings that never came near the extravagant claims of the recruiting agents back in London. Lucy Clifton's journal covers the months of March to July 1841 when hopes were high at Australind, yet it reveals the inevitable tensions among a small group of women thrown together in a community dominated by men. Mrs Daisy Bates, a friend of Georgina's, put her own gloss on the lot of pioneer wives and daughters half a century later:

> *When one considers the many difficulties that beset those cultured women who had elected to accompany their husbands 'into the unknown', one marvels at their courage and endurance in facing the terrible realities of domestic life in those early days. No servants, no comforts, no conveniences of any kind except what their own ingenuity supplied. That most necessary article in domestic economy – soap – was frequently unobtainable, and they had to learn to make soap from pipe-clay; tea and sugar rose to famine prices at times; water could only be got by sinking wells, the attachments to which were the ordinary rope windlass. Just imagine the so-called fine ladies of the present day drawing their own water, baking their own bread, cooking, washing, mending, making a dinner out of the scantiest of materials; keeping their little homes, their children and their husbands neat and trim, and looking sweet and contented at the close of the day's work!*[7]

John Wollaston fixed carts, ploughed the land, and spread muck as well as the gospel, but George King brought no such 'hands-on' approach to domestic problems; he had no grown sons, little time, and probably no liking for manual toil. Jane King must have suffered enormously as a result. At the end of 1848 relief was at hand, not only for her but also for King's beleaguered brothers in Christ. When he failed to receive a (promised) S.P.G. missionary assistant to share his burdens, he suffered a breakdown in health and the colonial surgeon recommended a change of scene.[8]

George King gave one of the reasons for his resignation as an ongoing 'painful struggle within his soul' – whether to choose the good of his churches or that of his children.[9] Through no fault of his own (and despite his prodigious labours) he had seen his stipend steadily eroded, with warnings of further significant reductions. As he told his superiors in London, it was a simple matter of choice: either he met the expenses of his horse's keep or denied his offspring 'many of the common comforts of life to which they have been accustomed'.[10] The cost of living was shockingly high in Western Australia and 'common comforts' were rare. The humble cabbage cost seven times more than it did in Ireland (King's own vegetable garden had been given over to growing fodder for his horse) and bare essentials were not always available, and exorbitantly priced when they were. It must be said, then, that the George King who stepped ashore at Sydney in 1849 hardly resembled the optimistic forward-looking young man who left London in 1841. The years in the Swan River had brought an increasing sense of disillusion, and at thirty-six the parson felt undervalued and was dogged by a deep and perpetual discontent. During the last days of his mission to the Swan River colony there had been much to occupy his mind. His parish was vast and lonely; it was made up of communities scattered over an area of some 900 square miles. Peregrinations were tedious and lasted a week at a time. Did Parson King seek his God and a renewed sense of mission as he gazed over the restless ocean and through the towering jarrah? Or did he stare fixedly before him, thinking of financial problems and constantly brooding on his wrongs and rights?

The tensions created by George King's disposition, his overbearing behaviour and unrealistic expectations should not be allowed to detract from his considerable achievements in the west. The simple mud-wall and thatch churches at Mandurah and Pinjarra and the stone church of St John in Fremantle were a considerable testimony to his endeavours, and on that basis alone his seven-year mission could be called a success. In Fremantle,

King's pastoral duties were paramount and demanded his wife's full support. As well as the Sabbath rituals, he conducted day and Sunday schools, concerned himself with the Aboriginals, and took divine service in the gaol.[11] The outlying congregations were small but still needed his attention. In Fremantle, of course, it was different: one hundred worshippers turned up on a Sunday at St John's, where the pulpit – described by Wollaston as that 'great elevated' affair behind the altar – provided the parson with a chance to salve his wounded self-esteem.

Like the living at York, the house and land King expected at Fremantle had failed to materialise. From the beginning he was forced to fend for himself, and he made sure his employers knew it: 'after residing a month at a very expensive lodging I took a cottage in the country with two acres of land, which I expect will be sufficient to feed my horse, at a yearly rent of forty pounds.'[12] His congregation was expected to contribute to his support but was hardly in a position to do so. Even so, from 1 June 1846, his annual salary of £250 was reduced drastically to £200. A further reduction would, he was warned, take effect from 1 June 1847.[13] Such domestic calamities reinforced George's bitterness, and his preoccupation with finance increased.

Coinciding as all this did with his deteriorating health, the uninhibited answers King made to the Society's standard questionnaire in 1846, three years before his eventual resignation, reveal his dissatisfaction with his lot and his envy of his colleagues. There was still no parsonage, although government had offered 'a site for a house which is not worth a farthing for yr Missionary'.[14]

It was a time of severe retrenchment, and King, like everyone else, was feeling the pinch. The South Australian copper mines of Burra and Kapunda were draining the Swan River colony of its workforce, and pushing up prices as a result. As for parochial support, there was little hope of anything significant 'owing to the general poverty of the people'.[15] King, however, took it as a sign of moral strength that he had not 'availed himself of the resources of the country'. Unlike the other five clergymen in the colony (he pointed out to his superiors in London), he owned no cows, sheep or land – although one can't help thinking that his situation would have been far better if he had. John Wollaston, for example, had seized the opportunity to buy 115 acres, a house and farming equipment from an expatriate American whaling captain, and set himself as a small-time farmer in order to feed his family.[16]

King lacked Wollaston's stoicism and resourcefulness, and many of his problems were self-inflicted. His tendencies towards indiscretion and attacking his fellow churchmen, regardless of the merits of the case, were increasingly evident by the time he decided to leave. So too was the unwillingness to compromise that would dog his subsequent career. An introduction was provided to Archdeacon Williams in New Zealand on behalf of 'our dear friend the Reverend Geo. King' and 'his enfeebled health', and in January 1849 the Kings, whose children now numbered five, sailed for New Zealand via Adelaide and Sydney.[17] When he stepped ashore in Sydney a month later, the group who met him included Bishop William Broughton, Australia's senior Anglican churchman.

CHAPTER THREE

My Father's House

Like its fellow in the Swan River colony, the Anglican Church in New South Wales had a perennial problem with attracting personnel. In the early days expatriate parsons were legally obliged to look for guidance to the Bishop of London (a good four months away), until in 1814 they were included in the newly created bishopric of Calcutta (a fraction nearer).[1] For another thing, working in a penal colony perceived as running on rum was unlikely to bring advancement in the socially conscious Church of England.

Since settlement in 1788, the colony had seen a succession of parsons garnered from varying sources facing the challenge of personal survival as best they could. Like Sydney town itself, the Anglican ministry developed along irregular patterns, taking the lie of the land into consideration and adapting to local conditions. It made for a motley crew. Ten years later, reinforcements arrived in the form of missionary refugees from the island of Tahiti. This proselytising flotsam included Rowland Hassall, a carpenter by trade, who was in turn storekeeper, volunteer sergeant, and superintendent of government livestock in the area known as the Cow Pastures. Hassall's son Thomas was the first Australian candidate for ordination, and combined his ministry with raising sheep. His extensive travels saw him nicknamed 'the galloping parson'.[2]

The creation of the New South Wales Legislative Council in 1824 brought some degree of self-government to the colony. That same year New South Wales became an archdeaconry under the same Thomas Scott who was shipwrecked off the Swan River Colony (see Chapter Two). His successor was William Broughton. Broughton's career, both as archdeacon then bishop, was marked by appeals to London for chaplains and funding for churches and schools. By 1849, the year of George King's arrival, Sydney had recovered from the harsh economic times brought on by the end of transportation in 1840. Trade, or rather the lack of it, was no longer a major preoccupation of the populace in general, but Bishop Broughton still had serious problems with supply and demand.

The bishop's particular line of business in promoting Christian values, as represented by the Church of England, made the dearth of ordained salesmen in the Sydney diocese a very real concern. As a result, Broughton fell into the habit of redressing the shortfall whenever opportunity presented, and of fishing replacements from a rather problematic pond. One of the earlier catches he netted was Robert Knox Sconce, a graduate of Oxford University, and it was Sconce's resignation that indirectly opened the way for George King.

Sconce was a simple layman with 'the deepest sense of reverence for the Church of England' when he arrived in the Port Phillip District of New South Wales in 1841, aged twenty-three. He had no particular vocation.[3] Succumbing to Bishop Broughton's urgent advances – as usual, God's anointed were desperately thin on the ground – Sconce was persuaded to take holy orders, and in March 1844 was appointed minister of St Andrew's cathedral-church, or 'procathedral' as it was known, a makeshift structure on a prime site in the centre of town. He remained convinced of papal supremacy, however, and before long was heard referring openly to the Church of England as a 'fragment of St. Peter's see'.[4] Sconce's doubts concerning Anglican doctrine finally came to a head in early 1848 when, after ten days spent in prayer and earnest consultations with the equally doubting Thomas Makinson, vicar of St Peter's, Cooks

River, both men resigned their licences as Anglican priests[5] and were welcomed with open arms by the opposition.

Broughton had formally opposed the creation of the Catholic diocese of Sydney five years earlier, and he suffered tremendous loss of face. Sconce's replacement, Thomas Naylor, also proved unsatisfactory, for when George King arrived en route for New Zealand Naylor was desperately ill and unable to carry out his duties as St Andrew's parish priest. King must have seemed a gift from Heaven and, acting with his customary decision, Broughton immediately urged him to stay.

Parson King also knew a good thing when he saw it. Although much earlier he appears to have set his sights on New Zealand,[6] here in Sydney, there would be no vast mileages to cover in order to spread the word of the Lord, and as minister of the town's chief church he could expect to mix with his intellectual and social peers. Seizing the moment, George King settled into his new role, first as curate of St Andrew's then as the parish's *locum tenens*.

With an alacrity that in retrospect seems distasteful, the Kings moved into what Georgina remembered as 'a high house in Liverpool Street, Sydney' that later became St Andrew's parsonage,[7] while the Naylors and their brood of nine shifted for themselves as best they could. In July, Naylor obtained leave of absence for eighteen months and sailed for England, and there he clarified the situation considerably by dying.[8] King now assumed the vacant living of St Andrew's on a permanent basis.

The foundation stone of St Andrew's Cathedral was laid by Governor Lachlan Macquarie in 1819. Governor Richard Bourke laid a second in 1837. In 1842 all construction was halted due to the widespread recession, at which point only the south-east wall was showing any real promise. The stand-in cathedral was wooden and was a perfect example of the temporary made permanent. (It remained in situ until 1868, when the cathedral at last opened and the old church was demolished to give way to the portico of the present Sydney Town Hall.[9])

George King noted in his memoirs that '[A] man could step over the foundations of the Cathedral, and no work was being done about it, nor any contract for work in contemplation'.[10] Before long he adopted the project as his own and threw himself into it wholeheartedly: 'While thus attending to the Spiritual wants of the Congregation, I directed my best energies to the erection and completion of the new Cathedral.'[11] Soon the newcomer was making a name for himself in the increasingly regulated Anglican community of Sydney.

In 1852, three years after clasping George King to his bosom, Bishop Broughton left for England in a bid to empower the Australian bishops in the matter of ecclesiastical law. The right to call synods remained the monarch's prerogative as head of the Established Church, a fact that the local bishops viewed as detrimental to the efficient running of their affairs. Broughton died in London in early 1853 with the matter of Australian church freedom still unresolved. He did, though, leave behind a structure to guide the faithful, and unless (like Robert Sconce) one chose self-immolation on tricky points of doctrine, a cleric's life could proceed uneventfully towards a hallowed grave. (It was as well that Broughton did not live to see the dispute that developed between his successor Frederic Barker and his protégé George King – a clash that would rock the diocese of Sydney to its foundations and cause the Fremantle differences between King and his superiors to pale into insignificance by comparison.)

Barker, who was only the third choice for Broughton's replacement, was vicar of Baslow, a picturesque village in the English Midlands where he was born in 1808. He was a perennial opponent of Roman Catholicism and a former Liverpool Evangelical. Gone were the days when he 'preached fifty-two sermons in a month', but he did go out to Australia 'in a firm Evangelical spirit'. After considerable delay he arrived in Sydney in May 1855, and the twenty-five years he spent there provided him with ample opportunity to exercise 'an acid humour to which colonial pretensions gave much scope'.[12] The Duke of Devonshire had been Barker's close neighbour in Derbyshire, and Sydney's new bishop knew how to recognise a proper 'toff'. Nonetheless, even for him the pretensions of the incumbent of St Andrew's would in time cease to be a laughing matter.

Unlike the renegade Robert Sconce, George King's Anglican beliefs were firm. He had nothing of the 'Roman' about him, and at first sight he appeared as unremarkable as any other member of the team awaiting Bishop Barker. Yet in 1858 the pair became involved in a war over rights and privileges – a war intensified by Barker's push for a church constitution and King's publicly expressed belief that the bishop's powers were already excessive.[13]

Barker's cathedral church of St Andrew, or 'the procathedral' as it was generally known, stood on what had long ceased to be Sydney's second burial ground. The two roles of this modest weatherboard building should have caused no problems, but did. For Barker, it lacked the charm of his fourteenth-century church of St Anne at Baslow, but it was *his* cathedral and his rightful seat as Bishop. For King, it was *his* church and equally his province.

In July 1858, Barker proposed to appoint a dean to administer a cathedral that as yet was non-existent. The position – unlike the building – would by no means be nominal. The dean would receive a stipend commensurate with his position and take precedence over King whenever diocesan ceremony so required. King found the prospect of playing second fiddle untenable. (And, if a non-existent cathedral could have a dean, then King felt he should at least have been appointed a cathedral canon.)

Bishop Frederic Barker was no Chaplain Wittenoom, stiff and uncompromising in matters of secondary importance. Unlike Wittenoom in Western Australia, the bishop patiently tried to explain that the death of one senior churchman, the newly deceased venerable Archdeacon William Cowper, necessitated the appointment of another (who just happened to be the dead man's son), and that, given time, the present anomalies over church and cathedral would be removed.

Dean Cowper (also 'William') was a newcomer to the diocese (although highly experienced elsewhere), and with the new appointee in line to preside over a rare ordination ceremony, King was not prepared to wait.

> *Your Lordship would appear to look forward to the remote day when the cathedral will be consecrated as a suitable time for taking the claims of its then existing Minister into consideration, but long before that day according to present appearances, and human calculation, the voice of the present Incumbent may be hushed in the silence of the grave.*

Far from being silenced while in the land of the living, George was not prepared to give in without a fight.[14]

Anyone reviewing the subsequent documentation might be forgiven for seeing the whole sorry business as a protracted game of chess. A series of letters in the *Judgment of the Bishop of Sydney in the case of the Rev. George King, M.A., Licensed Minister of St. Andrew's, Sydney*, published under the headings of 'King to Bishop' and 'Bishop to King', reveals the successive moves, with the pawns a group of ordinands backed by Barker on the one hand, and a larger group of local parishioners unflinchingly loyal to their parish priest on the other.

The two opponents were evenly matched: Barker, whose towering presence – he was almost 6'6" in his socks (less mitre) – earned him the nickname of the 'High Priest', confronted George King, who stood equally tall on the principles of his position. (Taller, perhaps, since one of his supporters saw fit to inform a meeting of 'wiseacres' that 'in moral and intellectual qualities Mr. K. was AS superior to his Diocesan as Heaven is above Hell'.[15])

As King pointed out:

I cannot but regard my own status in the Church under the authority of a Dean as very much lowered from my original position here, nor can I look forward to the arrangements for the future without a feeling of humiliation which to me is very distressing.[16]

He offered to quit, and then attempted more of the emotional blackmail at which he proved singularly inept: he would only leave if he were given 'a parish where I shall be able to continue the education of my children'.[17]

Barker stood his ground. Patience, urged his Lordship, as if exhorting a child:

I have already informed you that if when the Cathedral is opened you occupy your present position, I shall regard the minister of St. Andrew's as a very proper person to form one of the Cathedral body. The difference between us at this period ... is one of time only ...

No affront was meant to King's dignity, he continued; nothing had changed with the appointment of a dean.[18] Barker's tone throughout the prolonged exchange was friendly but firm, although with time he was less inclined to patience.

And so it might have continued, this inglorious stalemate (the case was even discussed inconclusively in the highest court in the colony) until George King chose to sweep Bishop Barker unceremoniously from the board.

Locking the door of a procathedral against one's bishop when that gentleman and his officials are turned out in full fig, was by no means the wisest of career moves, as the Reverend King discovered. When Bishop Barker found his entry barred on 21 September 1860, he declined to send for a blacksmith but chose to force the issue in a far more dignified manner. Tired of conducting services elsewhere in order to spare the feelings of his turbulent priest, he deliberated long and hard, and at last summoned King to appear before the church's governing body. There, King was to show why his license should not be revoked.[19]

Barker's solution was masterly. By no means a vindictive man, he rose above the temptation to exact revenge. Instead, he revoked the original licence granted King by Bishop Broughton in 1849 and issued a new one of his own, in which he set out the conditions under which King was to continue to function.[20] Thus, the future positions of bishop and priest were sharply defined.

CHAPTER FOUR

The Beginning of Wisdom

Before George King and Bishop Barker famously locked horns over the matter of precedence, the family had settled comfortably into life in Sydney. Georgina King was three and a half when her family moved into their large house within easy distance of the procathedral, which came to them rent-free after the parson's representations to Governor Fitzroy one evening over dinner.[1] As an affable post-prandial gesture, it was in keeping with the character of the governor, a man noted for his easy manners and social skills, and this story of a 'personal gift' (as George King always termed his parsonage) is a fine one.

Whether or not the story was actually true, not everyone would have liked iron founders living at the bottom of the garden, but Bubbs and Co's Foundry at the back of the parsonage grounds became a place of pilgrimage for young Georgina:

> *My eldest Brother Will took out the nails of the lower part of the paling fence between our grounds and the Foundry, and I could move them aside and go in and out. I just slipped them aside, when anything of interest was going on.*[2]

Georgina's early years were spent in zestful discovery, and she was often punished as a result. Although Will, two years her senior, encouraged his sister's escapades, the sorties through the garden fence into Bubbs' inferno were frowned upon in other quarters. Frequently they earned her a diet of bread and water, but already Georgina bore suffering in the name of science as a badge of honour, rather than a disgrace.[3] George King knew something of minerals and his second daughter was sufficiently interesting, even as an infant, for the parson to egg her on in the face of his wife's disapproval: 'My Father told me that when I learned to read I would find out all about iron.'[4]

Iron became an obsession with the tiny Miss King.

> *The men at work used to tell me all about what they were doing, and they were so good to me, and showed me how they cast iron in moulds, and how it came out so easily, as iron contracted in cooling, and the furnace fascinated me, and I used to go as often as I could to watch the men.*

So wrote Georgina in her memoirs seven decades later, recalling the child who did indeed teach herself to read 'in order to find out about such things'.[5] Her father dubbed her 'his little philosopher', sensing already her burgeoning love of the natural world; sympathising with his daughter's thirst for knowledge, and encouraging her by bringing her precociousness to the attention of his scientific friends in Sydney.

The former Port Jackson was no longer an insalubrious penal settlement. Its better-off residents had acquired many of the pretensions of civilisation, and a range of recreational opportunities beckoned to the moneyed, leisured and scientifically inclined. Thanks to the efforts of Alexander McLeay, colonial secretary from June 1825 to January 1836, Sydney now boasted a 'Colonial Museum' and a library (the latter going by the grand name of 'The Australian Subscription Library and Reading Rooms'). The Botanic Gardens, once termed the 'Governor's cabbage-patch', now contained the rarest of rare plants, and could be seen and appreciated by anyone who cared.[6] The 50 acres of natural and cultivated gardens surrounding McLeay's new house out at Elizabeth Bay were also open to the public. Meetings of the Philosophical Society of Australasia – every bit as 'exclusive', 'secretive', 'solemn, narrow, aloof and highbrow' as its illustrious inspiration, the Royal Society of London[7] – were open to anyone who was sufficiently pedigreed (and male). The School of Arts and the Mechanics' Institute were open to the lower orders, unless they preferred something less demanding – intellectually speaking – such as theatres, grog shops, and the other traditional pursuits still readily on offer.

In 1851, the year the Port Phillip District of New South Wales became the Colony of Victoria, Charles Fitzroy, the governor of New South Wales, was appointed governor-general of Australia. The University of Sydney was founded, with chairs in classics, mathematics, chemistry and experimental physics, while the Reverend W.B. Clarke and Dr George Bennett continued to dominate the world of natural science as they had done for many years.

Both men were on the committee of the Australian Subscription Library in Bent Street. They were also on the committee of management of the Australasian Botanical and Horticultural Society. Most important perhaps, as far as Georgina's story is concerned, was their connection with the Australian Museum in College Street, an institution that passed as the fount of all public knowledge, and which opened at no charge every Monday and Friday between the hours of 10am and 4pm.[8] George Bennett was the museum's first secretary and curator; W.B. Clarke the second.

For the early years of its existence, the collections of what was first called the 'Colonial Museum' migrated around the city, and for four years (from 1836) the 320 or so specimens (arranged and classified by Bennett) occupied the former residence of the colonial chief justice in Bridge Street. Then, sometime after 1840, they were transferred to the Court House in Woolloomooloo. In 1849, the year of the Kings' arrival in Sydney, this moveable feast came to rest in its present position opposite Hyde Park, where the original building forms part of the north wing opposite Park Street.[9] Both residents and visitors to Sydney turned up to stare at dead birds, reptiles, insects, and, in time, even the skeletons of whales. The King children must have been as familiar as anyone else with the 'Specimens of

Natural History and Miscellaneous Curiosities' on offer,[10] but what better way to receive enlightenment than first-hand from the former curators themselves?

William Branwhite Clarke was in his fifties when George King took up his duties at St Andrew's procathedral. The glory days of fieldwork were behind him, days when he found gold, explored the wondrous rock formations of the Illawarra, and became a controversial expert on the colony's coal.[11] Since swapping the saddle for regular Sunday sermons, Clarke's enthusiasm for geology remained – as did his perennial annoyance that business still took precedence over natural science in the colonists' minds. Clarke, like King, was instrumental in founding St Paul's College, an Anglican foundation at the new university,[12] and he was counted a King family friend.

No life is without its twists and ironies, and it was Georgina's mother rather than her father who unwittingly directed the young girl towards the many disappointments that lay ahead. Georgina recalls how Jane used to take her to see Clarke, for so long the de facto government geologist and since 1846 the incumbent of St Thomas's in West Street, North Sydney. Clarke has been described as displaying 'the simplicity of a child, and a fund of never failing humour',[13] and a visit to his North Shore parsonage out at rural St Leonard's was an adventure in itself. In old age, Miss King remembered him with great affection, and to a small child the engaging cleric must have seemed an ancient seer – especially if he already cultivated the flowing beard of later years.

Every seriously scientific nineteenth-century gentleman worth his salt had his cabinet of curiosities or 'Wonder Room', and the Reverend Clarke was no exception. Since arriving in New South Wales in 1838, Clarke bestrode colonial science like a colossus – spreading himself rather too thinly to make a real success of anything, as some would have it.[14] In his day he had covered vast tracts of New South Wales, and delved deep into many a geological stratum. Of this, his collection was ample proof. In Clarke's study, lined with his scientific library and containing umpteen display cabinets of Australian minerals and fossils, the little girl pressed her nose against the glass cases and was instantly entranced. She was particularly captivated by what Clarke called his 'Devonian water lilies', in actual fact a fossil 'lily-shaped animal' and not of the vegetable world at all,[15] and which occupied pride of place in his collection as evidence of prehistoric forms of life.[16] While he was unlikely to have given the child any of these precious 'flowers' to hold, let alone keep, Clarke most certainly fostered Georgina's growing interest in geology into her adult years.

Dr George Bennett was to play an even more important role in her life. The man was a phenomenon: handsome, charismatic, much married, and possessed of boundless zeal in the cause of science. Born in 1804 in Plymouth, Devon, Bennett answered the call of the sea in his teens. Smitten by 'sea-fever' at the age of fifteen, he left home to spend two years in Mauritius and Ceylon. On his return he studied medicine, first in his home town, then in London. From 1828 to 1835 the sea reclaimed him, and he made two vastly significant voyages to Australia and the South Seas as a naval surgeon-naturalist, at the end of which his scientific name was made. By the time he settled in Sydney in 1835 at the age of thirty-one and married a lady of some social standing,[17] the 'surgeon-naturalist' had become a naturalist quite simply, and only money concerns forced him back into medical practice full-time. It was in his capacity as family doctor that the Kings came to know him, and he became a frequent visitor to the Liverpool Street parsonage, both in a professional and private capacity. If his skills as a doctor were appreciated, then as a published authority on the colony's natural science his visits were equally prized – and eagerly reciprocated by the Kings.

Before visiting England in 1859, Bennett occupied a large house at 172 Elizabeth Street South, adjacent to Hyde Park.[18]

On his return, and with a new (third) wife whom he met on the voyage back to Sydney, he moved into 167 William Street, Woolloomooloo. And what a house it was! Only a stone's throw from the Australian Museum, it has been described as 'a combination of an art gallery, a miniature museum and private zoo'.[19] This was nothing unusual in Sydney – after all, the Macleays of Elizabeth Bay had been at it for years – but Dr Bennett's wonderland was just around the corner from the Kings' family home. The doctor's rooms were crammed with expertly stuffed animals and birds, a matter of interest to Mrs King, a talented amateur taxidermist.[20] Rare birds like cassowaries, or mooruks lifted from New Britain, wandered freely through the house and into the kitchen, 'keeping the cook in a state of excitement', 'dodging about under the tables, chairs and sofas', chirping and whistling as they went.[21] (Bennett's cassowaries ended up in the zoo at London, but the platypuses in his possession were not so lucky. Five weeks after their capture at the end of 1858, the two 'water-moles' were dead 'and the ladies of England lost an opportunity of beholding these really "darling little ducks" of quadrupeds'.[22])

'My Mother tried to suppress my originality',[23] Georgina recollected. Not so Dr Bennett. Handsome still though in his fifties, he was a true magician conjuring up visions for the mind of an intelligent child; and as she grew up, Georgina King's ambition – in science, at least – would know no bounds. 'I always wanted something real in my life', she stated,[24] and as her family became established in Sydney society and George King became a figure of some note, from mentors such as Bennett and Clarke, and, indeed, from King himself, the encouragement Georgina would always thrive on was never lacking.

CHAPTER FIVE

The Dwellings of the Wilderness

Until the unpleasantness with his bishop, George King's star had been rising in the Anglican Church of New South Wales. He was undoubtedly popular in the parish of St Andrew's, where he had restored morale after the unsettling Sconce ministry and driven the cathedral building project for a good ten years. In 1853 he was one of the first elected Fellows of St Paul's College, an Anglican foundation intended to counter the effects of the new university's purely secular teaching.[1] In 1860 King – a 'very humane man' who 'sympathised so much with defective children and people'[2] – was involved in founding what would became the New South Wales Institute for the Deaf and Dumb and the Blind, with the governor of New South Wales as patron.[3] (He had been less successful in his bid to 'evangelise the aborigines' by setting up a similar institution for them in 1853.[4])

Fellowship of St Paul's brought equal status with the university professors, while the committee of the Institute included John Frazer, the merchant and philanthropist, James Reading Fairfax of the *Sydney Morning Herald*, and Christopher Rolleston, the auditor-general and a trustee of the Australian Museum. The 'Ladies Visiting Committee' comprised the wives of some of Sydney's most distinguished churchmen, lawyers, industrialists and politicians, and included Jane King. George King's famous stoush with Bishop Barker brought loss of face and damaged his professional prospects, yet his standing with the lay community remained unchanged, as it did among his oldest colleagues. His charitable work reinforced the approval of his peers. This meant that in a town with a population nearing 80,000, the Kings moved in the very best circles, both sacred and profane. Their children were accustomed to the society of men and women of wealth, integrity, intellect and principle.

Throughout the dispute with Bishop Barker, George King's concerns were shared between his dignity and his family. While vigorously defending his position, he put forward the rights of his children to receive a decent education, children 'for whose advantage he must live more than for his own'.[5] As in other respects, he was guilty of exaggeration: the King family comprising five daughters and two sons was now complete, and only the youngest child, George Eccles Kelso, or 'Kelso' as he became known to his family and the wider world, was still at school. The daughters were educated informally at home.

With five girls to provide for, as well as the daughter from her earlier marriage, Mrs King was increasingly aware of what the marriage market required. Isabella Stewart, Jane's firstborn, married unexceptionally in 1857, but the second King daughter was certain to be more of a problem. As Georgina entered her teens, her mother Jane – the 'old-fashioned conventional, conservative Mother of the age' – tried to fit her awkward offspring into a universally accepted mould,[6] one where young women were biddable and anxious for marriage. It was no easy task. Red-haired 'Miss Georgie' showed all the Celtic pugnacity of her father, and not for nothing did Will King nickname his sister 'Ginger for Pluck'. Of the few formal portraits of Georgina known to exist, one from her early thirties shows her as part of a sorrowful quartet; another depicts an unremarkable woman in solid middle age. She was big-boned and undeniably strong.[7] Where she gave her love, she was blindly loyal. But despite Georgina's good points – which were few enough, given the requirements of society at the time – Jane King had her work cut out to make her daughter marriageable. Given Georgina's total lack of conventional interests, not surprisingly, her mother failed.

On the subject of Georgina, the King household was divided. 'Little George', as she was often known in the family, was a precocious and spirited child who caused friction between her parents – with her father proud of 'his little philosopher' and her mother alarmed by the individuality she displayed. Georgina and her brother Will were close companions, but Rebecca May or 'May' (or indeed 'Cassandra' as Georgina dubbed her for her gloomy outlook on life) became Jane King's confederate and a constant thorn in Georgina's side. 'I was very much misunderstood by my eldest sister May, who made my life a very hard one', she wrote.[8] 'Dr. Bennett said he noticed when we were children that my sister May was hysterically jealous of me and we were such different types.'[9]

From the evidence of her autobiography, Georgina perceived herself as a natural target. May came actively between her and her ideas of pleasure, and there was little love between them. Georgina King in the role of 'victim' would become a familiar figure to those who knew her in her middle and later years, but as a small self-willed tomboy, she could always escape from her tormentor. Bubbs Foundry, that bewitching place, drew her back time after time (until it moved to other premises), and escape into a world of fire and molten metal was always possible.

In adolescence, revelling in 'Greek mythology and all the Grecian and Roman muses and myths with my brother Will' and sharing 'a delight in the study of Shakespeare' were deemed legitimate occupations,[10] but when Darwin's *On the Origin of Species* reached Sydney in 1860, it was another matter. The book horrified Rebecca May and Georgina noted with some glee that 'May who always made a religious profession . . . could not bear to hear about it'.[11]

That same year St Andrew's parsonage was painted and renovated, and the Reverend King took his brood over the water to 'Lyndcote', a grand three-storeyed house on Hunters Hill rented from the steamboat owner Charles Edward Jeanneret.[12] Soon enough the hill would lose its exclusivity (twenty years later it was covered with suburban sandstone villas set in a common blaze of rioting roses and bougainvillea), but in the early 1860s the area was at peace with nature, with very few houses and space enough for Georgina to avoid the carping May. It was also a source of pleasure:

> *My father had often to go to Sydney by steamer for his various duties, and I used to take the boat across for him on his return, for I could row well. We kept a boat when we lived in Sydney and I learnt to row when I was very young.*[13]

Such peaceful moments on the Parramatta River were regrettably few, however, and throughout Georgina's teenage years May buzzed about her like a sanctimonious wasp. Jane King's attempts to direct Georgina away from controversy were gentler. Mrs King was a keen and industrious gardener and created gardens wherever she lived.[14] Like so many other women of her day, she was a strict disciplinarian with a strong work ethic and expected a great deal from Georgina in the way of honest toil around the house and grounds. Tall, athletic Georgina laboured for the family; May's work took place among the poor, bringing her deference from the needy and reinforcing her overbearing attitude at home.

While Georgina writes affectionately of her mother, there is a sense that Jane King neither understood her, nor wished to. If Jane's main aim was to keep her awkward daughter in check, then she succeeded, for Georgina did not rebel: 'As I grew up . . . I was her slave in many ways, from, as I thought, a sense of duty.'[15]

Meanwhile, the 'squabble' with Bishop Barker bore increasingly bitter fruit. With the revocation of the licence granted by Bishop Broughton and the issue of a replacement by Broughton's successor, King found his stipend diminished by the not inconsiderable sum of £25 – the reasons why enlivening the pages of the *Sydney Morning Herald* for over a week in July–August 1862, as King quibbled over points of law with the diocesan registrar.[16]

Again, he came off second best. Having cast aspersions on his bishop's rectitude, King's removal from St Andrew's followed. On 15 February 1863, as the cathedral moved steadily (if slowly) towards completion,[17] King was sent to a living in the country. He spent the rest of his clerical life in outlying parishes and (one supposes) in an increasing climate of bitterness as he watched others receive preferment in his stead.

For eighteen months Georgina's father had bombarded his bishop with letters, and she had witnessed the invigorating powers of the pen. So much so that many years later she would employ the same tactic in the course of her own difficulties with another ruling clique.

Georgina was nearing eighteen and May was in her early twenties when the Kings moved to distant St Peter's, Cooks River, once the living of Thomas Makinson, another tiresome priest. The move was as inevitable as – in the disgraced parson's eyes at least – it was undeserved. Cooks River drains into Botany Bay, and when Captain James Cook discovered it in 1770 the bay's foreshores were reed-lined and marshy. The hinterland of what was originally given the unpromising name of 'Sting-ray Harbour' was a vast expanse of sand dunes and lakes, raised a little above sea level and watered by perpetual streams. While these deceptive 'meadows' (mistakenly described by Cook as some of the finest in the world) proved useless for farming, plentiful subterranean reserves of fresh water encouraged other activities. Simeon Lord set up a woollen mill as early as 1815, and tanning and other textile works followed.[18] In 1855 the government resumed the land and set up a pumping scheme to supplement Sydney's inadequate water supply. Even though factory closures had caused serious unemployment,[19] by the time the new incumbent of St Peter's took up his duties, industry was advancing along the shores of Botany Bay and up the stream (by now dignified with the name of Cooks River).

The parish of St Peter's is situated between present day

Tempe, Marrickville and Mascot, about two miles from the river and three from Botany Bay. The church was built in 1838 on a flat and scrubby site that even then was unprepossessing.[20] Today it abuts a busy arterial road, with its foundations rocked by thundering traffic, traffic that in 1863 consisted of horses, carts and drays, or people availing themselves of what was quaintly termed 'shanks's pony'. Tempe was named after a delightful Greek valley famed for its singing birds and sylvan shade, and in 1863 was still as rural as any provincial outpost; Mascot featured cow pastures and market gardens. The area was healthier than Sydney, a town where the Tank Stream continued to pour its abominations fulsomely into Sydney Harbour, yet, isolated from the intellectual and social stimuli he was used to, George King brooded over what he perceived as further 'persecutions' at the hands of his bishop. While the factories steadily inched inland and brought employment to many of his congregation, King himself faced his future gloomily, in the manner of a patrician exiled from the hub of imperial Rome.

CHAPTER SIX

In Spirit and in Truth

Of all the Kings' neighbours in the parish of St Peter's, the Michael Metcalfes were the best known. A merchant and customs agent, Metcalfe was also the bursar of St Paul's College, where, like King, he was a Fellow. Metcalfe was an active High Church Anglican and deeply involved in fundraising efforts for Saint Andrew's Cathedral. He was also a valued contributor to the finances of the church in New South Wales generally. Mrs Agnes Georgianna Metcalfe, who was on Jane King's 'Ladies Visiting Committee' at the Deaf, Dumb and Blind Institute, would be a witness at Rebecca May's wedding. Metcalfe's mother-in-law, on the other hand, preferred to concern herself with the world to come and devoted herself to the ouija board or 'planchette'. Whenever she came on a visit to the Metcalfes', Georgina was invited to watch the spirits at work.[1]

Magnetism, mesmerism and spiritualism were a flourishing vogue in 1860s and 1870s Australia. Spiritualism appealed to all levels of Victorian society, a society 'assailed by death – if not on a daily basis, then all too frequently'.[2] Since the practice sought to reconcile religion with science, it could be taken seriously – not only by the easily gulled but by rational people, too (Alfred Deakin, a future Australian prime minister, was a devotee in his youth). With advice on forming 'spirit circles' at home readily available, even the most respectable households succumbed to experimenting with the paranormal. The residents of St Peter's were no exception. Old Mrs Robinson, Mrs Metcalfe's mother, had taken a shine to Georgina, and her invitations gave the girl a chance to conduct her first adult scientific investigations – for, while 'Everything about magnetism and electricity and animal magnetism attracted my earnest thoughts', like her father, when it came to the supernatural she was a natural sceptic.

The Northern Irish bogs of George King's childhood reeked of superstition, but there was not much of the druid or the mystic about the Reverend King, a graduate of Trinity College, Dublin. He was twelve when his great-uncle, an ex-colonel of dragoons and 'a great warrior in his day' died in the fullness of his years. Less grief-stricken than curious, and remembering the ninety-year-old soldier's tales of encounters with the 'Arch-enemy' in the form of 'a gigantic black dog' – an apparition common in benighted parts of Britain even today – young George resolved 'to seize the opportunity of testing the reality of these supernatural visions' at the dark gravel pit reputedly frequented by the massive hound.[3]

The test took place on the very day his uncle died. He gazed one last time on the old fellow's face, lingered with his bereaved relations until the ghostly hour of midnight, then set out on his faithful steed for 'the darksome mouth' of the putative canine's den. There, he 'looked all around, but not the shadow of a dog, great or small, appeared within view'. George got a nasty fright, however, as he continued homewards on his lonely ride. Before long 'the rattling of a loose iron chain' was heard, 'clinking along the macadamised road'; at the same time 'something which appeared as large as an elephant' loomed up and moved towards him. This proved to be only a dray-cart laden with peat, but young George was not disposed to linger. The next morning he was congratulated by his family on surviving 'such a weird & unhallowed adventure', and that was the end of superstition as far as he was concerned.[4]

A quarter of a century later, Georgina came to share her father's views on the paranormal, and would apply her own brand of scepticism to phenomena such as these, although animal magnetism *did* claim her interest for a while and she was always ready to visit the Metcalfes. That Metcalfe, a convinced Christian, should allow his female relations to dabble in spirits of a supernatural kind is not at all surprising: with spiritualism all the go, who was he to seem outmoded? So his wife, his mother-in-law – and the local vicar's daughter – whiled away the evenings, shivering deliciously as, in turn, they put their fingers on the glass and reached out across the ether. Georgina's opinions on table-turning, spirit-rapping or any other form of spiritualism are not on record, nor does she say whether she witnessed any of the more 'normal' manifestations of the paranormal, and her participation in séances was short-lived.

One evening Sir Julian Salomons, a notable Sydney barrister, joined those who sat hand in hand around the table in a darkened room. Afterwards 'I made a remark about animal magnetism', recalled Georgina, 'when he said, "I have just read that in a new book I have received from England, and you could not have seen it. I shall send it to you".' When Salomons proved as good as his word, 'my sister May would not let me read it and returned it to Sir Julian Salomons by Mr. Rogers who was afterwards my brother-in-law'.[5] Deprived of the book by May and her offsider Rogers, a Gold Medallist in chemistry and experimental physics at the University of Sydney who should have been more open-minded, Georgina's investigations now took her on a different tack.

One day Dr Charles Fisher, the homeopathic physician who attended her younger sister Helena, informed Georgina that she possessed what was known as 'Odic Force'. 'Od', according to Baron von Reichenbach, its discoverer, was 'intermediate between electricity, magnetism, heat and light, and recognisable only by the nerves of sensitive persons'. It pervaded all nature 'wherever chemical action is going on' – and that included graveyards.[6] Knowing that she had 'such high perceptive powers that it amounted to a sixth sense', and that 'only one in millions had it', led Georgina to exercise her investigative talents in an obvious direction.

> *The church at St. Peter's was in the centre of the grounds, and the parsonage was on the far side and the burial ground was*

on the near side. When we lived there we often used to walk round the church in the evening with friends, and one evening I saw a blue light over one of the graves, but no one else among our party saw it, and I kept seeing it every time I walked in its direction.[7]

Did 'Miss Georgie' see ghosts? Many people thought so, but Georgina herself had a natural explanation, bound up with the famous disappearance of Frederick Fisher (no relation of her sister's doctor) and the subsequent appearance of his ghost.[8] 'I have thought it might have been a similar escape of gas that was seen by the person who indicated Fisher's remains hovering over the place where his body was found in the water hole' – for the gas would escape through water, as well as earth, and might be taken for a ghost. 'Since then I have been an advocate for cremation', sniffed the fastidious Miss King, satisfied with the results of one of her first scientific enquiries. (After her death in 1932 she was, indeed, consigned to the flames.)

She was less satisfied with the behaviour of her elder sister. 'Whenever she saw me reading she used to say "some unorthodox book"', Georgina complained. 'And I was thirsting for knowledge . . .'[9] Like the proverbial elephant, Georgina neither forgot an injustice nor did she ever forgive, but looking back on those days in St Peter's parsonage she wrote: 'People long ago used to call my sister May my "opposing force", perhaps I needed an "opposing force".'[10]

The two sisters could not have been more different. Georgina was always so sure in her conviction, while May 'was always imagining something was going to happen'.[11] On 11 January 1868 something *did* happen, and we can only hope it turned out to be to the gloomy May's liking: she married Francis Rogers, and went to live in the Sydney suburb of Burwood. Free at last of May's attempts at interference and control, Georgina returned to her reading and began to seek a direction for her life.

CHAPTER SEVEN

Stages in the Odyssey of a Soul

When Darwin's *On the Origin of Species* reached Sydney in 1860, Georgina King was in her mid teens; she may have been in her early twenties before it truly captured her attention. Others older and wiser than the young woman would agonise over the implications of the cataclysmic *Origin*, and most of them were 'creationist' (or orthodox) in outlook. While they admired Darwin as a scientist, they were unequivocal in their rejection of his ideas.[1] W.S. Macleay was one who acknowledged the challenges set by the Evolutionists. Writing from Elizabeth Bay to his friend the Viscount Sherbrooke, the scholar and naturalist confided:

> *The naturalist finds himself on the horns of a dilemma ... It is far easier for me to believe in the direct and constant Government of the Creation of God, than that he created the world and then left it to manage itself, which is Darwin's theory in a few words.*[2]

While encouraging his second daughter to develop her scientific bent, George King was dogmatic when it came to points of canon law. He would have been the unlikeliest of converts to Darwinism, and who else in that household would have openly dared question the word of God and the teachings of the Bible? Georgina's early reading on the subject of Evolution was done in secret, and as the new movement gathered force in the 1870s, she was equally discreet.

Writers such as Herbert Spencer (1820–1903) and Thomas Carlyle (1795–1881) backed Darwin, the great new name in science. The philosophy elaborated by Spencer was in tune with

Evolution. Well before Charles Darwin could steel himself to publish his groundbreaking ideas, Spencer promulgated the theory that circumstances determined the evolution of man and society. His *First Principles* was published in 1862, the earliest of a series of works designed to 'trace how the law of evolution was gradually realised in life, mind, society, and morality'.[3] Spencer's sole distinction these days is (arguably) that of lying in London's Highgate Cemetery opposite the equally *passé* Karl Marx. He was prolific and his later work is abstruse – this, after all, was someone described by Carlyle as 'the most immeasurable ass in Christendom'.[4] Carlyle, for his part, brought hope to 'the thousands whose faith in dogma had been shaken';[5] '[Carlyle] was my first love – Herbert Spencer was my second – as mental affinities', Georgina declared when putting her youth into its mid-Victorian context, and she claimed both as her favourite authors.

'Carlyle's Sartor Resartus was a great comfort to me and helped me along in many difficulties . . . He (Carlyle) was my ideal, and I always looked for a Carlyle in my life when I was young.'[6] But there were few, if any, eligible young men like Thomas Carlyle living in Sydney in the 1870s – or if there were, they were already married or bespoke. Frank Rogers, May's biddable fiancé, was hardly one of them, and we know little of Layman Harrison, who married another sister, Martha King, other than that he was a partner in a firm of auctioneers. (His family had been neighbours when Georgina was a child, Mr Harrison helping her master her letters.) Both Harrison and Frederick Humphery, Helena King's husband, were good brothers-in-law to Georgina, and the law, once the men were widowed, would have permitted nothing more. So Georgina read and reread Carlyle's *Sartor Resartus* (first published in book form in 1836) and dreamed of a substitute for the irascible Scottish writer, a lover who would take her away from an atmosphere of repression, jealousy and active dislike.

Sartor Resartus, Carlyle's story of a 'patched-up tailor', is to some extent an autobiographical work. In Part One, Professor Diogenes Teufelsdröckh pursues a philosophical discourse on clothes. Clothes, for this unusual 'tailor', represent the misleading notions that may come between us and our recognition of the truth. All 'symbols, forms, and human institutions' are 'clothes', or 'the garments of the idea', and, like clothes, can easily be mended, discarded or replaced.[7] Part Two, in which Carlyle draws upon his personal experiences, is an imagined biography of Teufelsdröckh himself. The small Scottish market town of Ecclefechan where Carlyle was born, and Edinburgh where he received his tertiary education, are transposed to Entempfuhl in an imaginary Germany. The whole book is a portrayal of spiritual crisis. For anyone struggling to find a belief system beyond the recognised spiritual avenues then available, the book was an invaluable reference point.

A Thomas Carlyle forced to accept his tendency towards intellectual scepticism and spiritual denial to some extent mirrored Georgina's own dilemma. In her twenties, the thoughts that preoccupied *him* became *her* constant companions. Diogenes Teufelsdröckh could not bring himself to espouse orthodoxy; he dedicated himself to 'a life of spiritual affirmation', but was 'unable to base this affirmative spirit on the traditional religious beliefs that had supported his father'. It was this aspect of the book that Georgina probably found most appealing, for the professor's beliefs were founded 'on his own will, his imaginative response to nature and the inspiration provided by the lives of great men'.[8]

In choosing science over religion, Georgina reacted in much the same way. She sought guidance from a series of older scientific mentors, each distinguished in his field of expertise, and revelled in her natural surroundings *on her own terms*. As with her solitary struggles with Euclid's *Elements*,[9] she was always ready to grapple with difficult ideas and to interpret them to her satisfaction – an attitude that would never change. Like Thomas

Carlyle, she dwelled on 'the individual life and its problems, the search for happiness, the law of duty, the aspirations of the soul'.[10] She watched her sisters marry and gradually distanced herself from the accepted norms for a young woman of her time. Like the afflicted Teufelsdröckh, she came to believe that freedom of choice was more important than the pursuit of happiness; should suffering be her lot in life, then she would bear it as a free spirit – an indomitable spirit ready to defy the tyranny of evil.

'The tyranny of evil', as Georgina might have termed the establishment forces with which she clashed in her middle years, did not concern her yet. Rather, it was death that came to mock her. One by one, those she loved were struck down in quick succession. Long-faced, miserable May Rogers stares out glumly from the portrait taken when she was a white-haired old woman, her role as 'Cassandra' vindicated – for in the years between 1871 and 1878, weddings and funerals mingled in a ghastly *danse macabre* that left the King family devastated.

On 16 November 1871 Rosetta Jane King, Georgina's youngest sister, died aged twenty. On 1 June 1872 Martha West King was married to Layman Harrison (the year the Kings moved to the parish of St Thomas, Enfield). On 20 January 1875, when Georgina reached that defining thirtieth year of a Victorian woman's life, the marriage took place between Helena Anna King and Frederick Thomas Humphery, merchant, financier and later MLA. Helena died two years later on 22 July 1877 aged twenty-five, leaving a little boy, and a baby daughter who did not long survive her. William King, Georgina's beloved 'Will', died on 29 November that same year, aged thirty-four. On 3 October 1878 Martha West King Harrison also died, aged thirty-one. Her two small children joined the King household.[11]

May Rogers continued in good health, as did George Eccles Kelso King, the entrepreneurial younger brother. In 1870 he joined the staff of the Bank of New South Wales after a stint in

Queensland as a jackeroo. In December 1877, the twenty-three-year-old became CEO of the Mercantile Mutual Insurance Co. He subsequently had two wives, one of them an heiress, and a long and distinguished career in the course of which he was knighted. This left Georgina as the only child living at home.

Tall Georgina with her red hair and odd ideas had failed to find a husband, and 'Little George' (she was sometimes simply called 'George') was destined to care for her parents in their old age. In her day there were three possible options for middle-class women. In her biography of Georgina's friend Rose Scott, Judith Allen lists them as: 'Spinsterhood and caring for parents and community; marriage without children and with service to family and community; and marriage with service only to immediate family, largely consisting of numerous children.'[12] Spinsterhood was definitely the worst option from the point of view of social status, but possibly not too dire for Georgina. She and her mother would inevitably clash, but there is no doubt that father and daughter had a good relationship and that she was his companion of choice. So, having seen four of her siblings drop like flies over a period of seven years, Georgina may have become resigned to her lot – certainly, on the evidence of her memoir, she did not see herself as someone to be pitied:

> *When we were reading* The Coming Race *by Bulwer-Lytton, my father who indulged me very much used to call me Zee, for fun, after one of the characters in the book. He said I was never to marry but to be the old maid of the family. He thought there were great possibilities for me as I had such originality.*[13]

Edward Bulwer Lytton's 'science fiction' novel was published in 1871. The women characters were stronger than the men, and 'Zee' or 'Zy', a true heroine of the genre, was quite literally larger than life with an intellect to match – a notion reinforced, perhaps, by those intimate moments shared on the Parramatta River. Dr George Bennett also advised Georgina against matrimony: 'he said I had talents and individuality which would not be developed if I married.' (All the same, had that illusive Carlyle substitute turned up in Sydney, 'I would not have regarded my father's and Dr. Bennett's advice – I would not have grumbled about him as Mrs. Carlyle did', she admitted years later.[14])

Originality. Talents. Individuality. These two men surely had her interests truly at heart. Bennett, the Kings' doctor, realised what we of the twentieth-first century often fail to remember: that marriage for a woman was a hazardous business. (Bennett lost two wives before he took a third.) Both men knew that multiple childbirths had a stultifying effect on the mind, as well as taking a frightful toll on the body. Jane King had eight children, all of whom survived into adulthood, and her tremendous achievement in ensuring this probably made her fairly dull to live with. 'I took natural science as my liege Lord instead', Georgina stated simply, when faced with the prospect of conventional marriage or being true to herself.[15]

Georgina had helped her mother with her younger siblings when their nurse left to be married; and she was good at it, apparently. 'My father thought so much of what I did for the children', she wrote,[16] and in her old age she worked hard on behalf of the children of Sydney. But it was in 1877 that life began to assume the tragic aspects that never entirely went away, and she was to have experience of motherhood if only at second hand.

'While my youngest sister Helen lived I had her loving sympathy for she understood me so well. She had such a bright intellect, and was so cultured.' Thus Georgina wrote on the first page of her autobiography, revealing the traits she found attractive in a woman. 'She married the Hon. F.T. Humphery, M.L.A. and he was a good kind brother to me.' What better solution when Helena died so tragically after delivering her second child than for Georgina to take care of her children, fulfilling a deathbed promise? Now, although she was marked out for spinsterhood by her father – and by inference to be her parents' mainstay in their declining years – she took on some of the aspects of a wife. And at the same time she found a substitute for her dead brother, William, who had shared so much of her life and interests. Able to indulge her intellect instead of being worn out by childbirth, she found that she had a genuine liking for children and the company of a congenial brother-in-law whenever his business interests allowed.

Baby Hilda Rose did not survive her mother for long. Anxious for his infant son, Frederick Humphery built a cottage at Springwood in the Blue Mountains, and the trio moved away from sorrowful memories and set up their little ménage. It was here, in the very mountains explored by Louisa Atkinson – the first woman to make her mark publicly in New South Wales science – that Georgina began her own botanising, and 'collected 32 varieties of ferns there, and had them in flower pots'.[17]

'Childhood, education, search for a vocation, love, spiritual doubt and darkness, the inaction which follows upon loss of faith, the reascent to light and assurance – these are the stages in the Odyssey of a soul'[18] – and by the time she moved to Springwood, Georgina King had passed through almost all. The happy times might have lasted forever, for she had no ambition other than to stay. She had no reason to look to Frederick Humphery for marriage. These were the times, remember, of the 'Table of Affinities' which forbade 'Marriage to a deceased wife's sister'; times when sexual relations between such a couple were considered incest, the ties acquired through marriage being as binding as the ties of blood. When, in 1882, after six years of harmonious cohabitation, Frederick took another wife, his sister-in-law was shattered. It was as if her sister died anew. Worse still, she lost little Esca Morris, who was – and always would be – 'the darling of my life'.[19]

CHAPTER EIGHT

Brotherly Love

As Helena King Humphery lay dying, she extracted a deathbed promise from her older sister to take charge of her two children.[1] Georgina, a capable woman of thirty-two with no obvious prospects of marriage, had no reason to refuse. Besides, for years Helena had offered Georgina staunch support against the more reactionary elements in their family and there was a debt of gratitude, as well as one of duty, to be paid. All but four years of Georgina's life had been spent in or near Sydney where, as the Reverend King's daughter, she moved in the best of social circles. She had her mentors Clarke and Bennett too, and a sense of purpose, yet when her brother-in-law built a cottage retreat in the Blue Mountains for his surviving child, a little boy, Georgina took to country life with no apparent regrets.

The days when the blue-hazed western mountains represented a tantalising enigma were gone. Inland New South Wales was opened up to pastoralists in the early 1800s and geologists began searching out the secrets of the mountain rocks. The liberating railway followed. When it crossed the Nepean River in 1867, thousands of travellers came to marvel at the zig-zag approach to the mountains at Glenbrook, a sight that became essential viewing for visitors from overseas.[2] Mount Victoria (later known as the 'Simla of New South Wales') was reached in May 1868, and by October 1869 the second even more miraculous descent – again by zig-zag – down the western escarpment into Lithgow and on to Bowenfels was complete.[3] It was at Glenbrook that Georgina first saw geological theory tested in the field. The child who had taken such pleasure in W.B. Clarke's

'Devonian water lilies' was in her early twenties when she rode the famous zig-zag in 'about 1870 or 1871 in the same train and carriage' as Clarke, and listened intently while he explained the complexities of the Lapstone Monocline to her in person.[4]

The Great Western Railway made access to the Blue Mountains an easy affair.[5] Industry quickly took advantage, as did Sydney's entrepreneurs. In places like Mount Victoria, Medlow Bath and Katoomba, guesthouses and grand hotels began to mushroom (for, after all, a change of air was 'essential to well-being'; 'mountain sunlight was healthier (the rays could impinge directly)'; and gum trees gave off 'an antiseptic vapour that could be inhaled from the cliff tops'[6]). Soon the great sandstone plateau became Sydney's playground, a place where even the poor could fill their tortured lungs with good, clean mountain air in summer – if only for one day at a time.

The railway had been fully operational for over a decade when in 1878 Frederick Humphery removed his son and sister-in-law to Springwood, a small town twelve miles east of Penrith. It owed its name to Governor Macquarie, who camped there on his way 'to visit the new discovered country to the westward of the Blue Mountains' in April 1815,[7] when of course it was only forest. In 1878 the population of 200 consisted mainly of small farmers and railway workers, with a butchery, baker's and store.[8] Trains from Sydney stopped there, although the little town was never as popular as Weatherboard (the stop for Wentworth Falls) or the dismal-sounding Crushers. Nonetheless, Springwood had various gentrified estates, several gracious homes, and its share of the local elite. Sir Henry Parkes lived at 'Faulconbridge' from 1878, and Charles Moore, merchant, auctioneer and alderman, had his residence at the mansion he named 'Moore Court'.

Whereas Sir Henry helped shape a nation, Moore 'improved' on a more parochial scale. During his time as Sydney's mayor,[9] he had the abominable Tank Stream covered over, and created a public park from the sandhills of Sydney common. When he moved into his Springwood home in 1876 he started improving the town. He was Irish, like the Kings; and, like them, he was a backbone of the Sydney Anglican church. He knew of Frederick Humphery in the latter's capacity as official assignee of insolvent estates, even if he did not know him personally in Sydney (which seems unlikely). In Springwood, certainly, Humphery and his little family were to be close neighbours and the Moores' friendship with Georgina continued long after she moved away.

Moore Court, built on a Crown grant obtained in 1875, was initially a modest affair. The two-storied annex that followed befitted a local squire instrumental in founding the Springwood public school (in 1878), and who donated the land and most of the money for the Anglican church (completed in 1889). Rate books for the period do not exist, but Humphery's cottage was possibly built on the Moore Court estate itself, under some kind of leasing arrangement. (Not that buying land would have been a problem for Georgina's brother-in-law, for in addition to his official appointment, Frederick Humphery was a commission agent and owned several cattle stations in Queensland.)

There is no trace of Humphery's cottage in Springwood, and Charles Moore's home was demolished years ago. Commemorated in the present Moorecourt Avenue, the house when Georgina knew it was set in extensive grounds of 34 acres, within easy walking distance of rainforest gullies to the north and south. More poetic souls might head further west, to the grander hotels of Katoomba (the glamorous new name for 'Crushers'), where, for the 'weeks and months' necessary for coming to grips with the mountains, they could 'let the majestic colouring and clothing of the sunset sink into [their] being' and 'watch as nature weaves the robes of imperial purple and royal gold'. As the promotional material at the time chose to put it, visitors could expect to watch, transfixed, as

> *... down in the gorges the pale-grey mists and the deep blue shadows are prepared; while every salient point, every*

unshadowed ridge is flooded with fiery light; while the bare crags gleam and glow as if in process of transmutation, and the gnarled and stunted trees of the summit stand out in spectral light.[10]

Less sensitive travellers – or those more pushed for time – were just as likely to settle for Springwood. Here, visitors left the train in their hundreds to experience a gently manipulated nature, and take to the light tracks leading through the sassafras trees to fancifully named destinations with rustic bridges and idyllic bathing pools. It is still possible to retrace their steps as they headed in their Sydney Sunday best south from the Royal Hotel to 'Fairy Dell', or perhaps north to 'Madoline Glen'. Scented satinwoods, lilli pillis and black wattles still follow the watercourses and climb the slopes, and tall, shapely sassafras fill the air with fragrance. Ferns and fungi lurk in crannies; lichens mask the stones. After rain the rock face streams with water and droplets fall from the glistening canopy above . . . 'I collected 32 varieties of ferns there and had them in flower pots', Georgina tells us in her memoir.[11] It was in places such as these that she loved to wander and collect the plants of which she was so proud – and today even the most jaded modern eye can detect a little of the magic.

Life in the cottage proved idyllic after the fractious family life she left behind her, and Georgina was provided with an independence that would have been impossible at home. She found fulfillment in keeping house and looking after little Esca, benefited from her brother-in-law's connections in the area, and had ample opportunity to cultivate her own. In fact, by the time Humphery remarried, his sister-in-law's 'networks' would spread as far west as Lithgow, Bathurst and Orange, facilitating her collections for Baron Ferdinand von Mueller and Sir Frederick McCoy in the 1890s. Esca meanwhile became 'the darling' of her life. The bond created between the two in those early happy years was of the strongest, and the pain of the continual bereavements of the 1870s, when one by one her siblings were taken from her, was dulled.

For Georgina, who by now had crossed the threshold between eligibility and spinsterhood, the little ménage proposed by Frederick Humphery lessened pain of another kind and met her needs as a single woman. She had seen her sisters suffer and die in childbirth; she had seen the effect of frequent maternity upon her own mother. She herself exemplified the dilemma that confronted the Victorian woman: a choice between domesticity and intellectual pursuits. In her case, the choice appears to have been made for her, with her mentor George Bennett advocating subservience to science rather than to a husband, and her father designating her to be the family's old maid. What has been written about her friend Rose Scott applies equally well to Georgina:

> *. . . a woman's place was still the home in the restrictive sense. A woman who did not choose to marry was the target of slurs that she could not. A woman who wanted to develop her mental powers above those of a hen or a doll was unsexed. She was a warning to minxes who rebelled against the frowsy sentimentality that encrusted biological facts.*[12]

To what extent Georgina did choose spinsterhood for herself we cannot tell, but for as long as she lived in Springwood she was in control of a household and her unmarried state was not derided. She had a child of her own to nurture and cherish without having to pay the sexual dues of a wife. Naively, she supposed the situation would never change.

Years before, Dr Bennett told her that she had 'the strength of character to carry through all difficulties', and now in the face of such a cruel separation from Esca and her life in the Blue Mountains (when Frederick finally remarried), she proved a worthy pupil. She packed up her bags and, rather than return to her parents' house in Ashfield whence the Reverend King had removed following his retirement from St Thomas's, Enfield, she set her sights on Europe, taking a trip very likely financed by her grateful brother-in-law. There, she visited her Irish relations and undertook a modified version of the Grand Tour, and all the while the 'little philosopher' remembered her childhood lessons. Always observant and questioning, she took in her new surroundings. She looked, she read, she enquired. Georgina King may have left Australia brokenhearted, but she returned a woman of thirty-eight and a scientist in the making.

Part Two

The Changing of the Guard

CHAPTER NINE

Coming of Age: The Australasian Association for the Advancement of Science, 1888

For anyone with Georgina King's ambition, the 1880s would seem to have been the perfect moment to make one's name. The century following European settlement was one of gradual enlightenment and change. From the motley crew of felons, officials and opportunists discharged on the shores of Port Jackson in 1788 had emerged a second and third generation of colonists who more and more considered themselves 'Australians'. This sense of being 'at home' in an erstwhile alien environment permeates the writing and painting of the day. With increasing familiarity, landscapes became less threatening and more recognisably Australian. No longer did mighty English oaks masquerade as gums: the bush was represented in its natural beauty, not depicted along heavily nostalgic European lines. Early poets did still incline towards 'perfumed bowers' and 'gliding streamlets' (not to mention 'soothing zephyrs')[1] but once they 'grew into' their surroundings, then bushfires, bushrangers – or simply 'the Bush' – became common topics, allowing the likes of Ben Hall and 'Bullocky Bill' to enter the national psyche through the medium of song.

In science, too, the mood began to swing away from subservience to Britain. Before the various philosophical societies of Australia and New Zealand were formally linked by the creation of the Australasian Association for the Advancement of Science (AAAS) in 1888, it was accepted that institutions all over Europe should claim their share of Australia's natural bounty, and many early collections were housed in herbaria as distant from Kew Gardens as Berlin and St Petersburg.[2] For years colonists like George Bennett in New South Wales and Captain James Drummond in Western Australia sent specimens to scholars in the Old Country – Bennett through his enduring friendship with Richard Owen, and Drummond because he was strapped for cash. Surgeon-naturalists on official Royal Navy expeditions pursued their scientific (and social) interests when on terra firma.[3] Independent adventurers collected and conveyed specimens to Europe for classification, description – and sale. Australia's curious flora and fauna became, in short, 'Big Business'.

Georgina returned home from Europe in 1883 to find the popularisation of science and technology well under way. Enlightenment had slowly been reaching out to the masses for years and mechanics' institutes and schools of art were burgeoning. 'Popularisation' should not be confused with 'democratisation', however. Lectures were seen as a means of 'improving' the working classes, just as well-meaning ladies tried to wean them off the grog. It was the 'Victorian way' and 'Society' encouraged such advances, especially when promoted by the men who succeeded W.B. Clarke and George Bennett as leaders of Sydney's scientific pack.

In the old days, naturalists and natural philosophers had formed societies where they might voice their ideas and formally express their thoughts in writing. The origins of the Royal Society of Tasmania go back to 1839, those of Victoria's Royal Society date back to 1855. The Royal Society of South Australia grew out of the Adelaide Philosophical Society of 1853. If one discounts an earlier version that 'expired in the baneful atmosphere of distracted politics'[4] in 1822, and several others that failed to sustain the interest of their members (see Chapter Twelve), the Royal Society of New South Wales emerged from the Philosophical Society (formed in 1855), and was given permission to change its name in 1866. It counted among its members several of the 'new men' of Australian science: professionals and paid servants of colonial government, not gentlemen dilettantes, men who no longer believed in a system where their contributions were all-important but where they had no voice. Rather, they considered themselves independent of British science – custodians and assessors of their natural world *by right*.

Australian science was in the ascendant, at least as far as outsiders could tell, but in the Royal Society of New South Wales, discontent was running high. Publication in scholarly journals was (and is) a slow business at the best of times, and money was another issue. 'We are thrown entirely on our annual subscriptions', Vice-President W.B. Clarke warned members at the society's inaugural meeting in 1867, and one guinea a year per person simply would not cover the cost of publishing that individual's contribution – in its entirety, anyway, and possibly not at all.[5] The wait for domestic recognition was a frustrating one for those publishing scientists who, rather than listen to the pronouncements of other people, preferred to see their own ideas in print.[6] The efficiency of Australia's transcontinental telegraph only made things worse, for after 1872, news from Britain arrived in a matter of hours, highlighting scientific achievements in the Old Country so very far away.

The Australasian Association for the Advancement of Science (AAAS) did not come into being overnight; it owed its creation to the assiduous efforts of Professor Archibald Liversidge over a period of some fifteen years. Recognising the need to promote the interests of colonial science in its own right and on its own patch, this bachelor, for whom work made up for the lack of a wife, has long been acknowledged as one of the visionaries of Australian science. There is a certain irony that Liversidge, the driving force behind a body intended to make colonial science independent of British institutions, was himself an Englishman. He reached Sydney to take up his post as 'Reader in Geology and Assistant in the Laboratory' at the University of Sydney in 1872, the same year the Overland Telegraph began its operations. Trained at the Royal School of Mines and the Royal College of

Chemistry, he was appointed to the chair of geology and mineralogy in 1874. (He 'knew nothing about geology', Georgina commented in her memoirs,[7] and while this was one of her not uncommon exaggerations, in the matter of formal qualifications Liversidge was certainly not alone: T.W.E. David had an Oxford degree in classics; William Stephens, appointed in 1882 to a lectureship in geology and physical geography as well as to the chair of natural history, a new creation, was by training a classicist and mathematician.)

As Edgeworth David did later, Sydney's new professor of geology set scientific circles humming. 'We never got a move on till Liversidge came', noted Dr Carl Adolph Leibius, when Liversidge as joint honorary secretary (Leibius was the other) woke the Royal Society of New South Wales from its slumbers;[8] and, whatever the state of his geological knowledge, he went on to build a reputation as 'the greatest organiser of science that Australia has ever seen'.[9]

In 1888 the widespread branches of colonial science in Australia and New Zealand united for the first general meeting of the AAAS. It was a sign of increasing self-confidence, and members came to Sydney looking for full cooperation and mutual support. A defining moment in our history, too, as colonial science prepared to stand alone. On the eve of proceedings, members and guests gathered informally in Sydney University's Great Hall. High overhead the roof with its carvings in the Gothic style aped its English antecedents, but there was nothing sham about the gathering below. Over the checkered marble floor, dappled with light from the opulent stained-glass windows in the mediaeval style, moved gentlemen scientists and professional savants, accompanied by their wives and daughters. The whisper of rich silks mingled with the hum of expectant conversation while portraits of British 'greats' gazed blindly down on colonial aspirations.

On that last Tuesday evening of August 1888, new men prepared to strut their stuff and old men came to watch. Among the latter was Dr George Bennett, who in deference to his past achievements (if not his present contributions[10]) had been elected joint honorary secretary of the AAAS and a member of the general committee.[11] Bennett was now the unchallenged patriarch of colonial science (W.B. Clarke had died ten years earlier, in 1878). At eighty-four and magnificently white haired, Bennett was still an impressive figure; as a friend of Sir Richard Owen, the 'dinosaur-designer' and implacable foe of Darwin, Bennett was a living link with the achievements of the past. By 1888, in fact, the doctor, whose endeavours on Owen's behalf have become the stuff of scientific legend, was considered something of a dinosaur himself.

The first congress of what would become the Australian and New Zealand Association for the Advancement of Science (ANZAAS) in 1930, began next day on Wednesday, 29 August 1888, and continued until the following Monday,

> *[t]o give a strong impulse and a more systematic direction to scientific enquiry; to promote the intercourse of those who cultivate science in different parts of the Australasian colonies and in other countries; and to obtain a more general attention to the objects of science . . .*[12]

The previous evening, Miss Georgina King, who at forty-three was well past her youthful bloom, had been more than happy to share the attentions lavished on the superannuated physician as Dr Bennett's attentive companion. Now as a bona fide member of the scientific congress[13] she found herself caught up in the wave of enthusiasm electrifying the great mock Gothic hall, and listened intently as H.C. Russell, New South Wales government astronomer and AAAS president, proclaimed the new association's aims.

The programme that followed ranged from 'Astronomy, Mathematics, Physics and Mechanics' (Section A) through to 'Architecture and Engineering' (Section J). Natural history, mineralogy and meteorology were well represented, while anthropology found a place on the 'lunatic fringe'. The section for geology, Georgina's especial interest since those childhood visits to Clarke's parsonage at St Leonard's, was well attended. Fifteen papers were read – only one short of the largest section, biology, and a mark of the popularity enjoyed by this relatively new science of the rocks. In addition to the lectures, the AAAS meeting 'progressed majestically' through a week of ceremonies and *converzationes*, while excursions were undertaken to the Jenolan Caves, the Prospect Dam and 'the Sewage Farm at Cook's River'.[14]

Five years had passed since Georgina King's homecoming from her European tour. Money appears to have been no object while she was on her travels, and in this one detects the generous hand of Frederick Humphery. Keen to recompense his sister-in-law's devotion towards his orphaned son, he would have hoped to assuage her grief at the way in which the little Springwood household was broken up. In this he succeeded handsomely: by any standards it was a magnificent experience for someone hitherto confined to the eastern edge of New South Wales. Georgina travelled widely, covering the length and breadth of Great Britain and yachting on the Clyde in Scotland. A prolonged sortie into Ireland followed, where she was feted by her cousin, the Dean of St Patrick's Cathedral, Dublin, and chaplain of the Chapel Royal. In Belfast she met her wealthy Ewart relations who had significant interests in the Irish linen industry. She visited the north of the island and the great basaltic mass of the 'Giant's Causeway' projecting into the sea off County Antrim. On the homeward journey she visited Paris, Turin and Rome before joining her steamer at Naples.

Stimulated by her experiences overseas and apparently reconciled to the loss of little Esca, when she attended the inaugural meeting of the AAAS in August 1888 she was ready to strike out in new directions. The social skills acquired as an urban parson's daughter, together with an increased self-assurance resulting from her travels overseas, served her well at the congress and at home. It was a poised Miss King who gave an afternoon tea party for some fifty guests at 'Ashfield', the house she shared with her parents at Homebush in Sydney's southern suburbs, where George King had retired in 1879.

Unlike the company described by Thomas Carlyle in Georgina's beloved *Sartor Resartus*,[15] the group she assembled in her pleasant garden was not quite the 'choicest party of dames and chevaliers'.[16] Nor did they engage in 'trustful evening conversation' (this, after all, was late nineteenth-century Sydney where, even then, it paid to watch your back). Her contribution to the sparkling proceedings of that August week of the AAAS was intended as a brilliant beginning to her career as a geologist, a career in which the accredited geologists she courted would – she hoped – play a significant part. Georgina's consummate networking on this occasion was totally effective, and her party, she noted with satisfaction, 'was a great success'.[17]

'Embowered amid rich foliage, rose-clusters, and the hues and odours of a thousand flowers' as Diogenes Teufelsdrökh might have put it, sat William Woolls, the noted clergyman-botanist (now retired). With him were two distinguished government geologists: Robert Logan Jack of Queensland[18] and T.W. Edgeworth David who held an identical position in New South Wales. Jack was in town as president of the geology section at the congress. David was its vice-president and he gave two major papers.[19] It was these two men whom Georgina singled out to help further her aspirations.

CHAPTER TEN

A Toast to the Ladies

Despite the invitation to ladies to take part in the first meeting of the AAAS, a woman's place was still considered to be in the home. Gardening, botanical collecting and flower painting were genteel pursuits for a lady. Georgina's mother had indulged her interests in the natural world in this most conventional way while the family was in Fremantle and 'took great delight in the native flowers which she painted most beautifully'. She sent her paintings home to Grandma Mathewson in Ireland, a gentlewoman who, 'when botany was only in its infancy', had carried a hand lens about with her 'examining all the flowers she met with'.[1]

Western Australia is still one of the richest places on earth for botanists and lovers of wildflowers. Jane King's contemporary, Georgiana Molloy of Busselton, was a woman whose contribution to the knowledge of Western Australian botany was still celebrated by her European beneficiaries long after her untimely death in 1843. Mrs Molloy (1805–1843) arrived at Augusta in Western Australia's south in 1830 with her husband, Captain John Molloy, who founded the settlement. Among the profusion of glorious spring-flowering native plants, Georgiana turned to botany by way of distraction from her domestic worries. In December 1836 she was drawn into a network of collectors who sent plants and seeds back to James Mangles in Britain,[2] and so good did she prove at her task that she became a tremendous source of information for the taxonomists at Kew. For this she received no recognition in her lifetime nor, being modest about her talents, did she expect any. The only reputation enhanced by Mrs Molloy was that of her absent patron, Captain Mangles.

Through the efforts of this gifted woman, Western Australia's state emblem, the green and red kangaroo paw (*Anigozanthos manglesii*) was discovered and given a name – although obviously not her own,[3] for to men fell the pleasant duty of naming the plants the fairer sex had found. Had she lived longer than her thirty-eight years she might have gained a lasting reputation as a collector, although she was not considered eligible for the title of 'scientist' – that, like the term 'explorer', was a solely masculine occupation.

Women like Mrs Molloy continued a trend in vogue in late eighteenth-century Europe, when botany was considered a suitable accomplishment for young women – combining as it did exercise, the arts and a reverence for the works of the Almighty.[4] (Both Georgina King's mother and grandmother were products of this environment.) As the first professor of botany at London University remarked in his inaugural address:

> *It has been very much the fashion of late years [he was speaking in 1829] in this country, to undervalue the importance of this science, and to consider it an amusement for ladies rather than an occupation for the serious thoughts of man.*[5]

Things changed pretty quickly after that – the men grabbed the hand lens, and when they moved to centre stage botany became more of a professional culture. Women collectors, although classed as amateurs by virtue of their gender, remained central to the enterprise of classifying Australia's flora, yet the contribution of only one – Miss Louisa Atkinson, later Mrs James Calvert – was acknowledged in Bentham's preface to the first volume of the *Flora Australiensis*, published in 1863; the contribution of Georgiana Molloy was disregarded altogether.

At the time of Bentham's *Flora*, Ferdinand Mueller was the sole taxonomist working in Australia (other botanic garden directors sent their collections directly to the Kew Herbarium outside London for classification), and by George Bentham's death in 1882 the mantle of scientific imperialism had shifted to Mueller's slight shoulders. Rather in the same way that W.B. Clarke received the accolade of 'Father of Australian Geology', Mueller is seen as the founder of Australian botany. Despite the overseas honours that came his way, he did not wear his mantle with the insouciance of one 'born to the purple'. After all, his path to the botanical heights had been paved with professional difficulties and personal ridicule. In Melbourne, where clannishness along ethnic lines was sanctioned – provided it smacked of the Anglo-Saxon or the Celt – Mueller was referred to as 'the great Herr von Duffer' and his loyal staff at the Melbourne Botanic Gardens as 'a retinue of Teutons'.[6]

The list of women who supplied plants to Ferdinand Mueller is an especially long one, although Mueller's network was only in its infancy when the *Flora Australiensis* was entrusted to George Bentham in 1861. Mueller's own efforts in the field supported the ambitious undertaking based at Kew and greatly contributed to its completion. His possibilities as a 'faithful jackal' were seized upon, since the properties of a jackal were exactly what the botanising British required – the beast in human form has been seen for centuries as one 'who does the mean work for another'.[7] Colonials went on scavenging for years, grateful to be part of the mainstream scientific endeavour whereby, much in the same way their government imposed social systems on indigenous and colonising populations overseas, British botanists brought order (and orders) to the natural world.

In 1873 Mueller lost the unequal battle to keep his directorship of the Botanic Gardens while retaining his post as the Victorian government botanist, a position he had held since 1853. His network of collectors continued to develop, and by 1896 when he died it was amazingly diverse, covered most of the Australian colonies, and was made up mostly, if not exclusively, of women.[8] A letter to the Western Australian *Inquirer*, 11 May 1870, reveals a little of his modus operandi:

Dear Sir, Permit me to call the ladies' attention through your widely circulated journal to the very interesting employment of preserving flowers and seaweed. I have just received a communication from Dr Mueller M.D. of the Botanical garden in Melbourne who is very anxious to obtain specimens of the above from this Colony. Those who are disposed to amuse themselves at their leisure will find the best time for collecting seaweed is to take a walk on the beach immediately after a blow during the winter months.[9]

Fifteen years later Mueller once again asked for the help of 'ladies and gentlemen' in collecting specimens 'particularly at the remotest eastern and north-eastern settlements of W.A.' (this time through the pages of the *West Australian*).[10] The continued success of such appeals was not surprising. The fact that Mueller paid his workers goes a long way towards explaining the size and number of the subsequent collections, and the prestige in corresponding with a baron almost certainly helped. Mueller was assisted by his sister and nieces who lived in South Australia,[11] a colony where advertising worked as well as it did further to the west. Miss Jessie Louisa Hussey was one of the women who joined the network (from Port Elliot) and between the years 1893–1899 she supplied the botanist with over 2000 different species of seaweeds. The plants Mrs Annie F. Richards collected for Mueller from 1873 to 1894 reflect her policeman husband's postings: Fowler's Bay, Venus Bay and other locations on the Eyre Peninsula, plus Beltana in the upper Flinders and in the northern Mount Lofty Ranges.

Not all Mueller's correspondents were wives or single women helping out at home. There were also genteel ladies with a gift for botanical painting; there were those who earned a living from their art. Typical of the former was Fanny Ann Charsley of Melbourne,[12] while Marian Ellis Rowan, a gifted artist who won worldwide acclaim, combined her painting with a vigorous pursuit of wildlife in all its forms. Exhibiting her paintings with unprecedented success on four continents, and with the means to travel, Ellis Rowan had no need to earn her living from her brush. The Scott sisters, Helena and Harriet, however, painted as professionals and brought a knowledgeable eye to the specimens they sent Herr Doktor Mueller. Helena Forde nee Scott was a devoted friend of Louisa Atkinson (later Mrs James Calvert), a talented amateur artist who, although 'a lady', wrote articles on the bush and country life for the *Sydney Morning Herald* and the *Sydney Mail* for which she presumably was paid. There were other ladies of quality and social standing connected with Mueller's botanical work, but Louisa Atkinson is of the most interest to us here, linked as she was to the individuals who encouraged Georgina King to make a serious scientific study of the natural world.

As Georgina grew up, into the newspaper columns entitled 'Science Notes', 'The Cultivator', 'Mines and Mining', 'Facts for Farmers', and 'Science-Invention', crept an insidious little voice – 'A Voice from the Country' – the voice of Louisa Atkinson, a woman who surely broke the mould. A King family friend, the Reverend William Woolls, introduced Louisa to Mueller and also to the Reverend W.B. Clarke and other respected men of science. In her brief adult life she combined the eye of a collector with the mind of a naturalist, going further in her conclusions than was expected of one of her sex.[13] Given the position of women at the time and their exclusion from scientific circles, Louisa Atkinson's success as a naturalist might seem surprising – until we remember that she dealt directly with Ferdinand Mueller in Melbourne. Mueller was nothing if not appreciative in dealing with his correspondents and collectors, and the fact that George Bentham made 116 mentions of Louisa Atkinson's specimens in the *Flora Australiensis* is a measure both of her skill and the baron's sense of justice and fair play. Georgina knew of the older woman's work even if she did not know her personally (Miss Atkinson did not live in Sydney), and it seems likely she took her as her model.

Certainly, by the time this first gathering of the AAAS was over Georgina had no doubts at all as to her own capabilities and chances of success. Thus, when Dr Bennett's protégée began her own forays into nature, and began to postulate her own theories and opinions, she expected to receive similarly equitable treatment from the gentlemen with whom she came in contact.

CHAPTER ELEVEN

A Place in the Sun

With one notable exception, Georgina's family was uncomfortable with the direction this single (and single-minded) woman was taking. Jane King and Rebecca May remained openly dismissive (the latter thinking that Georgina would be better off writing 'popular stories' *à la* Ethel Turner – they would at least bring in some cash[1]). Like George Bennett, however, Frederick Humphery recognised the active mind that set his sister-in-law apart from her stolid unimaginative siblings, and it was with both men's encouragement that Georgina set about tackling many of the scientific conundrums of the day.

During the years 1888 to 1893 she consulted Sydney's geologists on a plethora of geological matters. She wrote, for example, to Charles Wilkinson, New South Wales government geologist (with 'inquiries about the origins of precious stones', 'quartz reefs' and 'the matrix of gold'); and to Edward Pittman, chief mining engineer for the colony (on the nature of the geological strata of New South Wales). The answers she received were unfailingly courteous and often informative, but none of the experts she consulted – with the possible exception of T.W. Edgeworth David, an authority on the 'Origin of Kerosene Shale' – was prepared to offer her more than the time it took to answer one of her letters.[2] For his part, Henry Chamberlain Russell, government astronomer and meteorologist, with whom she maintained a lengthy correspondence into the mid 1890s, was pleasantly non-committal. 'You are always working at something and I am sure you must find a great deal of pleasure in it. How much happier one is with an object in life than without one', he remarked early in 1891.[3]

When Georgina began collecting specimens on behalf of 'serious' scientists, neither her mother nor her sister objected – to do so was both traditional and respectable, and if it took her away from Sydney no obstacles appear to have been put in her way. The money for travel was forthcoming (here again one suspects the generosity of Frederick Humphery) and Georgina was allowed occasional respite from her household duties, demanding elderly parents, and her carping married sister.

The two men who benefited most from her early expeditions were J.H. Maiden, curator of the Sydney Technological Museum, and Baron Ferdinand von Mueller. Like Mueller, Maiden came to Australia for reasons of health. Like him, he embraced his new country and its unparalleled flora with enthusiasm and explored ways in which trees and plants might be exploited for the common good. Maiden arrived in 1880 with the intention of staying only one year, long enough to set his health to rights. He had studied chemistry under Professor Barff at the University of London, and once Maiden reached Sydney, Barff's friend Archibald Liversidge offered him the position of curator at the new Technological Museum (now the Powerhouse Museum). There, as his biographers tell us,[4] Maiden established himself as an expert in economic botany, conducting research into the useful properties of Australian timbers and essential oils.

Georgina's donations to the Technological Museum range from 'Specimens of Fungus' and 'Native Bread, *mylitta australis* Birk' (gifted in February 1891) to a 'Collection of sponges containing about: 20 Specimens from Kiama, Wollongong, and one from the South Seas' (gifted in February 1895).[5] They also include seeds, eucalypt gum (or kino) foliage, fossils of various descriptions, and examples of native craft. What Maiden made of the eclectic sweep of Miss King's offerings we can only guess, but the curator was not slow in offering fulsome thanks, as well as exploiting her contacts in the Blue Mountains and her undoubted local knowledge:

Dear Miss King

I have been asked to make a display of Native flowers at the Horticultural Society's Show at the Town Hall on the 22nd & 23rd inst. As you have kindly helped me in past years, may I ask the further kindness of a box to arrive here late on the 21st or the very first thing on the 22nd.

I enclose a label which will bring the box freight free.

As flowers can be too common: I simply want them fresh.

Yours truly

J.H. Maiden, CURATOR

At the side of his letter Maiden added: 'Can you get me any from Springwood or Wentworth Falls?'[6]

The friendships Georgina forged so happily during the years in the Blue Mountains with Esca were evergreen, and she frequently returned to visit friends in Springwood. Thus, it was no trouble at all for her to comply with Maiden's requests. Each year the Australian bush bloomed briefly in vases for the populace of Sydney as Miss King obligingly produced her boxes full of springtime glory (a practice she continued long after Maiden took on the directorship of the Botanic Garden and was replaced as curator of the Technological Museum by Richard Baker).[7]

Georgina was forty-seven years of age when she became part of Baron von Mueller's celebrated network of collectors in 1892. She was staying at 'Moorecourt', the Springwood home of her friends the Moores, where the Reverend Hussey Burgh McCartney, son of Mueller's friend the Anglican Dean of Melbourne, was also a guest. McCartney was sufficiently impressed with his new acquaintance to bring her to Mueller's notice – deeming them to be 'kindred spirits' who should get to know each other.[8] He subsequently introduced them by letter, and Georgina met Mueller twice in Melbourne, in 1895 and again in 1896.[9]

The relationship between the couple flourished, and it would always have a special significance for Georgina. Others, too, would accord it the importance it deserved. On the first anniversary of the botanist's death Georgina's floral tribute secured 'first place after his relations' on the grave,[10] and she was also acknowledged as 'one of his true friends and co-workers' by his executor and devotee, the Reverend W. Potter (of 'Vonmueller', Arnold Street, South Yarra), in enlisting her help in establishing a permanent memorial for their mutual friend.[11]

In 1892 Mueller's New South Wales network already included Dr William Woolls and the Scott sisters, Harriet and Helena, all of whom were now living in Sydney and counted Georgina a friend. The 'star of the show', however, was still the late Louisa Atkinson (who had died in 1872), whose exploits made her Mueller's unassailable 'leading lady' and an enduring force in New South Wales. The fern gullies of the Kurrajong district brought Louisa her greatest successes, and may have inspired Georgina's earlier interest in ferns (see Chapter Eight).[12] Now she was all set to follow in the dead woman's footsteps (metaphorically speaking).

In *The Natural Art of Louisa Atkinson*, Dr Elizabeth Lawson uses the term 'arrogant lack of reflection' to describe Louisa's participation in 'the great scientific enterprise of her imperial-colonial world'. Like other naturalists, 'she clearly accepted the New South Wales bushland as a place for collection, dissection, classification, naming, description', and her enthusiasm was reflected in her writing.[13] Unlike Atkinson, Georgina did not bring the beady eye of a botanist to her work when she began collecting for Ferdinand Mueller. Her own undoubted enthusiasm was linked to a wish to be of service, rather than to vaunt her actual knowledge – which appears to have been fairly rudimentary. And, since Mueller's practice of immortalising the names of his helpers was well known (see, for example, *Epacris calvertiana*, named for Mrs James Calvert, the former Miss Atkinson) there was always the hope that, like Louisa, she might find something hitherto unknown and be suitably rewarded.

Georgina's first chance of recognition came through her collections of 'sea grasses' or Zostera while staying at the seaside resort of Coogee.[14] In fact, she may have discovered a new species. In his letter of 26 November 1896, Professor Sir Frederick McCoy told her: 'It was Professor [Jakob Georg] Agardh who named the new specimen after you & acknowledged your scientific labor, as himself the greatest authority on Algae.'[15] Unfortunately, this claim re the Zostera has proved impossible to verify. Through a mix up at the herbarium, the specimen was never sent to Agardh in Sweden and there is every reason to suppose that it went astray during the ransacking of Mueller's home that occurred as the botanist lay dying.[16]

Apart from the ill-fated seaweed and a specimen of the black-and-yellow flowered *Kennedia nigricans*,[17] the majority of plants recorded in Georgina's name at the Melbourne Herbarium are indigenous to the Blue Mountains of New South Wales. Although hampered by the petticoats and skirts that were the uniform of the Victorian female, and shod in sturdy high-buttoned boots, it was here that Georgina struck out in pursuit of booty for her newfound friend. Apparently combining the stamina of an athlete with the surefootedness of a mountain goat, this tall, strongly built middle-aged spinster lady tramped for miles over the wildest terrain from high heath to hanging swamp, leaning over cliff edges and venturing into gullies to grasp many an elusive prize.

She was, one suspects, enthusiastic rather than discriminating in her selections, preferring the colourful and brash where Louisa Atkinson with her superior knowledge targeted the modest and – importantly – the hitherto undescribed. Vigorous climbing plants such as *Kennedia rubicunda* (the 'dusky coral pea') and the 'bacon and egg' pea flower *Dillwynia* fell prey to Georgina's foraging, as did the equally showy *Hardenbergia violacea* ('false sarsaparilla') with its coiling stems and exuberant purple flowers.[18] Then there was *Sprengelia incarnata*, whose soft pink-and-white panicles provided a foil to the delicate blue sun orchid *Thelymitra ixioides*.[19] None of these plants was particularly uncommon. It was only when Georgina came upon a confusing specimen of *Boronia pinnata* that, like *T. ixioides*, she briefly blossomed in the sun.

On 16 September 1896 a letter arrived from Baron von Mueller.[20] The botanist was suffering from influenza and the letter was dictated. 'It will be pleasing to you when you hear that amongst the native plants sent by you some time ago is the Boronia floribunda on which your specimens shed additional light', Mueller wrote, and went on to explain a little of the plant's history. *B. floribunda* had been discovered in 1823 by F.W. Sieber, one of the foreign collectors who targeted Australia so successfully in the early 1800s (see Chapter Nine). George Bentham dismissed it as a dimorphic form of *Boronia pinnata* in the *Flora Australiensis* of 1863, but now that Georgina had given him the opportunity to examine a fresh specimen, Mueller was able to confirm that *B. floribunda* was indeed a species in its own right. In conclusion, Mueller explained the basic differences between the two species, telling Georgina what to look for in future, since 'Sieber does not seem to have found fruiting specimens which will now fall to your share —'[21]

A week later Mueller was thanking her for the specimens she sent him from the Hawkesbury River. He enclosed 'sketches of the flowers of both [species] so that you will easily understand to discriminate these plants and find out more localities, for it seems restricted to your region'.[22] He was already planning a 'preliminary article' for the Linnean Society of New South Wales, and when this was duly written it was delivered to Elizabeth Bay House by Georgina, to be read at the society's meeting at the beginning of October. The ailing Mueller confidently expected that 'the essay can be extended when later in the season the fruit of B. floribunda can in full ripeness be obtained'. 'Can I reckon on your kindness in this also', he enquired.[23]

As happened later with the sea grass or Zostera, things now

went awry. For Georgina, the timing was wrong, and even less auspicious for the baron – for neither he nor Georgina had any premonition that this work would be his last. What Mueller considered 'influenza' carried him off within a couple of weeks, and he died on 10 October 1896.

'Notes on *Boronia floribunda*, Sieber' was published the following year in *The Proceedings of the Linnean Society of New South Wales, 1896*.[24] In it the now defunct Mueller paid tribute to 'the zealous amateur lady naturalist of your colony' who 'forwarded splendid specimens of *B. floribunda* to me from the Hawkesbury River, her plant proving to be the genuine one of Sieber'.

But by then Mueller's successor, J.G. Luehmann, had unwittingly ruined the effect of Mueller's appreciation. 'Is it not remarkable that Dr. Woolls never noticed B. floribunda?' he wrote to Georgina in January 1897.[25]

> *There is no specimen in our herbarium from him, but we have it from Mrs. Rowan (who paints the Australian flowers), from Botany Bay collected by Baron von Mueller 40 years ago, and a specimen from Middle Harbour without the collector's name as well as several of Sieber's original plants.*

Far from 'rediscovering' a long lost flower and being covered in associated glory, Georgina had come full circle, back to her role as a mere collector: 'You would much oblige by sending me some fruiting specimens of this plant', Luehmann requested in conclusion.

CHAPTER TWELVE

Science and Societies

The Royal Society of New South Wales in the 1890s was home to the time-honoured tradition that still exists in Academe today – one by which a dominant clique ensures that those who know their place put down those who do not. Cliques and factions were as old as the colony itself, for colonial science was elitist from the start. The Agriculture Society, founded under the aegis of Governor Lachlan Macquarie in 1818, wilted and withered on the vine when free settlers refused to mix with former convicts.

From its first meeting in June 1821 at the Sydney home of Justice Barron Field, the Philosophical Society of Australasia continued this unfortunate trend. As well as Field – a paradox of a man with 'a violent and unforgiving temper' who loathed convicts yet spread the word of God to native Australians[2] – the society comprised 'seven men prominent in the colony's affairs; mercantile, medical, legal, political and geographical'. Taking the ultra-elite Royal Society of London as its model, it proved every bit as 'exclusive', 'secretive', 'solemn, narrow, aloof and highbrow' as the original.[2]

Sir Thomas Makdougall Brisbane (1773–1860) was one of Wellington's successful generals and an astronomer and meteorologist of note. When he became president of the Philosophical Society of Australasia, the organisation should have received a tremendous boost. Instead, it became remarkable for its divisions. A year after succeeding Macquarie (in November 1821), Brisbane fell victim to the same backbiting as his predecessor. He and his fellow liberals found themselves in one camp, the

Reverend Samuel Marsden, Justice Field and their 'exclusivist' convict-hating cronies in the other. Before long, Governor Brisbane was referring to the 'slander and malevolence' that 'constantly stalked abroad' in New South Wales.[3]

Matters on the scientific front improved with the recall of Brisbane in 1824 and the arrival of Alexander McLeay as colonial secretary (or second in command to Governor Darling) in 1826. McLeay brought a sense of decorum to a circle acrimoniously made up of 'us' and 'them'. He was a Fellow of the Linnean Society and a Councillor of the Royal Society of London. He was a friend of Sir Joseph Banks and Sir William Hooker, director of the Royal Botanic Gardens at Kew. McLeay had wealth, political influence and prestige, and, along with his wife and six daughters, he brought with him his fine natural history collections and an enormous interest in his new surroundings. With such a leader, Sydney science found itself 'on a bit of a roll'.[4]

Macleays (the spelling preferred by Alexander's sons) would dominate New South Wales' science for the next two generations. White and resplendent, their house at Elizabeth Bay resembled a nobleman's palace; in the gardens were to be found 'the plants of every climate from Rio to the West and East Indies, China and even England'.[5] It was a manmade paradise (Alexander McLeay was said to have spent £3000 on the lawns alone), and its owner remained as impervious to the dissensions fermenting outside his extensive grounds as he was to his numerous debts.

In the 1840s the scientific community fractured once again. Science became a matter of national pride, not the province of the privileged few, and two distinct factions emerged: that of the wealthy Macleays and their adherents; and that of the *professional* men dependent on the public purse, and theirs. As these professionals took the ascendant, yet another scientific society was formed.

The Australian Society for the Encouragement of Arts, Science, Commerce and Agriculture saw the light of day in January 1850. More comfortably known as the Australian Philosophical Society and its members as 'philosophers', the new body was well supported but again failed to prosper. This time it was the presence of gold, rather than the absence of harmony, that was the major cause. From 1851 members took themselves off to the diggings, while the 'Linneans' of Elizabeth Bay, who had no need to go grubbing in the earth for riches, continued to command the true flagship of scientific enterprise, the Australian Museum.[6]

With the arrival of the new governor-general of the Australian colonies, Sydney's self-styled 'philosophers' were in for a bit of a shock. Sir William Denison, a man with a keen interest in science, engineering and sewerage, arrived in Sydney in January 1855. After an uncomfortable eight years as lieutenant governor of Van Diemen's Land (renamed Tasmania in 1856), dealing with convicts, ex-convicts and awkward local leaders, science Sydney-style presented very few problems for Sir William. Before long the failing Australian Philosophical Society was given a shot in the arm (and a kick in the pants). By 1856 it was calling itself the Philosophical Society *of New South Wales*, with Denison presiding over regular monthly meetings.

Meanwhile, under first William Sharp Macleay then his cousin William John, Elizabeth Bay House remained the focal point of science as practised by the Linneans (the term denotes an interest in the descriptive and taxonomic aspects of natural history). In 1862 W.J. Macleay co-founded the Entomological Society of New South Wales, a society that provided work for Georgina's friends the Scott sisters (see Chapter Ten) and made them honorary members. In 1874 he would also found the Linnean Society of New South Wales.

Eleven years after Denison's intervention, the Philosophical Society changed its name one last time. The Royal Society of New South Wales, as it was now to be known, held its first meeting on 9 July 1867 with the inaugural address given by the Reverend W.B. Clarke, that venerable survivor of its earlier incarnations. The aims of the society as stated by Clarke were as follows:

> *We must strive to discern clearly, understand fully, and report faithfully; to love truth in things physical as in things moral; to abjure hasty theories and unsupported conjectures; where we are in doubt, not to be positive; to give our brother observer the same measure of credit we take for ourselves; not striving for mastery, but leaving time for the formation of the judgement which will inevitably be given, whether for or against us; contented if we are able to add but one grain to that enduring pyramid which is now in course of erection as the testimony of nature to the truth of Revelation.*[7]

If Georgina King is to be believed, 'truth' and 'things moral', as aspired to by the Royal Society of New South Wales in the 1860s, had little to do with the society as she knew it in the 1890s. 'Slander', 'malevolence' ... the nastiness experienced by Thomas Brisbane in the 1820s, and echoed in the tensions between the amateur and full-time (modern professional) scientists in the 1840s, had been simmering along nicely ever since then. Spite and malicious gossip were still very much the norm. While as a woman Georgina was excluded from membership, with her connections in Academe she was as well placed as anyone to know of the unpleasant state of affairs prevailing within the magic circle. She knew of it personally, too. During the first five years of the 1890s, whenever she tried to have her geological papers read on her behalf at the society's meetings, the 'scientific clique' (as she called it) at the society's centre blocked her at every turn.

Nonetheless, encouraged by friends like Ferdinand Mueller and determined to honour her promise to Dr George Bennett,

Georgina worked tirelessly on behalf of science. When she developed her own network ('I am devoted to science, and have many collectors in all parts of the country'[8]) the specimens and artifacts that came her way were impressive in their range. 'Mr. Eric Ross of Delta Downs Queensland', for example, sent Georgina cores from a diamond drill operating at Croydon, and possibly the dilly bag 'made of grass and stained by the natives of Gulf of Carpentaria' that were added to the Technological Museum's collection in 1894 also came from him. ('Is it made from grass fibre? It looks much more like some bark fibre', queried J.H. Maiden, the curator.[9]) That year Georgina loaned a terracotta Mexican image, and part of a plaster ornament retrieved from the ruins of Palenque by a missionary friend serving in Central America. (These were retrieved the following year when relations between donor and curator cooled – gifts from Georgina being usually the expression of personal warmth rather than philanthropy on a grander scale.)

Throughout her life she was sensitive – too sensitive – to slights, and as her father's daughter and a witness to his various struggles against superior forces she had learned the importance of natural justice. As a result, she invariably insisted that credit be given where credit was due – as was not always the case in certain quarters. 'Dear Mr. Maiden', she wrote on one occasion:

> *I am sending you the marine Carboniferous fossils in five wooden boxes in a large box. I wish you to give Mr. Sydney Dodds of Vermont Malbring, via Maitland the credit of those that came from Mount Vincent, although I settled by a number of Books with him long ago for them, nevertheless it will encourage him to have them presented as by himself – and he was not well treated by the Mines Department. I innocently defrauded you of some which Mr. Dodds had intended for the Technological Museum when I introduced him to Mr. C.S. Wilkinson. Please give Mr. Thornton the credit of those he got for me also – they are so marked.*[10]

Although their household was a modest one, the Kings could afford to employ a general servant, Hannah Thornton, whose father is mentioned above. Like Sydney Dodds, the main subject of Georgina's letter, Robert Thornton, worked at a colliery outside Newcastle, and, when it is pieced together from an examination of Georgina's papers, his story is further evidence of her generosity of spirit. 'The daughter of a coal miner, named Thornton, came to live with us as a domestic about 1892', she writes in her autobiography:

> *... and through her I found that her Father was a perfect genius, in collecting and preserving Wood Moths, and their natural history, from when he was a boy ... I bought a number of the moths from Thornton, and gave them to Dr. Maiden for the Technological Museum.*[11]

Notes on the life history of the wood moths would cost Miss King a further '£1.0.0.' and these she donated to the museum as well.[12]

W.W. Froggatt, the Technological Museum's entomologist, was a member of the Linnean Society of New South Wales. When he came to write up the wood moths in the society's journal he was the soul of courtesy and circumspection. He acknowledged that his account was not only 'Chiefly compiled from the Notes of Mr. R. Thornton, of Wallsend, N.S.W.', but that the collection of these very wood moths was made available to the Technological Museum 'through the liberality of Miss Georgina King, of Homebush'.[13] He sent a reprint of his paper to Georgina, and, as in the case of *Boronia floribunda*, this kind of acknowledgement was all that she wanted. When it came to her geological research, however, nothing short of total public recognition would do.

In the autobiography she lodged in the Mitchell Library a few years before her death, Georgina King emphasised the influence on her life of forces she calls 'environment', and what her contemporaries termed 'environmentalism' or 'environmental determinism'. Looking back as she prepared her personal vindication, there was no doubt at all in her mind that her work had been dictated, not so much by natural and man-made surroundings, but by the people and events that shaped her behaviour from a very early age. She had been marked out for a mission. Not by destiny, but by a series of circumstances and mentors for the part she was intended to play. Thus, when confronted by the obstacles placed in her path by the committee of the Royal Society of New South Wales, Georgina King – who from birth was blessed (or, some might say, 'cursed') with her father's strength of character and taste for contention, and dubbed, remember, 'his little philosopher' from the age of three – was not easily deterred.

CHAPTER THIRTEEN

Gold Standards

The history of gold in Australia is marked by murder and mayhem. Happily, though, for the conflicting Georgina King and Archibald Liversidge, deceit, not bloodshed, was involved. The story of gold discovery arguably begins with Paul Edmund de Strzelecki, a self-taught geologist (and self-styled Polish count), who arrived in the convict colony of New South Wales in 1839. During the course of extensive fieldwork, he detected traces of gold in iron pyrites near Hartley in the Blue Mountains, and in quartz near Wellington on the Fish River north of Orange. It was a discovery he agreed to keep to himself in the interest of public order. That same year saw the arrival in New South Wales of Georgina's mentor, the Reverend W.B. Clarke. Clarke was impoverished and suffering from the effects of a rheumatic fever – a fever that failed to prevent a series of punishing field trips that resulted in a similar discovery of gold. ('Put it away, Mr. Clarke, or we shall all have our throats cut', Governor Gipps famously urged him in 1844.[1]) That gold also came from the quartziferous slates near Hartley, and from the Bathurst region.

Clarke, a small man who added to his presence with a flowing 'Old Testament' kind of a beard, quickly became a giant in Australian geological circles. Described as 'tenacious and often a sharp controversialist', he is rightly considered the father of Australian geology,[2] and – importantly for this story – he spanned both the formative period in Georgina's highly irregular scientific education and the work she undertook later. Even from beyond the grave (he died in 1878), she was influenced by his teaching and held him in the highest esteem.

Strictly speaking, the Reverend Clarke was an amateur. Yet by no means can he be considered unqualified for his preferred area of activity. At Cambridge University he was a student of Professor Adam Sedgwick, and it was through Sedgwick – an expert on Palaeozoic fossils and a leading proponent of the Devonian system – that Clarke was introduced to geology, in those days a new and exciting field of study. Parting ways with a chronology of the Bible that fixed the Creation at 4004 BC, geology was beginning to emerge as a science based on physical evidence gathered from fieldwork, and like so many other prospective churchmen, Clarke succumbed to its lure. He was elected a Fellow of the Geological Society of London in 1826 at the age of twenty-eight, and by the time he left England for Australia as a missionary for the Society for the Propagation of the Gospel he was a highly skilled field geologist and natural historian.

Initially discouraged by Governor Gipps and his fear of murderous gold-hungry convicts, Clarke swung into action once the governor was dead. By 1847 he was advocating an official survey of New South Wales and drawing the public's attention to the possible presence of gold. Alas, when a geological surveyor was appointed in 1849, it was not the Reverend Clarke,[3] and when gold was 'officially' discovered in May 1851 Clarke received no recognition (the role of discoverer has traditionally gone to Edward Hammond Hargraves). Clarke now acted as the government's scientific adviser and served as geological surveyor from September 1851 to July 1853. Such was the force of his personality and public persona in fact, that his position as de facto 'colonial geologist' went unchallenged until his advancing old age.

Then, into Clarke's twilight years stalked Archibald Liversidge, seeking supremacy in everything to do with gold. One day Dr Charles Leibius, a former president of the Royal

Society of New South Wales, confided to Georgina that the supposedly 'shy and retiring' Liversidge was not always what he seemed. Not only did he 'torment' and 'browbeat' the ancient cleric 'whenever he tried to do original work at the Royal Society of New South Wales',[4] but (Georgina continues):

> *Dr. Leibius told me that when Dr. Helms was demonstrator to Professor Liversidge the former had not time to copy some University examination papers and he took a photograph of them and afterwards found that the latter had altered the marks.*[5]

Leibius by all accounts was 'genial', 'sincere' and direct. That he was willing to indulge in tittle-tattle with a maiden lady is a lesser-known aspect of his character. It is possible that he had no liking for Liversidge: the pair were joint honorary secretaries of the Royal Society of New South Wales at the time when Liversidge began whirling like a dervish, and the oft-quoted comment that 'we never got a move on until Liversidge arrived' may have been rueful, rather than laudatory. In 1893, and especially given Dr Leibius' revelations concerning Liversidge, Georgina had her own reasons for doubting 'the nature of the beast'.

As the man largely responsible for the foundation of the Australasian Association for the Advancement of Science (see Chapter Nine) Archibald Liversidge was one of the leading lights of the Royal Society of New South Wales. Circumstances would also turn him into one of Georgina King's principal *bêtes noires*. Liversidge was twenty-six when he joined the Royal Society after his arrival in 1872, and he is also credited with that society's rapid resurgence. One of its most productive members, and with an interest in chemical mineralogy, he had delivered no fewer than forty-two papers by 1894, when Georgina was struggling so desperately for recognition. The third edition of Liversidge's *The Minerals of New South Wales* coincided with the 1888 centenary, but nothing of similar scope followed this magnum opus. Rather, Liversidge is mostly remembered for securing a proper recognition of science within the community at large.[6]

Even before Archibald Liversidge became professor of chemistry and mineralogy in 1882, his research into the metallurgy of gold became almost an obsession – one of his very first papers (1876) had been entitled 'On the Formation of Moss Gold and Silver'. Interest in precious metals, particularly gold, may have brought him to Australia in the first place,[7] and it is tempting to compare the fledgling School of Chemistry in the early 1880s with the arcane world of alchemy in the Middle Ages, its enthusiastic new professor a latter day Paracelsus in search of the 'elixir of life' and the equally elusive 'philosopher's stone'. Yet despite invoking numerous powerful forces (scientifically speaking), Liversidge was fated to remain as much in the dark as anyone when it came to 'the origin of gold'.

When Archibald Liversidge put pen to paper in 1893 and went on to share his thoughts on gold with his scientific peers, all was quiet on the western front of New South Wales. The heady days of the gold rush were well and truly over and the formerly swinging towns of Hill End and Sofala were all but deserted. Gulgong, that erstwhile 'Hub of the World' (as it styled itself in the 1870s), had gained an incongruous respectability, but for professional geologists in Sydney gold was a hot topic still. In 1893 Miss King was working on various scientific papers under the encouraging eye of George Bennett, and she, like Liversidge, had the subject very much on her mind:

> *When writing these papers for Dr. Bennett, I thought of what the Rev. W.B. Clarke said about the Golden Springs and Lewis Ponds alluvial Gold – That he was not satisfied, but could not draw any definite conclusion about their origin.*[8]

The fact that Archibald Liversidge was 'bullying' and 'browbeating' Clarke at the time cannot have helped the parson's deliberations, and it was left to Georgina years later to tackle the tricky subject. In July 1893 she visited an unmarried friend who taught at a private school in Bathurst. It was far from a social visit: while 'Professor Liversidge, Professor David, Mr. E.F. Pittman, the Government Geologist and myself were all trying to find out the origin of cubic crystals of iron pyrites', Georgina enlisted the help of her friend Miss Keyes of the quaintly named Pixie Ladies College and set off to 'get behind Mr. Clarke's brain in the matter'.[9]

This was easier than it might seem. Georgina's network in the west proved as reliable as it was elsewhere and the help she enlisted was undeniably first rate. Miss Keyes' sister, the second Mrs Thomas Geake Webb (the first had died in 1872), lived at Byng, twelve miles east of Orange, about three miles off the present Great Western Highway between Orange and Bathurst from the turning at Lucknow. Apparently named for the unfortunate Admiral John Byng, who was shot for neglect of duty in 1757, the tiny hamlet was once known as 'Cornish Settlement' as well. The area was settled in the late 1820s by dissenting emigrants from 'the Delectable Duchy' in England's far west, the first of whom was William 'Parson' Tom. In 1828 Tom, a Methodist lay preacher, settled on a land grant on the left bank of the very same Lewis Ponds Creek mentioned by W.B. Clarke. He called it 'Springfield' and brought up a family of thirteen children – including eight strapping lads (the shortest of whom was a mere 5 feet 11 inches, the tallest 6 feet 4).[10] In 1847 Tom began building a fine two-storied house in the local sandstone mined from a quarry nearby. This he also called 'Springfield'.

Parson Tom's daughter Emma married Thomas Geake Webb in 1854 and her husband subsequently purchased the property. Two years after his first wife's death he married Jane Keyes, the sister of Georgina King's school-teaching friend. In July 1893 the second Mrs Webb (who by now was a widow) introduced Georgina to her late husband's brother-in-law, another William Tom, this one the discoverer of the Ophir goldfield. Now aged sixty-nine, he lived in the original family home and held memories of the gold rush days that were evergreen – and bitter.

Georgina must have been fascinated by everything Tom told her: the man was a living link to Australia's golden past and she so wanted to be part of any present discoveries. It was to the pleasant vale of Byng that the legendary Edward Hammond Hargraves travelled in early 1851, planning on how to make good his disappointments on the Californian goldfields. Making his way past the recently established Carangara copper smelter and following the high hawthorn hedges, Hargraves came to 'Springfield', where he crossed the traditional Cornish welcome stones set at Parson Tom's front door. In hindsight it is difficult not to see him as some latter day serpent in this Wesleyan version of Eden, and the story that unfolds tells of a similar dispossession.

Hargraves had pursued a number of occupations (none of them, it must be said, with any particular *éclat*) and was determined to find enough gold in New South Wales to claim the government reward for discovering a 'payable' goldfield. In February 1851, while on the way to the Wellington district (where 'Count' Strzelecki had noted the presence of gold in 1839), Hargraves stayed at the Guyong Inn kept by the widowed Mrs Lister just up the road from Byng. There, in what was considered to be copper country, he was shown samples of gold-bearing quartz 'and found the impetus for the goldrush he was hoping to engineer'.[11] As a result, he spent some time prospecting at Lewis Ponds Creek north of the Tom property, with the widow Lister's son as his assistant. Many hands make light work, as the saying goes, and Hargraves – who had no particular intention of dirtying his own – decided to enlist more to help. Hence his visit to the Toms.

By now, the younger Toms were pretty well scattered throughout the colony but Hargraves found two of them at home. James, twenty-nine, and William, twenty-seven, listened intently to the smooth-talking stranger with his alluring tale of hidden wealth. He then 'encouraged the Toms to go on with the search, taught them how to make a "cradle", and to conduct sluicing operations', recalled their younger sister Selina many years later. She related, too, how the brothers found a nugget 'that proved to be worth £70 and that led to the opening up of the first payable goldfields on the Turon'. To these this pious family gave the name of 'Ophir', after the mine that yielded the gold to adorn King Solomon's temple.[12] And so began the series of 'rushes' that were to shake the western district of New South Wales periodically for years to come. Tom showed Georgina the original cradle fabricated to Hargraves' design; and that first nugget he'd found at the root of a tree. He described the diggings, the terrain and what to watch out for, and Georgina – ever the alert and attentive pupil – went away enlightened.

William Tom failed to make a fortune, although he performed a vital role. In 'Sunrise', the first family homestead – 'a five-roomed house made of ready-cut laths and covered with plaster' facing east – Georgina King listened to the old man's tale of betrayal. A great log burned in the ten-foot-wide fireplace but chill winds still stole through the lathwork – much in the same way that Hargraves had insinuated himself into the confidence of a family wise in the ways of the Lord but ignorant of the ways of men. To Hargraves had gone the enduring glory – and £10,000 with it – but (Tom told his lady visitor with a noticeable touch of pride) he and his brother and John Lister, the widow's son, hadn't let it go at that. They had fought back and made the government sit up and take notice of their claims to justice. In 1853 they had been awarded £1000. But when it came to public recognition ... the old man shrugged and his lips twisted in a bitter smile. At the end of the day, as Georgina would come to agree, it was the lack of recognition that mattered – and for that, one had to fight.

Georgina's 1892 paper ('Had Eastern Australia a true Devonian Period?') contained the comment that Australian scientists 'had been working along European lines' when she 'discovered that our formations were different, and that we had no true Devonian period'. In July 1893, in the course of her visit to Byng, the discoveries she made were 'even greater':

> *and there I found the cubic crystals of iron pyrites, on the surface of the soil, in intrusive granite and in soapstone, just beside the intrusive granite, and in various basalts, and in Serpentine. Not far from the surface near, a very pretty specimen of auriferous quartz was found.*[13]

'Before the Geologists took my discoveries as their own, they had always said that our alluvial mineral wealth was owing to the denudation and erosion of other formations and that there had been tremendous rainfalls', Georgina writes.[14] And they were wrong! She had indeed 'got to the back of Mr. Clarke's brain': much of New South Wales's mineral wealth was 'intrusive' and 'had been erupted during the Tertiary Period'.[15] By postulating that dramatic volcanic action, rather than slow and persistent erosion, was responsible for the colony's alluvial mineral riches, Georgina King, an intuitive (if untutored) amateur, dared diverge from the accepted 'wisdom' of the time as promulgated by the professional geologists of New South Wales. It was a position she steadfastly maintained, but her discoveries – so generously shared with the Royal Society's membership – brought her no benefit at all.

Elated by her discoveries, Georgina bounced back to Sydney for a poignant reunion with her surviving mentor:

> *I went to see Dr. Bennett on my return from the West, to show him my specimens, and tell him all about what I had found, and seen, and he was delighted and told me to persevere. I saw him again just a fortnight before he passed away, Sept. 1893, and he held my hand till I promised to go on working at science, for he said I had a mission to my country, for he knew the geologists were wrong in their conclusions. It was this promise that made me work on all those years, surmounting all difficulties.*[16]

These discoveries made up part of a paper she handed to Archibald Liversidge in September 1894 – and subsequently published as a newspaper article in July 1895 under the title 'The Palaeozoic Carboniferous Formations in New South Wales'.[17] It was against Liversidge, for whom she admittedly had no respect or liking, that Georgina levelled her first serious charge of plagiarism and theft:

> *In September 1894, Prof. Warren took a paper of mine, that I had written about my discovery that our mineral wealth was intrusive and found in eruptive rocks, with the specimens I had collected illustrating my discoveries, to Prof. Liversidge for the Royal Society of New South Wales. Prof. Liversidge sent them back to me and replied, 'I have read your paper and examined your specimens. It is hardly suitable for the Royal Society of New South Wales. I am sorry I cannot do anything with it for you.'*[18]

The paper in question, 'Had Eastern Australia a true Devonian Period?' had been circulating among members of the Royal Society since May 1892 (see Chapter Fourteen) and Sir Frederick McCoy, FGS, FRS, professor of natural science at the University of Melbourne, had checked this latest version for its author. On 5 September 1894, and possibly by coincidence, Professor Liversidge exhibited 'The Structure of Gold Nuggets' at the society's monthly meeting. At the same venue a month later (on 3 October), the professor read the 'Preliminary Note' by means of which he set himself up as an authority on 'The Occurrence of Gold in the Hawkesbury Rocks about Sydney'.[19] At the society's *conversazione* in December 1894, Professor Liversidge showed photographs of sections of gold nuggets, native gold, gold in quartz, calcite, serpentine, and so forth, which just happened to be similar to the specimens collected by Georgina. It was the latest in a series of such coincidences and she came to the sobering conclusion that, 'unable' to help Miss King, Professor Archibald Liversidge had – quite literally – helped himself to her ideas.

Long before 'The Palaeozoic Carboniferous Formations in New South Wales' appeared in print in the *Sydney Morning Herald* in 1895, it proved a veritable 'gold mine' to Messrs Liversidge, David and Pittman. The manuscript version of the article (reproduced in full in the Appendix) provided any number of helpful clues on a comprehensive range of subjects. Between April 1892 and October 1894, the trio – in 1893–1894 the society's vice-president, honorary secretary and councillor respectively – had ample opportunity to examine it at their leisure, and to pick the eyes out of Georgina King's research. Although she had made great headway in geological matters, she had learned nothing about human nature.

William Tom waited two years for monetary recognition for his endeavours; W.B. Clarke was forced to wait for ten.[20] They were dealing with bureaucracy and the money eventually was handed over. Georgina naively equated education with honesty – a mistake belatedly pointed out by Professor William Warren (see Chapter Fourteen). She not only made the discoveries, she obligingly pointed the way. Her findings soon became common knowledge. H.C. Russell of the Sydney Observatory had heard about her visit to Orange;[21] he knew that Professor McCoy had seen her paper and was taking an interest.[22] As well as approaching J.H. Maiden at the Technological Museum on 22 August 1893 to explain the nature of her work, and asking him to analyse a soil sample, she sent him 'some cubic forms of iron found sprinkling the hill and in soap-stone in the hill' at Byng and told him:

> *The iron was ejected in cubic forms and some came down in a shower like hail while some remained in the soap-stone. All the hills or mountains appear to burst forth with lava & thermal springs in the neighbourhood of Byng at the early part of this Tertiary period. Mount Canoblas was not the only one that was in activity then. I never heard of anyone remarking this before, and I have much to investigate on the subject.*[23]

Georgina received no answer to her queries until November 1893,[24] yet the contents of the communication probably did not remain a secret from the brotherhood for long. Maiden may have had a word on the sly with his Royal Society colleagues, but this seems unlikely – he was a family friend of the Kings.

There is another possibility to be considered. Maiden did not conduct chemical analyses himself; this was the province of Henry George Smith, the museum's laboratory assistant. Smith began work at the museum as a ticket writer and painter, but improved his lot in 1884 by attending evening classes in science held under the auspices of the Board of Technical Education – of which Archibald Liversidge was a founding member. Smith duly joined the Royal Society of New South Wales, and knew Liversidge in that particular context as well. So did he drop a word in his erstwhile mentor's ear, or indeed, in Professor David's? It would explain why the contents of the paper were not new to Liversidge in 1894 – he may have been privy to Georgina's research since August the previous year . . .

Archibald Liversidge read nothing to the society between his presidential address for his term of office 1889–1890 and a paper 'On some New South Wales and other Minerals: Note No. 6' in 1891. On the evening of 6 September 1893, however, six weeks or so after Georgina's return from the west, he read no fewer than five papers on gold to his fellow members. They included 'On the Origin of Gold Nuggets' and 'On the Condition of Gold in Quartz and Calcite Veins' (plus a re-hash of the 1876 offering on 'Moss Gold').[25] He was quite blatantly staking his claim to El Dorado – and, like William Tom of Byng, Georgina King was accorded no private thanks, nor public recognition.

CHAPTER FOURTEEN

The Long Arm of Coincidence

During the period 1892–1893 Georgina submitted several versions of her paper 'Had Eastern Australia a true Devonian period?'[1] for consideration by the Royal Society of New South Wales. The paper is wide-ranging and covers the major preoccupations of Australian geologists of the time.

Coined in 1839 after the English county of Devonshire, the term 'Devonian' of Georgina's title refers both to a system of rocks below the Carboniferous and above the Silurian formations, and to the geological period to which these rocks belong – dating back, in the case of the Devonian, to some four hundred million years before the present. All three periods belong to the Palaeozoic era, when the earliest forms of life developed, and cover a time of great volcanic upheaval that resulted in the folding, uplifting and granite intrusion to which the paper refers.

In Europe, the Carboniferous system – as the name suggests – indicates the presence of coal,[2] while in Australia the question of *where exactly* (geologically speaking) coal occurred was still a matter of much debate.[3] Georgina's paper discusses, among other things, the differences between the European and Australian coal-bearing strata and the significance of fossil flora. To writing it, Georgina brought the same approach that would inform all her work in science: that of benefiting her country. She hoped 'to be useful in helping in the determining of the ages of our auriferous quartz reefs and metalliferous deposits, which will assist in the investigation of the occurrence of our mineral wealth'.

She was never one to let an interesting topic pass her by. In addition to the perennial fascination with iron that dated back to her childhood, her preoccupations prior to the inaugural AAAS congress of 1888 included 'the cause of the tilting of the earth's axis' and 'the heat given off by falling rain'.[4] A voracious reader, she regaled her friends with the facts, half-facts and theories that produced a 'rich medley' of ideas – as would later also be said of Georgina's friend, Mrs D.M. Bates. By the early 1890s Georgina had developed theories on subjects such as 'the occurrence of gold' and 'the origin of precious stones'[5] (theories that led to the experiences already related in Chapter Thirteen).

Georgina attended the first congress of the AAAS a confident, well-travelled woman, and her subsequent reflections on what she had seen in Europe – notably the differences between European and Australian geological formations – brought the major step of presenting her research to the Royal Society of New South Wales. She had been urged to work on her discoveries herself rather than entrust them to anyone else, but with a typical generosity of spirit she outlined exactly where others might see these things for themselves.

Since women were excluded from membership of the Royal Society of New South Wales, Georgina had no choice but to rely on the patronage of others. Once the Devonian paper was in the hands of the committee, she hoped that it would be read on her behalf at one of the monthly meetings. First she sent the paper to Dr Carl Adolph Leibius, a past president of the society and an acquaintance living in nearby Burwood with whom she often swapped scientific gossip. This was in May 1892. While telling her the paper was unsuitable, he would, he said, keep it until they could meet to discuss the paper more fully. (He had already shown it to E.F. Pittman of the Department of Mines for his opinion.[6]) Then in October 1892 she sent the paper – presumably revised – to another acquaintance, Henry Russell, currently president of the Royal Society (officials were elected at the annual general meeting held on the first Wednesday of May each year). 'I suppose it will come before the Council of the Society in due course', he told her.[7]

In February 1893 Georgina felt impelled to ask Russell why there had been no progress. He replied:

> *You know our Council consists of 20 persons and some are very critical about papers submitted and I fear yours would not be accepted . . . Of course my view of what would guide the Council may be very wide of the fact but you asked for my opinion.*[8]

Soon after, Georgina was advised by an academic friend to revise the paper – advice that Russell thought 'bad'. Since the Royal Society was in recess between December and May (this was the middle of March), nothing could be accepted until its first regular meeting in June. Besides, he continued, 'you do not, at least I presume you do not, yet know why it has been rejected'. It would be unwise, he told her, to rewrite 'until you know what to alter',[9] advice Georgina appears to have accepted meekly enough, even though by then the paper would have been out of her hands for over a year.

'Had Eastern Australia a true Devonian Period?' was to bring a flurry of papers from the pens of others, but its first obvious impact on what she came to call the 'corrupt scientific clique' (and what we might more diplomatically term 'the Opposition') brought a clumsy attempt to draw her in, albeit in a secondary role. William Warren, president of the Royal Society for 1892–1893, was also Challis Professor of Engineering at the University of Sydney and an acquaintance of Miss King. When he informed her 'that if [she] attended any of the classes of the Professors, [her] discoveries would come out as their pupil', the overture (on his part, at least) was well intentioned. Nonetheless, it hit a very raw nerve. For, added Warren, this was her only chance of recognition – 'as [she] had no elementary knowledge, Professor Liversidge said'.[10]

In addition to the impressive mental capacity she shared

with her ally Daisy Bates, Georgina was possessed of an equally strong sense of pride. She was infuriated. The biographical details of Daisy's early life are vague (all that can be said for sure is that she was born in Ireland), but she was an educated woman, fluent in French and German and a gifted writer.[11] How she acquired these talents is disputed and even her first biographer seems uncomfortable at the lack of proof for Daisy's claims,[12] yet whatever form it took, it *was* a *formal* education. Georgina, on the other hand, had never attended school and taught herself to read and write.

To be educated informally at home was the lot of her generation, class and sex, but while no great sums of money were invested in her education the same cannot be said of time. She was, after all, designated to be the 'old maid of the family' – which meant not only to be a household drudge but a congenial and interesting companion for her father in his old age. Like another friend, Rose Scott, Georgina King benefited from the 'tutelage and intellectual input'[13] of a group of knowledgeable older men who – in Georgina's case, anyway – encouraged her to observe her natural surroundings and form her own opinions. When the University of Sydney admitted women to its classes on an equal footing with men, Georgina was in her thirties and about to leave on a defining trip to Europe. When she returned, and entered into territory viewed by the 'professional men' of Sydney as theirs by right of employment – and gender – she saw no reason why lack of formal qualifications should in any way hamper her work. Faced with the dampening and discouraging reception given that work in 1892 and 1893, the bright intellectual flame so assiduously fostered by Messrs Clarke and Bennett would surely have flickered and died, had it not been for the innate pugnaciousness gifted to his daughter by the battling Parson King.

'I wrote to Prof. Liversidge', Georgina says, 'and asked him why he said I had no elementary knowledge after flattering me. He replied to me that I had been misinformed.' Such fudging was all very well but by no means was it the end of the story. Trouble came when she learned of the content of the address given by the new president (the kindly Professor Warren) at the AGM of May 1893. In it he summed up the society's activities for the preceding year covering the months between June and December 1892, and gave an overview of the scientific state of New South Wales.

To date, the litany of Georgina's complaints spanned a matter of some twenty years, from when she was W.B. Clarke's acolyte in her early twenties to now, when she was in her late forties. The complaints rose to a crescendo with the paper under discussion in this chapter – a paper that at the time of Warren's presidential address in May 1893 had been circulating among the society's officers and council for some twelve months. Three men appear to have benefited from the contents of the paper, all of whom bore office in the Royal Society of New South Wales at the time in question and were prominent in their respective fields. They were professionals paid to 'bring home the bacon' on a regular basis, and all three had the opportunity and the incentive to help themselves to the ideas contained in the freely circulating paper, 'Had Eastern Australia a true Devonian Period?'. On the evidence available to us at the time of writing, that is what they did.

Edward Fisher Pittman (1849–1932), the New South Wales government geologist, was a graduate of the London School of Mines and served briefly in Victoria before returning to New South Wales and rising to the position of undersecretary of the New South Wales Department of Mines and Agriculture. Nowadays, his major publications are read for their 'historical interest' rather than their enduring scientific worth.[14]

Tannatt William Edgeworth David, a former colleague of Pittman's, was originally destined for the church and studied classics at Oxford University. Notwithstanding, he seized the opportunity to emigrate to New South Wales as a geological surveyor, and was a surprise choice for professor of geology at the University of Sydney in 1891. Even before his death, T.W.E. David (or Sir Edgeworth as he was to become in 1920) was elevated to the status of unofficial saint – in geological circles, at least.

The deceptively benign-looking but obsessive Archibald Liversidge, who denied drawing attention to Miss King's state of ignorance and whose work on gold has already been detailed, gave up all chance of a distinguished career in Britain to man the 'lonely outpost' of colonial science that was the University of Sydney in 1872.[15] There, he made a name for himself for his organisational ability rather than for his scientific achievements.

Georgina's charges of theft date from the time when she was still under the tutelage of the Reverend Clarke and they can be listed in the following manner:

> 1. (ca 1871) She details the loss of some 'precious stones and tin' and 'some encrinite stems' sent to her from Vegetable Creek in New England and lent to Dr Edward Ramsay, curator of the Australian Museum. These, he said, when she requested their return for examination by Clarke, 'had got lost among other specimens'. ('Autobiography', pp. 16–17.)
>
> 2. (April 1892) 'I sent in my paper by the late Dr. Leibius, "Had Eastern Australia a true Devonian Period?" to be read at the next meeting of the Royal Society of New South Wales. Instead of giving it to the Secretary to be read at the meeting, Dr. Leibius gave it to Mr. Pittman, the Government Geologist, who said it was not new ... When I went to Mr. E.F. Pittman, and asked him why he said the matter in my paper was not new he hung down his head and said nothing, but Mrs. Pittman said "Mr. Pittman has to look to those who butter his bread".' ('Autobiography', pp. 35, 36.)

3. 'My paper must have been given to Prof. David, for he had read a paper on the Coal Measures at the Science Congress, at Hobart, shortly before [January 1892] which he did not publish in the "Proceedings" [published at the end of the year].' ('Autobiography', pp. 38–39.)

4. 'In part of Prof. Warren's address to the Royal Society [of NSW] for that year [May 1893] there was this. "An examination of a Collection of Fossils obtained some years ago in the Vegetable Creek district of New England has led to the discovery in them of the shell Productus,[16] so that a very large area occupied by rocks containing these fossils will now need to be coloured on the geological map as Carboniferous instead of Silurian, as coloured at present." Prof. Warren told me that Professor David wrote that part of his Address, and why were not these fossils, from the Vegetable Creek district of New England, examined before Mr. Pittman got this paper of mine?' ('Autobiography', pp. 39–40a.)

Professor David may or may not have had second thoughts about coal measures after reading Georgina's paper (see 3. above and the Appendix), but the question about the marine fossils of 4. above was a pertinent one. Edgeworth David's acquaintance with Vegetable Creek is detailed in his 1887 memoir entitled *Geology of the Vegetable Creek Tin-mining Field, New England District*.[17] Called a 'detailed' investigation by one of his students (the geologist W.R. Browne) and 'exhaustive' by a friend (the schoolteacher and entomologist H.J. Carter), the memoir was aimed at the mining industry and mining adventurers. In his memoir David certainly examined the area in great detail, noting the existence and whereabouts of gemstones as well as the inevitable tin, and pronouncing on the region's great potential as others had done before him. David seems happy enough when treating of zircon, topaz, beryl, emerald, sapphire and such like, along with the gravel, basalt and the composition of the wash in which the metal was found. Yet when dealing with the plant and animal fossils found in crystalline rocks in, for example, the New England parish of Arvid,[18] the reader senses that the man is considerably less at ease. As he pronounces on the former beds of pebble conglomerate, chert and claystones, he is vague (noting 'black stains, due to obscure plant remains') and indecisive ('These fossils show the beds to be of marine origin, but do not afford conclusive evidence as to their age').[19]

David, of course, was an *economic* geologist. His remit at the time was to report on viable mine sites. While fossils were indicators of the same, he lacked palaeontological expertise. Information, however, *was* available that should have enabled him to make a pretty fair stab at pinning the 'casts of bryozoa, small lamelli-branchs and univalves' down to a couple of hundred million years or so, and to an approximate geological period. Charles Wilkinson, his boss at the Lands Department, was a known authority on fossils, but to David, tentatively making his way in an alien environment far different to his native Wales, consulting his superior may have been seen as a loss of face. On the other hand, there were books ... Archibald Geikie's *Class Book of Geology*, first published in 1886, follows that author's *Text-book of Geology* of 1882 in putting the bivalve lamellibranchs as early as the Cambrian period and certainly the Devonian, and there were other helpful works in circulation, notably those of the Reverend Clarke.

While David found no trace of the brachiopod *Productus* in his travels in New England, the crinoids that so delighted 'Little George' King in the 1850s were represented in the Arvid fossil beds in 1887 as 'a few joints of stems of stone lilies'. Georgina's reference five years later to the 'encrinitic remains' found in a New England tin mine may well have reminded David of his inadequacies, sending him off to the Australian Museum where Dr Ramsay was still curator (he died in 1894). So, was the 'Collection of Fossils obtained some years ago' by David one and the same as her own collection apparently 'mislaid' by

Edward Ramsay in 1871? A tenuous connection, perhaps, but there are others.

A more detailed examination of Warren's presidential address in 1893 produces further circumstantial evidence in favour of Georgina's claims (with a mention *en passant* of Archibald Liversidge and his investigations into 'the mode of occurrence and crystallization of gold'). Professor David's 'recent examination in company with Mr. E.F. Pittman, the Government Geologist, of the country in the neighbourhood of Rydal', is noted – an expedition that led to the discovery of a plant (*Lepidodendron*) of 'undoubted Devonian age'. This confirmed 'the views as to the geological age of the above plant in New South Wales . . .'[20] Another coincidence, perhaps, since the paper Georgina lodged with the president in October 1892 and which was perused without her knowledge by none other than Edward Pittman (see 2. above) contained helpful hints to anyone interested in the field of fossil flora such as 'Lepidodendron, found in the Devonian formations in New South Wales' and 'the Palaeozoic coal flora in New South Wales', including the Carboniferous 'glossopteris, &c.', found by the writer (that is to say, Georgina) on 'one of the highest mountains at Bowenfels'.

In 1894 David published his 'Note on Stratigraphical Distribution of Glossopteris in New South Wales'.[21] The previous year he and Pittman had jointly published two papers: 'On the Occurrence of *Lepidodendron australe* in the Devonian Rocks of New South Wales'[22] and 'Note on the Occurrence of *Lepidodendron* in Upper Devonian Rocks at Mount Lambie, near Rydal, N.S.W'.[23] This may or may not have been sheer coincidence, but it is interesting to note that the mountains where Georgina made her discovery of 'glossopteris, &c.' are also in the neighbourhood of Rydal, an area that Georgina knew extremely well through her visits to Mrs Andrew Brown, wife of the local 'laird'. There was no coincidence, however, in the questioning of a local businessman as to where Miss King 'got the fossils on the ridge at Bowenfels'. The enquirer was none other than Professor Edgeworth David,[24] and one has to wonder why he didn't ask Miss King herself.

'Men never speak the Truth to Women', Professor Warren told her during her tribulations.[25] They apparently saw no need to act honourably, either.

> *I said to Prof. Warren long ago, that I could not understand educated men, like the scientific men, who took my work and discoveries behaving as they did, and his reply to me was, "Miss King, you made a great mistake in thinking education elevates the individual".*[26]

The history of Georgina's paper appears to bear this out. There is no evidence that Warren had any particular educated individual in mind when he deplored the lack of ethics among his scientific peers, but Georgina could have supplied him with the names of three at least – Liversidge, Pittman and David. The trio enjoyed immeasurable influence, yet history reminds us that in any triumvirate one man is likely to outstrip the other two. It is easy to scoff at a man who felt impelled to sneak along in the footsteps of a woman, but there is no denying that by the end of 1894 Edgeworth David was 'cock of the Sydney walk', with a following that extended far beyond the purlieus of the university. He and Georgina might meet at social gatherings, but any friendly relations between the couple were over and soon forgotten. More importantly, after the shabby treatment dealt out in the matter of fossils and gold, Georgina King was ready to renounce her science for good.

CHAPTER FIFTEEN

The Changing of the Guard

Georgina King had a wide circle of acquaintances and friends, many of them male. Given her family associations, she was at ease in the highest ranks of Sydney society and with Anglican churchmen of note. She was on friendly terms with parliamentarians, and her networking among the landowners and mine owners of New South Wales was by any standard remarkable. Indeed, such connections made her an object of envy among the scientific parvenus of Sydney (if the behaviour of their wives is anything to go by). What told against her most was the temerity of her aspirations, and that was the crux of the matter: an unmarried, unschooled woman had dared trespass onto the territory of the dominant male.

A glance through the membership list for 1894 in the *Journal and Proceedings of the Royal Society of New South Wales* reveals the membership to be a decidedly unproductive lot (the number of papers presented at meetings is marked against a member's name and very few made any contribution at all). The society did not have a particularly good track record, either, when it came to original thought – Georgina was in a position to know, for she had friends and allies within the society's ranks. (Kelso King, who was elected to membership in December 1896, may or may not have been a lover of science; he was certainly no supporter of his sister.)

The Reverend Dr William Wyatt Gill was distantly related to the Kings by marriage. Before retiring to Sydney, he had lived for thirty years among South Sea islanders, working for the London Mission. The author of *Historical Sketches of Savage*

Life in Polynesia had been a member of the society since 1884. Rudely reminded of certain aspects of civilised behaviour upon his return, he warned Miss King to identify her work clearly when it appeared in public:

> *May I advise you now to stick to one signature underneath your clever articles? I know a case (in the old country) where a certain party quietly appropriated all the glory of being the (reputed) author of another man's anonymous book! It is impossible to fathom the meanness of some men's natures.*[1]

Dr Charles (Carl) Adolph Leibius, who was born in Württemberg, Germany in 1833, was another student of human behaviour, and he was always ready to provide those delicious little insights into Sydney science that were balm to Georgina's wounded spirit:

> *The Professors go in for private work and let their Demonstrators do most of their University work, and they make a great deal of money in this way to the disadvantage of private scientists – they do not read to keep pace with the times. Dr. Leibius was 25 years behind the scenes at our Royal Society and he used to tell me what went on there, and how publications from other countries and colonies were never opened or looked at.*[2]

With the deaths of both Dr Leibius and Dr Bennett in 1893 Georgina lost two staunch friends, but with Bennett there also died an era. The doctor had maintained contact with England and its men of science for almost six decades, sending back a steady stream of botanical specimens, both living and dead, to the Royal College of Surgeons of England, the Royal Botanic Gardens at Kew, and the Zoological and Linnean societies of London. Bennett was no mere collector – his scholarly publications spanned half a century (from 1831 to 1884) – and to Georgina King he was also an object of admiration – veneration, even.

Archibald Liversidge and others like him were unlikely to have shed a tear at Bennett's demise. The changing of the guard had taken place. Gentlemen scientists – *pace* William John Macleay of Elizabeth Bay House – were becoming as much an anachronism as the old doctor. Rather than being centred on stately private homes, the power base had shifted to public institutions such as the Technological Museum, the Department of Mines, and the Faculty of Science of the University of Sydney. The Royal Society of New South Wales stood as unofficial watchdog against unsuitable candidates for admission to the charmed circle of Sydney science, and after the setbacks of 1892–1894 Georgina stopped struggling for any kind of recognition. And for very good reason: as the saying goes, 'one door closes and another opens', and in Georgina's case that door was already ajar. She had found a new scientific mentor among the leading scientists of Victoria.

Georgina's geology clearly belongs to two distinct phases: the period when she was influenced by the Reverend W.B. Clarke (from her childhood until his death in 1878), and the years when she corresponded with Sir Frederick McCoy, professor of natural science at the University of Melbourne. Clarke fostered Georgina King's love of geology; McCoy encouraged her to promote her theories in the public domain. In hindsight, this association, however indirect, is more than a little ironic, as for decades McCoy and Clarke were at loggerheads over something as apparently uncomplicated as coal . . .

In the nineteenth century coal was a universal necessity. Nowadays, it no longer is a daily and tangible presence in our homes; power, heat and light can be summoned at the flick of a switch and are taken for granted. But for nineteenth-century Australian geologists, discovering the age of eastern Australia's coal deposits was the equivalent of the Arthurian search for the 'Holy Grail'. From as early as 1847, when McCoy was still palaeontologist at the Woodwardian Museum in Cambridge and Clarke was geologising half a world a way in outback New South Wales, he and the parson differed over this (to us) unglamorous subject, and for some thirty years they attacked each other's theories.[3] Clarke eventually fixed on the Permian period of the Palaeozoic era (280 million years before the present), a period that saw the rise of the reptiles and the first land vertebrates in Australia's east.[4] He insisted that 'the fossiliferous sandstone beneath the coal, the coal itself and plant fossils in the beds above represented one great unbroken series and belonged to the same geological age'.[5] McCoy, on the other hand, held that the different strata containing marine fossils, coal and plant fossils respectively, were separated by 'a vast geological time' – a contradictory view he maintained long after Clarke's views were widely accepted.

Sir Frederick's appointment to the University of Melbourne came in August 1854, despite him possessing no university degree. He was previously professor of geology and mineralogy and senior dean in the Faculty of Arts in Queen's College, Belfast, and that – along with his prodigious literary output – proved sufficient to secure him the chair. 'In the eighteen-fifties, in the first flush of McCoy's enthusiasm, the natural sciences were probably studied by a greater portion of the students at Melbourne than at any other British university', the official history of the university records,[6] although the professor's enthusiasm waned with his advancing years – and (some would say) earlier than that.

Dr Bennett approved of McCoy as much as he disapproved of Liversidge and his fellows. 'He was', Georgina explained in an early letter to McCoy, 'very angry with the scientific men for rejecting my work when he recommended it'.[7] There can be no doubt about the extent of Bennett's ire. He made several generous gifts to the University of Sydney, notably a stained-glass window for the Medical School in 1890, depicting no fewer than twenty-two coats of arms (his own included), and a set of Gould's ornithological works. The general expectation was that after his death his library in its entirety would follow. This was not the case. As Georgina puts it neatly in her autobiography:

> *... when the scientific men refused my original discoveries, he altered his 'will' and left his library to Mrs. Bennett. It came to his ears that the scientific men had said he was too old to give an opinion of my original discoveries, but he said he was not too old to alter his 'will'.*[8]

When Georgina told Bennett of her introduction to Professor McCoy, 'he took my two hands in his and said, "I am delighted to hear this, now you're in safe hands"'.[9] Two weeks later the doctor passed away.

From about 1925 onwards, Georgina, now in her eighties, carefully prepared her archive for a posterity she hoped would vindicate her claims. The papers and letters that are available for public scrutiny in the Mitchell Library in Sydney were carefully selected to represent her scientific endeavours and struggles for recognition. Letters that touched on her personal circumstances and were of a private and confidential nature we can assume to have been deliberately destroyed – such was the mindset of her generation. When Sir Frederick died, his rooms at the university were cleared and his papers were put into storage. Not realising this, Georgina wrote to his one surviving relative, a grandson, to express her sympathy at his loss and request the return of any letters of hers that he found at 'Maritima', McCoy's home in the Melbourne suburb of Brighton. This, Frederick junior did.

It was with mixed feelings, then, that in the course of our researches into Georgina King's life, we discovered a number of her letters surviving among the McCoy correspondence at the Museum of Victoria. The last one is dated 11 August 1898 (Professor McCoy succumbed to the after effects of influenza and a subsequent chill in May 1899), while the first bears the date 25 October 1893 and refers to the paper under discussion in Chapter Fourteen. Vouchsafed an insight into Georgina's tribulations, both in the wider world and within the confines of her family, we were confronted with the biographer's perennial dilemma. To what extent should we respect our subject's privacy? To what extent should we publish and invite charges of insensitivity and voyeurism? Given the extraordinary circumstances surrounding her life and work, and since history has failed to speak out for this courageous woman, we have allowed her letters to speak for her instead.

As well as providing relevant insights into Georgina's domestic circumstances, the letters from this important period of her life have enabled us to build up a picture of the stresses attendant upon her as a woman attempting science in nineteenth-century Sydney. A woman, in short, faced with the clannishness (or worse) that typified the Royal Society of New South Wales at that time.

By November 1893 Georgina had reworked her paper under McCoy's guidance. She thanked the professor for his help and the great trouble he had taken.[10] Then she told him:

> *When I saw Professor Warren a few weeks ago, he told me that if you recommended my paper he would see that it was not again refused by the Council of the Royal Society here, but last night he told me that he would have nothing to do with it.*

The reason was simple: 'Professors Liversidge and David had told him I was working without elementary knowledge.' There was more:

> *. . . he said that you and Baron von Mueller only complimented me on my work because I was a woman – in fact he told me he was the only one who was my friend and told me the truth, although I might not like him for it.*

Georgina would have nothing of it. 'The fact is I have done original work and the scientific men here who overlooked such work are jealous of me', she steadfastly maintained to McCoy and anyone else who would listen; and at 'Montesca', the house built by her parents for their retirement at Homebush, she continued to work at science.

Her mother's critical comments and the 'opposing force' of her sister, Mrs Rogers, did not go away. There was also the problem of her brother. The 'naturally goodhearted' Kelso had made a good marriage 'but his wife could not do a disinterested thing to save her life'. The former Miss Irene Rand whose father 'came in for about eighty thousand pounds through the death of his brother' saw no need to subsidise her sister-in-law's eccentricities in any way. 'She never allows my brother to give me a single thing – even for science, and I am narrowed very much in my allowance.'[11] When Sir Frederick McCoy began to take an interest in Georgina's work, her situation changed, though probably with no thanks to the Kelso Kings.

McCoy's museum at the University of Melbourne was outstanding and he controlled it absolutely 'as director, palaeontologist and zoologist'. He supervised a dozen staff, 'classifying innumerable boxes of new specimens', and corresponded widely with collectors and other museum directors overseas.[12] He had been part of the Melbourne Establishment for years, as a member of the exclusive Melbourne Club since 1856. The King women were typical of much of colonial society and were nothing if not snobs. Georgina might be obliged to keep the same old bonnet and the outdated remodelled clothes, but given her connection with Sir Frederick she did begin to enjoy an improved status at home.[13] Suddenly, funds for science were more readily available and fewer obstacles were put in the spinster's way. Yes, plain, put-upon Georgina had obviously made some kind of a conquest and her unwomanly ways were consequently overlooked, if not forgiven.

Although McCoy lorded it in the colony of Victoria, he had 'alienated the greater part of the geological community' in Australia[14] – never mind that he was awarded the prestigious

Murchison Medal of the Geological Society, London, in 1879 and elected a Fellow of the Royal Society in 1880. Or perhaps such achievements were part of the problem. In the 'Brave New World' of Australian science, McCoy's credibility (like that of the late Dr Bennett) was vested in the Old. The professor, like Georgina, smarted from his treatment at the hands of Sydney's scientific elite. His detractors claim, too, that he was no field geologist (although in old age he was game enough to 'finish a bit of the geology [at Woodend] left undone by the [Victorian] Survey'[15]). The unlikely couple finally met in Melbourne in May 1895, eighteen months after their correspondence began, and again in March 1896. The result was what Georgina termed 'an intellectual feast'.[16]

'Peppery when thwarted' but 'warm-hearted and friendly', Frederick McCoy had always been the university dandy. He was as spruce and dapper as ever at age seventy-seven and still carried himself 'with the grace of a dancing master' – although his reddish side-whiskers had 'paled to a lemon-tinted reminiscence of their former glow'.[17] Without bringing anything as modern as *sex* into the equation, there is no doubt that the middle-aged maiden lady was deeply smitten with the Irish academic,[18] and her devotion manifested itself in the most practical of ways. Over the next several years, fossils by the hundredweight, including specimens collected by an extensive network of mine managers in the Wallsend-Newcastle district, were dispatched to Melbourne for McCoy's Museum of Natural and Applied Science.[19] She even offered to make him a comforter and slippers (an offer he declined).

CHAPTER SIXTEEN

Rocks and Rock Hounds

Once she was done with Liversidge and his cronies, Georgina entered upon one of the most fulfilling periods of her life. Not only was there the joy of re-discovering *Boronia floribunda* for Baron von Mueller, there was the pleasure of organising her network and sending fossil specimens to their mutual friend Sir Frederick McCoy.

Georgina's flair as a 'rock-hound' was well known among the professionals. In July 1890, in the days when she was still on friendly terms with E.F. Pittman, she walked into the Department of Mines bearing a gift in the shape of a 'large block of coal merging into "Kerosene Shale" with a beautiful layer of fossil wood, from the Zig-Zag Mine'[1] on the eastern slope of the Blue Mountains at Lapstone. T.W.E. David, not yet appointed to the university, was no less surprised than Pittman, since the specimen contradicted his views as to where kerosene shale was to be found.[2] Georgina was a regular visitor to the Mining Museum in Macquarie Street and one day

> *I met Charles Cullen who used to be with the late Mr. C.S. Wilkinson, as his geological collector, then he afterwards had charge of the Mining Museum, and he told me that he had been asked to watch what specimens or fossils I was looking at.*[3]

That was in 1896, a year that saw her at the height of her success as a collector. She never went back and who can blame her? Not that she had much time to stand and stare – whenever her filial duties permitted, she was off on the hunt for specimens on behalf of Mueller and McCoy.

Georgina knew many residents of the Blue Mountains, and was extremely fortunate to have Andrew and Christina Brown, near Bowenfels in the western foothills, as friends. Although they lived some 90 miles from Sydney, it was easy to reach them by rail – a train leaving Sydney at nine in the morning reached Bowenfels at 2.45 pm. Once the western Zig Zag line was completed in 1867 and entered into use the following year, not only did it open up Bathurst, Orange and beyond, but it brought increased settlement to the Bowenfels district itself.

Andrew Brown, a young Scot from Perth, received his first land grant of 200 acres in 1824 and was soon 'a superb example of the old style squatter'. His 'drive and acquisitiveness' brought him thousands more, mainly in the Warrumbungle Mountains 200 miles to the northwest.[4] Coal was always known to exist in the heart of Brown's original grant of 'Cooerwull' and the railway's arrival made its exploitation easy.

Three villages – 'Lithgow', 'Eskbank' and 'Vale of Clywdd' – spread their terraced miners' cottages along the Cooerwull Brook (now known as Farmer's Creek) until they eventually merged into what is now modern Lithgow. Set against the mountainous sandstone backdrop of 'Hassans Walls', Lithgow's meatworks, iceworks, two copper smelters, a tannery and a brewery were all in production by the 1880s. Like the town, Brown's original home grew in scope, and the sequoias he planted would in time shade the burgeoning gardens. The cottage he built in 1830 is tiny, but the numerous outbuildings around the later 'Cooerwull House' attest to its builder's wealth and sense of style (they include a coach house, coachman's cottage and stables, as well as the foundations of a rectangular bathhouse).[5]

After Brown's death in 1894, Georgina continued to visit his widow and we can imagine her sitting in the small octagonal summerhouse in the elegant grounds, writing up her notes from her various sorties to mountain wilderness or mine. Or simply admiring a view that not even industry could spoil, although the peace around her was sometimes shattered by a steam train crossing Cooerwull land.

By the 1890s the Lithgow Valley Colliery Company had opened up two mines, the 'Lithgow Collieries' covering 1751 acres and the smaller 'Hermitage', covering 843. The company also owned a brick works, with its associated pottery supplying the domestic market until overseas competition finished it in the depression of 1898. One of the directors was Edward Gell, an architect by profession,[6] and it was Gell who came upon Professor David snooping his way along that high windswept mountain ridge above Bowenfels.

Coal created Lithgow. Hartley Vale, a company township covering 30 acres, owed its existence to kerosene shale. The New South Wales Shale and Oil Company began mining for kerosene shale in the original Vale of Clywdd in 1866, when the shale proved of such high quality that it was sent as far as San Francisco. For the first few years the shale was carted up Mount Victoria and put on the train at One Tree Station (now Mount Victoria), but once the Lithgow Zig Zag opened in 1869, a two-mile tramline up the mountainside connected with its siding at the mainline Hartley Vale station. Life became easier for workforce and visitors alike as a result.

The refinery plant built at Hartley Vale in 1885 flourished under the management of Mr J. Hall for years,[7] and he was still there in the 1890s. He was extremely helpful in dealing with Georgina's enquiries, for not only was the mine productive, it was a rich source of fossil plants. She visited the refinery in January 1896[8] and in March she delivered fossils to Professor McCoy in person.[9] Meanwhile, Mr Hall continued to tell his men to look out for 'Vertebraria' for Miss King,[10] and in November 1896 she returned to Hartley Vale. That second visit was especially fruitful and produced numerous specimens of Glossopteris – woody plants with tongue-shaped 'fern' leaves that had dominated the vast ancient continent of Gondwana in much the way that eucalypts dominate our Australian landscape today.[11] (Their roots were named *vertebraria* from their resemblance to the backbone or vertebral column.)

Matching Georgina's letters to the actual fossils she collected, and reading the occasional scrap of pencilled note that accompanies them, brings a touching immediacy to her accounts that computer printouts with their succession of figures, placenames and dates cannot hope to do. 'I taught myself to read by shaping the letters and putting them together', she tells us,[12] and her handwriting as a mature adult shows the same slow deliberation. It lacks the slick stylishness of (say) an expensively educated Edgeworth David, but it reflects the woman – ponderous, open and painstaking. That same thorough approach was brought to her November expedition – a 'delightful and most successful trip to the West', as she described it to Sir Frederick upon her return. A trip that resulted in several cases going to Melbourne of 'about three cwt. in all I think', including 'a marine boulder that was found in a creek near Cox's River'.[13] This time she did not stay with her widowed friend. While a hotel room closer to Edward Gell's pottery may have been less comfortable (Mrs Brown installed electricity at Cooerwull in 1896), there were advantages, and here we see Georgina at her very best. Four decades after her escapades at the Sydney foundry, she still had a way about her, and nothing was too much trouble when helping out Miss King:

> *I went to the Pottery and I saw Mr. Gell directly. I arrived at Lithgow on Wednesday afternoon – he also owns two coal mines near it – and he took me to the quarry and told a nice intelligent man to get me everything I wanted, and to do what he could for me. The man took a pick, and I had a strong Geological hammer and we worked away for two hours, when he helped me to carry the fossils to the Hotel where I stayed. He told me there was to be a blast in the quarry on Friday and he would make it*

lower on purpose to meet the shale where the fossils are found, and save them all for me. I went there at 6 o'clock on Saturday morning and was in delight, for I think I have got some treasures for you [McCoy], as well as plenty of the Vertebraria. I carried my basketsfull to the Hotel, and returned with a cart and took the rest away and got them packed (indeed I did it myself) in an ale case and brought them home with me, beside two baskets full.[14]

'I would like to have a peep at you when you are examining the fossils', Georgina added coyly in her letter to Sir Frederick.

On Thursday morning she visited the Vale Colliery at Lithgow, 'and went the 348 feet down the shaft and saw all that was going on there'. Then she equally intrepidly set off for the north:

On Friday I made an early start for Cullen Bullen,[15] *in a conveyance I hired at the Hotel, as I could not get a convenient Train there, and it is eighteen miles on the Mudgee Road and six miles from Wallerawang – A man who had business at Cullen Bullen drove me for the Hotel keeper and he gave me great assistance. I would not have missed this deposit of fossils for anything – These quarries have been made in the shale to repave the roads and on the surface a few inches down you come upon a wonderful find of curiously preserved vertebrarias, that lies above the deposit of shale. The coal mine is in the mountain before you come to this deposit of fossils which are mixed up with lime, clay, etc. We took all the fossils to the Hotel at Cullen Bullen and I got a case and packed it there and I put some fragments on the top of the box that were broken off as we carried them, but you can patch them together as they are interesting impressions in lime.*

Georgina had filled two cases already; the haul from Cullen Bullen made up a third:

The storekeeper said he would take the case himself to the

Railway station and see that it was sent on to me at Homebush. It will be numbered 3, and directly it arrives at our Station I will have it readdressed to you and sent on . . .

It was far easier for Sir Frederick to turn down scarves and knitted slippers . . .

Although Georgina's fossils reached Melbourne University by the hundredweight, her cherished relationship with Sir Frederick McCoy was not one-sided. His gifts to Georgina were less tangible but arguably more valuable than hers. He enhanced her standing with her family, for one thing;[16] he boosted her self-esteem, for another. He listened, he corrected, he instructed, he inspired. When Georgina informed Professor McCoy that her paper had been published in the *Sydney Morning Herald* in July 1895, she added by way of a postscript:

I would so like a conversation with you about a scientific subject which interests me greatly, for you would not misunderstand me. You grasp everything so easily with your splendid intellect and make things so simple for me – indeed you explain me to myself.[17]

Sir Frederick also offered his advice. He urged caution in her differences with the scientific 'Opposition': 'I do not know what to say about your taking Prof. Warren's advice about writing to the Herald in the matter of Mr. Pittman & Prof. David', he admitted, yet he did convince her not to go to the press with her story: 'Your time is too valuable to be wasted in personal controversies, which are not worth anything in comparison with the use you can make of it in searching out & illustrating scientific truths.'[18]

When T.W.E. David read his paper on 'Sill Structure and Fossils in Eruptive Rocks' to the Royal Society on 4 November 1896, McCoy tried to temper her increasing bitterness. Georgina wrote:

> *I sent the extract of it to the late Professor Sir Frederick McCoy, of the Melbourne University, telling him it would amuse him. He replied, "I was amused at the cool extract you sent me, and your old discoveries clearly elaborated by yourself will apparently make more Sydney scientific reputations than other people could have made for themselves. A graceful acknowledgement of the source of their knowledgement [sic] would not hurt them if they had the sense to see it."*[19]

Georgina's first pamphlet, 'The Palaeozoic Carboniferous Formations of New South Wales and the Occurrence of our Mineral Wealth', appeared at the end of 1895. It was a reprint of her August newspaper article ('The Palaeozoic Carboniferous Formations in New South Wales') that, in turn, was a version of the paper that went to the committee of the Royal Society of New South Wales between 1892 and 1894. The pamphlet would be the cause of a family row. To finance its publication, Georgina asked her brother to buy her diamond brooch for his daughters and keep the jewel in the family (it had been given her by her deceased sister Martha's now equally defunct spouse), but Kelso King refused.[20] Relations between the siblings were frosty for quite some time as a result.

At the end of 1896 she took McCoy's advice and that of Dr Wyatt Gill, and collected together what the professor called her 'incomparable contributions'.[21] Then she again ventured into print. This second pamphlet was entitled 'The Mineral Wealth of New South Wales and Other Lands and Countries'. Again, it contained her original article on the Palaeozoic, and two others – 'Modified Forces and our Mineral Wealth' and 'Our Coal Mines and our Mineral Wealth'. Like the first, it was printed for the author at Angus & Robertson's, and was offered for sale in their Sydney city bookshop.

Part Three

Ginger for Pluck

CHAPTER SEVENTEEN

De Profundis

The Reverend George King died in March 1899, and his wife, Jane, the following year. The parson had ruled his household absolutely (and was tight with his money besides), and Georgina was quite worn out by trying to please her nitpicking mother, thus her sense of loss was mitigated by an overwhelming sense of liberation. (She was, after all, free of all restraint for the first time in fifty-five years.) Like Rose Scott, the friend whose life so often closely paralleled her own and whose mother had died in 1896, Georgina immediately made the most of her freedom. Rose intensified her political work and Georgina chose to travel, still in pursuit of scientific knowledge. This would take her deep underground into the Jenolan Caves, an awe-inspiring network of tunnels and caves set in the limestone karst of the Great Dividing Range, some 50 miles to the southeast of Bathurst, which even then were a recognised attraction (a four-day excursion from the AAAS to Jenolan or Fish River Caves had set out as early as 31 August 1888, with T.W.E. David as one of the leaders).

Geology apart, Dame Nature in the Blue Mountains was at her most awe-inspiring. The Victorians were ever open to her wonders, and poets like William Wordsworth (always at his best when contemplating the more grandiose aspects of Creation rather than the lesser) lyrically egged them on. The Blue Mountains to romantically minded Australians were the equivalent of the Lake District to the English, and Jenolan Caves the ultimate in Nature's glories. From the evidence of her writings, it appears that Georgina King approached the caves with less than the reverence expected of members of her generation. Whereas most sought the Sublime and an accompanying Exaltation of the Spirit – and she herself, it must be said, was by no means unmoved by 'the lovely forms of stalactites, stalagmites, shawls and draperies that give such a beautiful appearance to the caves' – she went equipped with a hammer, not a book of verse.

Folklore promotes a convict runaway as Jenolan's discoverer, although the claim of Charles Whalan, a settler on the Fish River, 'to have been to the end of the world and seen the Devil's Coach House' is another fine tradition, one that dates back to 1838.[1] The 'Grand Arch', at the entrance to the northern system of arguably the best-known limestone caves in Australia, and the huge cavern so fancifully named by Whalan, quickly became a local attraction. Distance and logistics combined to keep almost everyone else away.

It was a long haul westwards even for the most intrepid of travellers, but the occasional party did come through by bullock dray or horseback from as far afield as Sydney. The nearest place of any significance was the prosaically named Bullock Flat, where the Whalan family was happy to provide overnight accommodation after a journey of 140 rough miles. The caves themselves were some 20 miles further on and the next day's ride brought the travellers to the steep descent into the Jenolan Valley.

From 1868 trips to popular Blue Mountains destinations such as the Wentworth Falls (alight at Weatherboard platform) and the Three Sisters (alight at Katoomba Station) could be made easily by rail. In 1872 the railway was extended beyond Bowenfels to Tarana, four stops further on. There, passengers alighted and boarded a buggy to proceed in comfort to within a couple of miles of the caves, driving through Bullock Flat to 'Two Mile Hill' where wheels were once again redundant. Only when a 'zig-zag' road was completed in 1879 did it become possible to continue all the way down to the caves by coach and horses. At the bottom, trippers were still obliged to camp.

A succession of articles on this 'Australian Wonderland', written for the *Sydney Morning Herald* in 1886 and republished in book form in 1889,[2] was written with the Victorian psyche in mind.[3] Guidebooks, too, stressed the notion of romance, and wild and rugged grandeur. The *Australasian Atlas* of 1888 made much of the 'succession of treasure stores, of palaces, of fairy playgrounds' – so much so that homely Bullock Flat was inspired to reinvent itself as 'Oberon' (the former Fish River Caves had already been transmogrified to something less redolent of the kitchen in 1884). With new caves being discovered at Jenolan on a regular basis, and given names such as 'The Jewel Casket', 'The Crystal Cities', and 'The Fairy's Retreat', the hard sell to the public in general was on in earnest.[4]

Given the constraints of distance and time, it is a tribute to the entrepreneurs of the Blue Mountains that access to the caves became so very much easier so quickly, and that comfort was assured. As cave-oriented tourism increased throughout the 1880s, it produced an almost irresistible package for the well-heeled middle class. When the 9 am train from Sydney reached Tarana at 4.15 pm, it was met by the Oberon coach. After an overnight stop at Oberon and a 'moderately early breakfast' next morning, a traveller could be at Jenolan and settle into its accommodation house by lunchtime. The rail and coach journey combined took about twenty-eight hours.[5]

Oberon soon found itself with competition. Anyone on the 5 pm from Sydney could leave the train at Mount Victoria, spend the night at one of its several hotels, and proceed the next day along a newly constructed buggy track built by the proprietors of the aforesaid establishments. The route was more direct, shorter, and how pleasant (said the promoters) to reach Jenolan in time for afternoon tea. Katoomba also vied for a slice of the action with the 'Six Foot Track', constructed in 1884 and officially opened in 1887. This much cheaper solution – four hours by train from Sydney plus another six on horseback – understandably failed to catch on.[6]

Georgina had learned a great deal about the Jenolan Caves in 1893 when visiting the Webbs of Springfield, Byng. While the old and embittered William Tom talked on about his dreams of gold denied, his four nieces and nephews told her of the caves they had first explored in 1881. ('Katie's Bower', part of the Imperial Cave, was named for Catherine Emma Webb, who as a fearless eighteen-year-old was present at the time of its discovery that year.) Only in 1901 could Georgina benefit from the improved infrastructure of this formerly remotest of regions and see the caves for herself – following in the footsteps of her good friend Miss Latta who had gone to Jenolan in 1896.

Miss Latta found that no longer was there any need to slip and slide down a rudimentary track and camp like 'mice in a cathedral' under the Grand Arch or in the Devil's Coach House,[7] with only the flickering of candles between them and the impenetrable gloom. No need, either, to walk the last few hundred yards to Caves House and risk wet shoes and stockings if the river was running high. By 1896 the road through the Grand Arch was completed, the bridge was in place, and every effort was being made to ensure all-round customer satisfaction. The caves on the regular tour had been widened, levelled and generally 'improved'. Some of the caverns and recesses were hung with light fittings, courtesy of the Electric Light Department of New South Wales and its steam-driven dynamo (first used under the Grand Arch in 1887 and replacing the magnesium lamps in use before). Entrance gates were installed and wire netting put in place to protect stalactites, stalagmites, pillars and shawls from unscrupulous 'souveniring'.[8]

Despite such modern interventions, the crystalline structures of the caves thus revealed – in more than their natural glory – could not help but thrill and overwhelm. Miss Latta, for one, declared herself 'delighted', as Georgina reported to Professor McCoy.[9] Not too delighted, though, to make scientific notes to relay to her friend: 'there was a band of iron or ironstone in the roof of the caves and during a storm they were beautiful for they were lit up with natural electricity.' 'Of course', Georgina told Sir Frederick, 'I suppose that it was due to atmospheric pressure and the large amount of oxygen in the carbonate of lime composing the caves which would also be a good conductor'. All in all, Miss Latta's information was enough to send Georgina off in pursuit of another theory.

As Georgina searched for the iron deposit mentioned by Miss Latta, she 'came upon a vent above the caves, with partly burnt rocks, containing marine fossils of the Palaeozoic age' – brachiopods, corals and crinoids undisturbed for perhaps 400 million years.[10] W.B. Clarke had taught his pupil well, and when she saw the 'Devonian lilies' of her childhood in situ, how could she resist? Despite regulations in place since 1872, Georgina set to and helped herself. When she shared her treasures with a friend in Sydney on her return, she made another discovery, one that quite simply took her breath away: sales of her self-published pamphlet, *The Mineral Wealth of New South Wales*, of which she was so proud, had been suppressed.

Robert Etheridge, who told Georgina about her pamphlet's fate, had been curator of the Australian Museum from 1895. He was a palaeontologist by profession, his interest in Jenolan Caves dating back to early 1891, when he was sent the skeleton of a thylacine (Tasmanian tiger) found in the 'Jersey Cave' by its discoverers, Jeremiah Wilson and Edmund Webb. As a member of the Royal Society of New South Wales, although not one of the charmed inner circle, Georgina's struggles would not have passed him by unnoticed. Since then, he and Miss King had struck up enough of a friendship for Georgina to entrust him with her finds. He thanked her, and informed her that he would 'write an account of the fossils and caves'. Then he told her that he had tried unsuccessfully to obtain her private publication, *The Mineral Wealth of New South Wales*.[11]

When Georgina investigated, what she found was this: the pamphlet, supposedly on sale at Angus & Robertson's, the university booksellers, since 1896, had never been on their books at all.[12] Worse still, it had not been removed by a shopkeeper's blunder, but suppressed through the deliberate intervention of a respected academic employed by the University of Sydney – none other than the professor of geology himself. To publish, she had been obliged to sell the valuable diamond crescent brooch given her by her late brother-in-law, Layman Harrison.[13] It had been sacrificed in vain, and her feelings can only be imagined.

By 1902 Edgeworth David had been professor of geology at the University of Sydney for ten years, where his wife, Caroline – no longer the tentative bride of a minor public servant – had consolidated their new social standing by spurring her slightly younger husband on to even greater things. Georgina's modest little geological publication had offended this upwardly mobile duo, and for some reason one of them or the other – or possibly both – had 'requested' *The Mineral Wealth of New South Wales* be removed from sale.

Georgina was sure she knew why. On 4 November 1896, as she had good reason to remember, T.W.E. David read his paper on 'Sill Structure and Fossils in Eruptive Rocks in New South Wales' before the Royal Society in Sydney.[14] The 'sills' in question were the flat bodies of intrusive igneous rock ordinarily found between beds of sedimentary rocks or layers of volcanic ejectamenta – those very 'unconformities' discussed in Georgina King's earlier research. Sceptical readers who come to consider the professor's paper more than one hundred years after the event will find little of Edgeworth David in it. Nor will they find any mention of Georgina King. Instead, references to the work of august Europeans are followed by 'some interesting rocks from Hill End' in the western district of New South Wales (as described by E.F. Pittman), and views on similar crystalline rocks in New England (as put forward by C.S. Wilkinson). The professor neatly explains the 'phenomena' that had puzzled Wilkinson, and also the 'apparent anomaly' that Pittman had come up with at the gold mining town of Hill End.[15] Then he seeks to substantiate his opening claim that his own 'special description' would 'revolutionize prevalent ideas, at all events in Australia' and 'satisfactorily [explain] the apparent anomaly of the occurrence of fossils in eruptive rocks'.[16] (He did convince Edward Pittman, who made a printed retraction of his 'erroneous conclusions' in 1899,[17] again with no reference to Georgina's work.)

David had certainly examined the areas in question – the western district in 1890, and New England where he worked alongside Wilkinson, his late chief at the Department of Mines between 1883 and 1887. Quite obviously stimulated by Georgina's fresh ideas, which by November 1896 had been available in pamphlet form for over a year (with an extended version newly out in print), David developed his earlier observations but at no time did he give her any credit. Words like 'now' and 'recent', and the phrase 'I now think', accompany his changes in direction, but he could not bring himself to admit as to *why* they had occurred. The 'graceful acknowledgement' that in Sir Frederick McCoy's opinion would not have hurt David was never forthcoming, for, of course, Sir Frederick was totally wrong. David was not man enough to admit that an amateur had upstaged him – and a female amateur at that. He simply hoped Georgina would let the matter rest, and had it not been for David's 'overkill' chez Angus & Robertson, that probably would indeed have been the case.

Sickened as she was by the connivings at the Royal Society of New South Wales, the years following the publication of her two pamphlets marked Georgina with a sadness of a more deeply personal nature. As well as both her parents, she lost yet more of the friends who had fostered her scientific aspirations and her sense of self-esteem. The kindly Mueller – 'He has been like a Father to me – all my investigations would have been useless had he not interest[ed] Professor Sir F. McCoy on my behalf and had my work on Geology locally established'[18] – succumbed to influenza in October 1896. The feisty if cynical Reverend William Wyatt Gill, who had warned her to be wary of plagiarism and literary theft, went to his heavenly reward that November. Sir Frederick and his wise counsel were removed in May 1899. So when Robert Etheridge told her what had happened to her second pamphlet, Georgina was left to rely on her own judgement and fight her battles alone.

To begin with, she acted like the lady she was. She told David in writing that she knew what he had done, and then got on with the business of everyday living. She moved into Sydney, continued to research and write, and attended meetings of the various clubs of which she was a member. Her interests widened to take in anthropology, and as a member then Fellow of the Royal Anthropological Society of Australasia she found the appreciation and regard she so much craved. As her work reached a wider audience and her reputation grew, she discovered that her enemy was not so much Professor David but his forceful and socially ambitious wife. Mrs David's involvement put a totally different complexion on the whole affair. From then on, she ranked high on Georgina's list of real or supposed enemies, to be distrusted as much as the men of Sydney's scientific clique – and events appear to have proved her right.

CHAPTER EIGHTEEN

Mrs Professor David's Husband and his Wife

The two women who were to become such deadly adversaries were equally strong-minded. Both were set on receiving their own particular form of recognition in the narrow little world of middle-class Sydney. On the face of it, Miss King had a definite edge – never mind her obsessions and her single state, hers was a well-established family and her place in society assured. She was a born lady with a common touch, whereas Mrs David was, quite simply, common.

Caroline Martha David first saw the light of day in a small coastal town in Suffolk, England's most easterly county, while her future husband was born on the great western peninsula of Wales. Distance alone would have made their meeting unlikely in Britain, while class differences would have made any kind of social relationship – let alone marriage – extremely unlikely, if such a meeting did transpire. Nineteenth-century Australia, on the other hand, was a country where couples of vastly contrasting backgrounds could, and often did, progress unchallenged to the altar.

The seaside town of Southwold boasted a sizeable herring fleet of longshore boats, and it was among its fisher cots that Pamela Mallett nee Wright delivered her daughter Caroline on 26 April 1856. Pamela, who had married 'beneath her', proceeded to have four children, the last born after her husband Samuel's death. The widow then took up with a man known only as 'Skinner' and produced another two children out of wedlock, adding a whiff of scandal to the stink of rotting fish. By this time

Pamela's family, who were of the respectable lower middle class, had cut her off.[1] When the future Mrs David sailed for Australia in 1882, Southwold was already on the up and up. In the 1890s, when the beaches of Norfolk and Suffolk became the chosen playground of the middle classes, the town would undergo a total social transformation – as did its absent daughter half a world away in New South Wales.

Understandably, Caroline David was never expansive about her mother and childhood. She did ensure, though, that her husband's rather more patrician background became common knowledge. T.W.E. David ('Twed' or 'Tweddie' to his wife) was born on 28 January 1858. His father, William, was rector of the Anglican church of St Mary at St Fagans, a picturesque village four miles outside Cardiff whose sixteenth-century castle now houses the Folk Museum of Wales. The thatched whitewashed cottages studded with diamond-paned windows show little signs of change since David and his two younger brothers roamed over Castle Hill, or ran headlong down to the River Ely – a river which famously ran 'crimson with blood' during the English Civil War of the 1640s.

Being of yeoman-farmer stock, the Davids were a fair few rungs higher up the social ladder than the late Sam Mallett, and pretentious enough to have their silver marked with the family coat of arms. William, one of a long line of 'David-ap-Davids' and a Fellow of Jesus College, Oxford, possessed an amateur's interest in genealogy, so 'Twed' grew up knowing that his mother's Irish ancestry included the Edgeworths, and the same James Ussher, Archbishop of Armagh, who in 1654 fixed the date of Creation so very precisely at 4004 BC.[2]

The youngsters' education reflected their contrasting backgrounds. 'Twed' was taught at home by his father, while Caroline attended St Edmund's, the local village school. The unpublished biography of Caroline David nee Mallett, written by Joyce Collins and held in the National Library of Australia as part of the David Family Papers, is rich in detail.[3] From 1870 to 1875, Collins writes, Caroline Mallett was a pupil-teacher at St Edmumd's. Bright as well as pretty, she was probably the teacher's pet, and her classmates soon exacted their revenge. Whoever branded Caroline Mallett 'the Suffolk Punch' showed a modicum of wit, and this nickname marked her all her life. A stocky build and sturdiness are assets in a carthorse (as her yeoman in-laws could have told her), and the 'hairy hocks' of the Suffolk Punch are other noted features. Applied to a girl with thick ankles, however, the wit is less subtle than downright cruel.

In 1875, aged nineteen, Caroline entered London's Whitelands College for teachers, along with sixty-four other young women, the daughters of tradesmen, artisans or superior household servants.[4] With her she brought good looks, a keen intelligence and a tongue honed to razor sharpness (her family baggage she wisely left behind in Suffolk). Under the guidance of the principal, the Reverend J.P. Faunthorpe – a man of obvious charisma, aged thirty-five – 'the Suffolk Punch' settled in and blossomed forth.[5]

Meanwhile, Edgeworth David moved from his father's tuition to Magdalen College School in Oxford. He entered New College, Oxford, in 1876, having won the senior scholarship in classics, and he, too, got off to an excellent start. Prizes came Caroline's way in French, drawing and school management, together with first class certificates in physical geography and botany, and she was proving her to be one of the most gifted and industrious students of her year.[6] Edgeworth, on the other hand was working – and playing – 'too hard'. He suffered some kind of breakdown (what Georgina King on a later occasion termed 'brain fag') possibly aggravated by his unwillingness to adopt the church career chosen for him by his father. He quit Oxford *pro tem* to take a trip per *Yorkshire* to Australia via Canada and back. In 1880 he took out an ordinary degree, his initial brilliance unfulfilled.[7] He returned to Wales unhappy with his prospects, and mooched around the Brecon Beacons indulging a newfound interest in geology.[8]

Caroline Mallett, for her part, was unstoppable. When still only in her second year, she was promoted head governess at Whitelands following the unfortunate death of her predecessor, a Miss Gillott. 'Tall, slim, warm-hearted and dark eyed'[9], perhaps she was *too* favoured and began to push her luck. Australia was no longer the place to send felons, but it *was* a handy destination for those likely to prove an embarrassment to families and employers alike. In an interesting parallel with Mrs Daisy Bates, who was likewise bright, attractive and *single*, Caroline decided to emigrate for what were given as reasons of health: 'her family was tubercular', a condition apparently that Daisy also feared. When Miss Mallett was appointed lady principal of Hurlstone Training College for female teachers in Sydney, perhaps that charismatic cleric, the Reverend J.P. Faunthorpe, gave thanks to his Maker and breathed a heartfelt sigh of relief.

On Friday, 8 October 1880, Lamont Young, an assistant geological surveyor in the Lands Department of New South Wales, landed at Bermagui on the colony's south coast to examine the Montreal gold diggings. By the following Sunday, Young and his companions had disappeared, never to be found, creating what has been known as 'the Bermagui Mystery' ever since. In 1882 Edgeworth David, who since graduation from Oxford had attended geology classes at the Royal School of Mines, learned that his appointment to replace the unfortunate Young had been approved. David and his future wife – later described by their daughter as 'delicate' but of 'indomitable spirit'[10] – first met on board the *Potosi* en route for Australia later that year. Their meeting has been much described, so has the renewal of their acquaintance on terra firma some time later, when David is portrayed as a determined swain in the pursuit of a blushing maidenly bride. (The reverse is just as likely to be true.)

The *Potosi* reached Sydney on 27 November 1882. In April 1885, and despite his prolonged absences on fieldwork,[11] David found himself betrothed. *Reader, I married him* . . . thus ends the classic Gothic romance of *Jane Eyre* – but in Miss Mallett's case marriage was just the beginning. Chance and a dead man's shoes may have brought David to Australia but there was nothing serendipitous about his future progress – or that of his wife. All her life Caroline David was preoccupied with status, and by pushing her diffident husband into professional and social prominence she was able to follow him on the upward spiral herself.

Aware that his intended was deficient in pedigree and likely to be termed a predatory 'adventuress', David wrote to his Aunt Sarah in a veiled bid for her support. *She was poor but she was honest* went the underlying theme, and there was more: people liked her; she had many friends in 'the best Society in Sydney' . . . he loved her . . . she loved him . . .

> *I know that she is really much too good for me but she says that she doesn't think so, and we are both certainly very much in love with one another, and so do you see any reason why we should not be married?*[12]

By the time his dear Aunt Sarah replied, the couple was married and, try as Edgeworth might, the ancestral shades of the Davids, the Edgeworths and the Usshers were yet to be placated. As the Reverend William David put it to his eldest son by letter:

> *The details you have so ingenuously given us of the process of your falling in love with each other were very interesting and amusing . . . From the description you have given of her principles and merits I think you most fortunate to have gained her affections, though my fondness and admiration of you is such that I don't think anyone can be too good for you.*[13]

Or did he mean *good enough*?

With Caroline (or 'Cara' as she became on marriage) standing behind him, prodding, the geologist in David came to the fore. It was a slow but steady progress, and the young woman supplied the strength of purpose that David arguably always lacked. (He would be slow in finishing projects, would rely on the partnership of others, and would be reluctant to confront the awkward matters of everyday existence.) 'The Suffolk Punch' now lived up to her maiden name of Mallett (a diminutive from the French meaning 'little hammer') and while her husband bashed away on his field expeditions, Cara David chipped away at Sydney's bastions of privilege to find her man his proper place.

The geologist was thirty-two when the Chair of Geology and Palaeontology at the University of Sydney fell vacant in 1890, and with a certain show of reluctance David threw his hat into the ring. His appointment the following May was surprising – he was a rank outsider with no form at all in the academic stakes – yet, bucking the trend to bring in new blood from the old world, the local forces were with him. Even so, David was still reluctant and (as his memorialist puts it), his wife's influence 'was largely responsible for his finding the courage to accept'.[14]

He now 'became more and more absorbed in his work, regardless of his own material interests and comfort' while she 'protected hearth and home'.[15] If Caroline kept the home fires burning, the same cannot be said of the flames of passion, and their descendants believe that it was at this time that the couple's sex life came to an end. The blame is attributed to Mrs David, then aged thirty-four and the mother of three young children. Sex had served its purpose – when she gave birth to their son in 1890 (they already had two daughters) dynastic obligations were fulfilled. 'Tweddie' was encouraged to divert his energies elsewhere and marital frustration found itself diverted into ambition and professional success. (As the partnership went from strength to strength, 'Twed' earned another nickname, that of 'Mrs Professor David's Husband'.)

In 1893 he took possession of a brand-new building complete with lecture theatre, laboratories and an academic assistant, and set about putting geology on as good an academic footing as the university's other science subjects. So well did he manage, that in 1894 he was invited to participate in a British-run expedition to test Darwin's theory on the origin of coral reefs.

In the same way that Professor Charles Lyell of King's College London had questioned Archbishop Ussher's theories as to the earth's age (Lyell reckoned it to be in the area of 240 million years rather than Ussher's more conservative 6000), Charles Darwin questioned Lyell on the subject of coral reefs: 'Travellers knew that coral polyps required warmth, light, and shallows, and many assumed that they encrusted *rising* volcanic rims. Even Lyell did.'[16] But what if Lyell were wrong? Darwin's own theory on the subject was formulated before he left Devonport, a twenty-two-year-old on board HMS *Beagle*, whose total nautical experience comprised a trip to Ireland and another across the Channel to France. *Beagle* reached the Keeling or Cocos Islands in the Indian Ocean on 1 April 1836, and Darwin's belief that the rims were *vanishing* rather than *emerging* was strengthened: 'As the land sank, the coral accumulated, rising to compensate, keeping itself at the optimum depth.'[17]

Sixty years later the Royal Society prepared to put this particular theory of Darwin's to the test, selecting Funafuti, an atoll in the Ellice or Lagoon group of islands (present day Tuvalu), as the example. Professors David and Anderson Stuart, who comprised the Australian executive, were invited along on HMS *Penguin*, but both men declined. David was particularly fortunate in his refusal, for thus he became associated with the successes of the second and third expeditions, rather than the failure of the first.

As proved so often the case with Edgeworth David, time and the admiration of his students – and *their* students later – have combined to credit him for the whole Funafuti effort. The expedition was first mooted when Dr Thomas Anderson Stuart visited England in 1891, and to him should be given equal credit for promoting the venture in Australia.[18] Words like 'drive', 'energy', 'arrogance', 'ruthlessness', and terms such as 'enormous fund of self-confidence' have all been applied to Anderson Stuart, the man who brought the Sydney Medical School into being, making him the very antithesis of Edgeworth David. They do, however, suit Edgeworth David's wife. For reasons best known to herself, Mrs David, who was a poor sailor, chose to accompany her husband on the second expedition. For more obvious reasons, upon her return she decided to write a book. Unlike Georgina King, she was too young to have been caught up in the initial excitement over Darwin's evolutionary theory, and remained unimpressed when she came across it later.[19] In her 'unscientific account of a scientific expedition' published in London and Melbourne in 1899, this was made quite apparent:

> *And what about Darwin's coral-atoll theory? Just so. And why was it necessary to prove its truth or otherwise? I don't think it was necessary myself . . . For weeks before starting I heard little else but our foolishness from some of our friends. The usual cry was, 'Well, what's the good of it all? If you were going to open up a diamond field, or a gold mine, or even a good guano deposit, I would take shares.' Of course there was no money in it, nothing but the desire to know, and it was consequently foolishness unparalleled.*[20]

Or was Cara's disdain for Darwin all a pose? Although the Davids returned to Sydney with the work unfinished (it was left to G.R. Sweet to complete the investigation the following year),[21] the outcome was already a resounding success. Using a diamond drill, and despite repeated setbacks, shallow-marine organisms were eventually found down to a depth of 340 metres: Darwin's hypothesis that coral atolls grew on slowly sinking platforms was correct. 'Foolish' or not, the 1897 expedition did more for the professor's future than any amount of gold nuggets.[22]

For all its laboured insouciance and contrived cynicism, Cara's *Funafuti: Or Three Months on a Coral Island* is a lively and readable account – not to mention a public relations triumph. 'David the Leader' was brought to public notice; Cara was revealed both as an amusing and talented writer and a tender and loving wife.[23] By enhancing David's reputation, the book also enhanced her own. Devoted mother, supportive spouse, she continued to look to her family's needs while fulfilling a growing list of social duties. In New South Wales 'the Suffolk Punch' had achieved her wish to be acknowledged as a lady, with a lady's obligations. More importantly – and never mind those unfortunate ankles – most (if not quite all) of Sydney was at her feet.

CHAPTER NINETEEN

The Law of Averages

The gentlemen of New South Wales had their clubs and societies, and from 1889, with the formation of the Women's Literary Society (WLS), the ladies of the colony had theirs. The WLS was an eclectic and elitist mix of privilege and progress with a membership drawn from old families, patrons of the arts and supporters of women's suffrage. At first, meetings took place twice a month at night at 250 Pitt Street, Sydney (a matter of some inconvenience to ladies living in the suburbs), and aimed at pursuing a determined programme of self-improvement. By 1893 the society had 120 members, many of whom had 'little or no formal education'.[1] During the 1893–1894 season, topics ranged from social issues ('Marriage as a Profession' – presented by Miss Robson) to 'Evolution' – given by Miss Scott. Georgina's favourite writers, Herbert Spencer and Thomas Carlyle, were represented in papers possibly read by Georgina herself.[2] Pioneering women abounded. Miss Louisa MacDonald, MA (London) was first principal of the Women's College of the University of Sydney. Miss Edith Badham, daughter of the Reverend Dr Charles Badham, professor of classics and logic, was principal of the Sydney Church of England Grammar School for Girls. Mrs Julian Ashton, wife of the artist and teacher, was a member of the WLS and a social writer for the *Daily Telegraph* in Sydney; she was also a foundation member of the Womanhood League of Suffrage of New South Wales.

Although educated at home and very largely self-taught, Georgina found it quite natural to mix with the leaders of Sydney's intellectual and artistic circles (she had done so ever since she was a child), and she felt totally at ease with even the more radical representatives of that society. Less comfortable was Mrs Caroline David, who was forced to guard her trenchant tongue in those early days in Sydney as she felt her way through the minefield of colonial etiquette.

Mrs David appears to have had no connection with the Womanhood League of Suffrage, a movement founded by members of the WLS in 1891. In any case, working alongside the likes of Rose Scott, Eliza Ashton and Mrs Dora Montefiore would hardly have been to Cara's taste (even suppose anyone had thought to ask her). Dora was a fanatical Jewish widow; the handsome upper-middle-class Rose was outspoken and controversial. Eliza Ashton was more outspoken still and soon incurred the wrath of the establishment by proposing 'a voluntary annual review by spouses' instead of the 'lifelong marriage contract'.[3] With three young children and a husband to get ahead in his profession, Cara was in marriage for the long haul; she had neither the time nor the inclination to fight for the rights of others less fortunate than her. Besides, as a good-looking, strong-minded woman of less than patrician origins, she preferred, whenever she could, to shine alone. In October 1900 Dr Mary Booth invited a group of women to her Hunter Street rooms to discuss the creation of the Women's Club, a club for working women, and all that changed. The response was overwhelming and Professor David's wife became known as a compelling public speaker and one of the town's 'movers and shakers'.

Among those invited to speak at a subsequent meeting of 100 held at the Women's College at the university were the indefatigable Miss Scott and Mrs Edgeworth David (who soon would become every bit as ubiquitous as Rose). It would, said the professor's wife, 'do brainy women good to mix with one another, and others who were not brainy would be none the worse!', and her remarks met with instant approval.[4] The new club came into being with Lady Beaumont, the wife of Vice-Admiral Sir Lewis

Beaumont, RN, commander of the Australia Station, at the helm. Cara David was elected one of four vice-presidents (Rose Scott was another) and took her place among a complement of real life 'ladies' on the committee of a society that (unlike the WLS) catered for 'middle-class women who worked' rather than 'middle-class ladies of leisure'.[5]

A year later the original membership had swelled to 176. Regular meetings were held in a rented room in a small street in central Sydney full of 'drunks and rubbish'. Situated off George Street, the oldest thoroughfare in Sydney, Rowe Street was also the 'waiting place' for members of the oldest profession – a fact of which the clubbing ladies were unaware. Once in the know, they overcame the objections of male relations and blithely went ahead – although, since it was 'a dirty little street', the committee had to 'write sternly to the City Fathers' about rats in the building itself.[6] A circle was formed for social and political discussion, another for lectures, and a third, called The Tuesday Club, was a debating circle 'with 30 regular members, each of whom must share in the discussion, having to stand for three minutes in silence if too shy to speak'. It was the debating circle that saw certain members of the Women's Club involved in a bid to quash Georgina King's buoyant spirit.

The seeds of the attempt were sown years earlier in August 1888, during the inaugural congress of the Australasian Association for the Advancement of Science (AAAS). Among those who took part was T.W.E. David of the New South Wales geological survey. Mrs David attended the functions with her husband and inevitably they met Georgina King, the protégée of Dr George Bennett, that grand old man of colonial science. Several 'scientific wives', including Mrs David, accepted Georgina's invitation to her tea party at the Kings' Ashfield home, but what Georgina naively took as friendship was nothing of the kind. She stood out from the other women present, not only by virtue of her inches and the colour of her hair, but by her obvious thirst for knowledge. As a result, the story that unfolded is not uncommon: the herd mentality prevailing, and the invidualistic spinster being marked down as a freak. That she might be superior not only in height, but in intellect – and breeding – was not allowed to come into the equation.

Not that the women were totally to blame. Natural antipathy apart – for centuries redheads have been seen as suspect, and not for nothing is the treacherous Judas Iscariot traditionally depicted with fiery beard and ruddy locks – hostility towards Georgina King was reinforced by the social practice 'of publicly and institutionally educating the men, but not the women'.[7] This practice was 'routinely extolled (by opponents of higher education for women) as enhancing the harmony of sexual relations by maximising the natural differences between the sexes, thereby increasing the attraction of opposites'. The truth was rather different. Once familiarity with a wife's body increased, so too did contempt for her undeveloped intellect; as a result, 'the experience of educated and intellectual men, expected to live intimately with uneducated women, could be alienation, loneliness and boredom'.[8]

A bored and lonely husband might be tempted to stray elsewhere – so unattached females with an intellectual bent were automatically to be distrusted. 'The women don't like you talking to their Husbands over their heads', Dr Leibius' daughter warned Georgina,[9] but what she failed to add was that her friend was seen as a self-opinionated old maid. One who monopolised men and showed up the ignorance of the women they married, something for which she would never be forgiven. Was Georgina rationalising away the hurt when many years later she stated, 'I chose Science as my liege lord' rather than a man of flesh and blood?

Miss King was human with a human being's failings (her inability to see herself as others saw her was one), yet she shared her father's strengths. She squared her shoulders against her perennial disappointments, spoke out against injustice, and decided to publish her work and let the enemy be damned. Meanwhile, the scientific wives continued to mock the ginger-haired Georgina, and in Mrs Cara David's case derision may have masked her apprehension. Only six years into their marriage, she seems to have virtually ceased intimate relations with her husband. If that was indeed the case, then she had good cause to be wary of any unmarried woman, however unlikely an object of desire (never mind that Georgina's designs were never on Professor David's body, only on the contents of his mind). Caroline David realised soon enough, though, that the threat from Georgina lay in the spinster's research and writing, and with that realisation a clash between the two women – both equally tenacious and equally determined to succeed in their own milieu – was inevitable.

Formally educated and bolstered by considerable academic success, Caroline David was at an apparent advantage (although the scars of her upbringing could never be totally erased). Georgina, on the other hand, a gentlewoman albeit of very modest means, was an autodidact deprived of a formal schooling. Nonetheless, Georgina's interest in geology and her obvious flair for obtaining specimens were clearly in her favour, as was her much-vaunted association with great Sydney personalities of a bygone era. Not unreasonably, Mrs Edgeworth David was envious of Miss King's social poise and excellent family connections. More than that, we believe that she saw Georgina's scientific pretensions as a threat – not to domestic equilibrium, but to her husband's smooth passage to the top of his profession. So Mrs David followed Georgina's progress with no little interest, and when Professor David produced his paper on 'Sills' with its obvious parallels to Georgina's already published research, Mrs David had reason to consider the implications. Her 'Twed' and his tendency to abrogate domestic responsibilities was something his wife could (and did) deal with in the course of her everyday existence; his need for professional stimulus was cause for rather more concern.

Since 1887 and the lukewarm reception given to his work on glaciation by the Geological Society of London,[10] Edgeworth David had been noticeably reluctant to 'go it alone'. Most of the papers he produced these days were for a local audience; they were published locally and frequently were the result of local collaboration. Cara was nobody's fool and thanks to life's vicissitudes, her native wits were scalpel-sharp. It mattered little that Georgina King whinged continually about her ill-treatment at the hands of the Royal Society of New South Wales. It was of no real consequence, either, that she should publish her work anonymously in the *Sydney Morning Herald*, or more recently under that uncomfortable pseudonym of 'Truth'.[11] Her 1895 pamphlet, too, had passed virtually unnoticed among the general public. When a year later there was a second (expanded) pamphlet appearing hot on the heels of David's 'sills and fossils', Mrs David feared it was unlikely to be ignored. Given the King woman's dogged character and her undoubted following, comparison with her husband's work must be avoided at all costs!

At this point let us indulge in a tiny flight of fancy, and imagine a conversation between the Davids along the following lines:

– *I tell you, Twed, that woman is becoming a positive nuisance!*
– *What woman is that, dear?*
– *Miss King, of course! Why, she's telling anyone who'll listen that you've stolen her ideas!*
– *Cara, my love, we've discussed all this before. Why would anyone believe her? I* am *the professor of geology, after all.*
– *Well, she says you have, and now she's published that ridiculous pamphlet to prove it! People are beginning to take notice, too!*
– *My dear Cara, we all have a right to publish our ideas, and Miss King obviously has the means to do it, as well . . . Although it's not as if people will buy the work of an untutored amateur . . .*

– But that's just the point! She's directing people to Angus & Robertson's and because they're the University booksellers, people think she has university approval. They think she has your *approval . . . I tell you, Twed, that if you won't do something about these ridiculous pretensions, then I must . . .*

After the publication of *The Mineral Wealth of New South Wales* in 1896, and secure in the knowledge that her work was in the public domain and her ideas safe, Georgina continued her research. She had a new group of friends, the amateur anthropologists of the Royal Anthropological Society of Australasia, and she frequently published in their journal, *Science of Man*.[12] Her work was esteemed; she herself was valued. Then, some time after her return from the Jenolan Caves in autumn 1902, Robert Etheridge informed her of her pamphlet's fate.

Unlike her father, on this occasion she reacted with admirable restraint:

When I discovered that my pamphlet had been suppressed at my publishers, a good Lawyer wanted me to bring an action against Prof. David, for he said I would get good damages. Other people wanted me to do so also, but I said it would spoil all my work, for I was working for my country, and it would be like a breach of promise. Money can't heal a broken heart, and my heart is in my scientific work.[13]

Instead, a devastated Georgina sent the apparent culprit a letter of reproach.[14] She was still smarting in September 1902 when the University of Sydney celebrated its jubilee, and the university's star turn, 'T.W. Edgeworth David, BA, FGS, FRS, Professor of Geology', gave an address entitled 'University Science Teaching'. In it he made the following remark: 'If honesty and integrity are so dearly prized in the humbler scientific workers, they are surely at least as much to be prized in those that sit in the high places of learning.'[15] The irony was obvious and only a saint could have held her tongue. When whispers began to circulate about one particular man's inhumanity towards one particular woman, it was too much for Mrs Edgeworth David. *That woman* as she hypothetically referred to Georgina, was becoming – no, had become – quite impossible. The problem must be excised . . .

In January 1903 the Women's Club moved to larger premises, still in Rowe Street. Admiral Beaumont weighed anchor and another president took over from his wife. Lady See and Lady Lyne, the two senior vice-presidents, were caught up in their duties as political hostesses, or were already ailing (the former died in 1904, the latter in 1903). With Rose Scott thinly spread over Sydney and campaigning in much of the state, it is easy to see how Mrs David, the fourth vice-president, gained ascendancy within the club.

While Georgina was holidaying at Katoomba in November 1900 she bumped into Mrs Edward Fisher Pittman. 'Oh,' exclaimed the good lady. 'This is the last place I expected to see you. I thought you would have gone to England.'[16] Such a departure would have been an ideal solution for the female half of the 'scientific clique', but of course Georgina stayed put. Not only that, she joined the Women's Club. So Caroline David marshalled her forces, prepared the ground, and set out to humiliate Georgina during one of the Tuesday debates she regularly attended.

Although the rules stated that all members of the debating circle participate or be penalised in the manner already outlined earlier, Georgina asked to be exempted.

> *I was very busy working at my science and I asked the Hon. Sec. Montefiore not to arrange for me to take part in any of the discussions, as I had not the time to take up the such matters, but I just liked to hear the discussions, as it was a rest for me, apart from my scientific study.*[17]

One has to say that the superior tone adopted by Georgina was enough to put any 'Hon. Sec.' offside, and she shouldn't have been surprised at what followed. She was asked not only to participate but take a leading role. The date was set for 4 August 1903, the topic 'The Rights of Minorities – Leaders Miss G. King, Miss Morice'. Concluding 'that it would not be a difficult question' she worked out what she would say.

> *When the time came I took my seat in the second row – Miss Morice in the front row opposite – other members came in and the President, Mrs. Harris, who stopped to speak to Miss Morice but never looked at me, took her seat, and the minutes were read. Then the President said the subject to be discussed is, "The Rights of Minorities", Miss Morice to lead . . .*

It should be pointed out that Georgina had arrived early that Tuesday afternoon and helped Secretary Montefiore to get the room ready. At no time while they were alone together did the secretary intimate that the order of speaker had been changed.

'That moment I felt some trap was laid for me', and she was correct in her assumption.

> *Miss Morice commenced by saying that Anarchists and discontented people should leave the country. And she went on, on this subject and said they were in the minority. Then when she had said her say, the President looked at me for the first time and said, Miss G. King to reply to Miss Morice.*[18]

Georgina's red hair might be fading but there was nothing dull about her wits. She spoke first about the poet Goethe's idea of the beautiful, 'a manifestation of the secret laws of nature'.

> *I said the apparition was revealed to so few, who were in the minority. I went on to speak of artists, poets, etc. all in the Minority, and that there was only one Shakespeare! and that when any great act was before Parliament or Council, it was the amendments formed by the Minority, that made such acts presentable. So the Minorities ruled the world.*[19]

This was not what the ladies had hoped to hear. Miss Morice got to her feet and went straight to the heart of the matter: some pamphlets (she said) had been given her and 'she had been asked to speak on them'. Seventeen years later as Georgina wrote this in her autobiography, the memory was as vivid as on the day it occurred and she knew exactly whom to blame.

> *Mrs. David planned it, and thought she would bring me into complaining about the way the scientific men had taken my discoveries. I had found out that my pamphlet, 'The Mineral Wealth of New South Wales', had been suppressed at my publishers. I knew she had laid a trap for me by giving Miss Morice the pamphlets, and saying that people who were dissatisfied should leave the Country.*[20]

Cara David had hoped to provoke Georgina into voicing a litany of all her grievances, making accusations and naming names. She would then have asked her to resign. The plan failed dismally, but the victim resigned all the same, if under protest. 'At the time I resigned', she tells us, 'I said nothing personal should enter the Club.' Asked to resign 'only for six months', she declined. 'I preferred to resign altogether, than be subjected, perhaps, to other annoyances, from Mrs. David' for 'Everyone but myself seems to be like wax in the hands of the Davids. If the corrupt scientific clique could only be broken up, there might be some hope of a reform, but they are all so afraid of each other.'[21]

The episode at the Women's Club was hurtful and definitive. The enemy had been flushed into the open with deleterious effect. Whereas before Georgina had concentrated her dislike on the professor, now she was filled with loathing for his wife. As time went on, the two became as one in her imagination. In reality their paths from now on rarely crossed, but the wrongs inflicted by the Davids imbued Georgina's life with a bitterness that gnawed away at her psyche like a rodent ulcer.

CHAPTER TWENTY

1903–1913: Miss King and the Queen of the Desert

Dear Professor Spencer,

Thank you for your letter of the 4th. I am inclosing a copy of a letter I received from the Prime Minister's Department, which with others was very aggravating, for they always speak as if anyone could protect our poor children of the bush, and 'that action will be taken to protect them', when as you well know, Mrs. Bates is the most qualified, and more mischief is done, than good, by people being appointed to such positions, who don't understand them.

You are on the spot, and can do so much, that is, if you have time . . .

Georgina King to Professor Baldwin Spencer, 9 May 1914

Georgina repudiated the Women's Club but she did not renounce her publications. Far from being shamed by the events inspired by her pamphlet, she saw them as a vindication of her work. In July 1906, four years after she discovered its suppression, Georgina republished *The Mineral Wealth of New South Wales*. The *Sydney Morning Herald* was particularly kind to her on this occasion and gave her work a favourable review (on 28 August 1906):

This pamphlet consists of articles published in the 'Herald' at various dates, insisting upon a theory of geology, which was counter to the then generally accepted theories, but which has since been adopted by its former opponents.

Miss King naturally feels aggrieved at one item in this reformation. She would naturally be glad to find what she first proclaimed to be the truth accepted generally, but equally naturally she expected that whatever credit was her due should be paid to her. We are not concerned to interfere in the disputes of scientists, which are just as acrid, if not quite so dangerous as the disputes of medical men, but in all reason it might be expected on behalf of a person who has thrown new light on any point in dispute that full acknowledgement should at least be paid to him. This apart, Miss King's contributions to the study of our mineral wealth are intrinsically valuable, and just now, when earnest attention is being awakened in our resources of this kind, their republication in pamphlet form will be of great benefit to those who have the wisdom to be taught. The present pamphlet contains several interesting and valuable articles, which were published in the 'Herald' since the first edition appeared.

The newspaper's board was more careful than Georgina ever would be over the matter of possible libel (on this occasion she indicted E.F. Pittman for 'recasting' her discovery re intrusive rocks in 1899 and again in 1901). Circumspect it might have been, but recognition by the *Sydney Morning Herald* was no less sweet for that, and in the years between 1903 and 1913 five of Georgina's articles, including one on Jenolan Caves, were published in the paper.[1] She was grateful for its support, for under the previous regime (as she knew from what the sub-editor, Mr Geoffrey Fairfax, told her) 'the scientific men had gone to the Editor, and asked him not to take any more of my writings'.[2] Thomas Heney, who took over as editor in 1903, and Samuel Cook, the manager, shared some of Georgina's interests: Heney 'cultivated native plants in his garden and collected Australian semi-precious stones';[3] and Cook, of course, had published his own articles on Jenolan back in 1886 – facts that undoubtedly helped her cause.

But in the end, even the generous William Heney had

enough and from 1913 the *Herald* declined to take any more of her work.[4] It was not surprising: Georgina maintained her perennial interest in minerals, iron in particular, but all the time she was moving away from the mainstream – some might say to the edge of the lunatic fringe.

Even before she resigned from a club that, according to Mrs David, rejoiced in an atmosphere of 'no wire-pulling and no squabbles'[5] Georgina's ideas tended to take her in all directions. When her parents died, she became deeply involved with the Royal Anthropological Society of Australasia, mixing with a group of people who nowadays are viewed by the scientific establishment as mainly dangerous cranks.[6] The society was set up in 1896 by Dr Alan Carroll, a Sydney paediatrician, and received the royal approval in 1899. Its patrons were state premiers, governors, and the governor-general. Its president was the lieutenant governor of New South Wales; its vice-presidents were respected and active politicians. All the same, it represented a science in its infancy and lacked the gravitas and big guns of, say, the Royal Australian Historical Society (with which it had a certain amount of uneasy contact). And there, among the society's individualistic not to say eccentric adherents, whose notions of anthropology appear to have 'combined racism with Lamarckian sentiments',[7] Georgina King found acceptance and a refuge from the Women's Club's own particular brand of nastiness and 'isms'.

She became a frequent contributor to the society's journal, *Science of Man*, and in February 1907 was elected a Fellow. Another Fellow was Mrs Daisy May Bates, the Irishwoman employed by the Western Australian government to research the indigenous tribes of that state and whose pamphlet, *Efforts made by Western Australia towards the Betterment of the Aborigines*, contained 'much useful information upon the efforts made by missions and other benevolent institutions to civilise and train the aboriginals by earnest men and women from the founding of the colony to the present time'.[8] This review, published in *Science of Man*, struck a chord with Georgina, who immediately took up her pen. By the end of the year the lady Fellows were corresponding regularly, though Georgina's letters to Daisy are regrettably not represented in either woman's archive.

George and Jane King were examples of those 'earnest men and women' who occupied themselves with what their daughter termed 'the children of the bush'. As she advanced towards old age, Georgina talked increasingly of her father's experiences when he 'studied the character of the primary aborigines of the bush in their native state in Western Australia',[9] and Daisy was more than willing to take notice. Although the Kings landed at Fremantle in 1841, and left again in 1849 when Georgina was only four and can have had few personal recollections, she provided a valued link between present investigations and the past. (Georgina's letters were a necessary element in 'beefing up' the articles on the Kings that Daisy wrote later – for while Mrs Bates worked hard at being taken seriously as a scientist, she had to eat as well.)

The story Daisy would uncover was unhappily all too common. George King did not aspire towards acceptance as a scientist; neither did he content himself with disinterested observations. Rather, he strove to change the 'native state' he witnessed into something more worthwhile. The Swan River settlers cared little for the natives' survival. They viewed these 'Indians' (as some called them) with the uttermost distaste, and the parson's unfashionable interest in their welfare met with scant approval among the community at large. 'I never witnessed so affecting a sight as this display of the degradation of humanity', Lucy Clifton, daughter of Australind's leader, wrote soon after she arrived at the fated settlement in 1841.

> *They do not look like human beings, so thin, so hideous, so filthy; oiled and painted, red faces and hair, and pieces of rush passed*

through their hair. They danced and distressed us all more; in fact I feel distressed at the idea of living among such a people, so low, so degraded a race.[10]

Lucy had condemned the native flora just as quickly, and again she changed her mind. Whereas she was moved to pity, King was moved to action.

The Methodists had moved into the area of native education already, and King decided to emulate his rivals in Christ. He had enough of the competitor about him not to wish to be bested, but we should also give full credit to his sense of natural justice. Ever quick to defend his own rights, he felt a deep shame for what the Aborigines were suffering at the hands of the colonists. 'We have usurped their well-stocked hunting grounds', he wrote, 'taken possession of their fisheries; & ploughed up the very staff of life, which the rich valleys naturally yielded, in the bulbs & roots so [con]genial to native life.'[11] His solution, although offered in all sincerity, was equally destructive, and the 'bread of eternal life' he offered in return in no way compensated for the loss of culture and tradition. (King, a man never noted for his sense of humour, failed to see the irony in that.)

He set up a mission school in a house lent him by the government and began to look for funds. Governor Hutt provided a grant of £50 per annum and eleven native children were removed from their parents (or 'collected', as King put it, once their parents' permission had been obtained) then schooled, to 'civilize & evangelize them'. The parson fostered an additional, more practical aim: 'to teach the pupils trades, according to their several capacities; *ultimately to establish them in life*, married to their fellows, so as to escape the many temptations to evil habits, by which, under other circumstances they might be surrounded.'[12]

After twelve months, when the children were deemed sufficiently domesticated, King prepared them for baptism, first buying off the girls' assigned husbands with a 'few pieces of

Reverend George King.
Courtesy of the Mitchell Library, State Library of New South Wales, PXA 1239.

Mrs Jane King.
Courtesy of the Mitchell Library, State Library of New South Wales, PXA 1239.

Georgina King.
Courtesy of the Library of the Royal Botanic Gardens, Melbourne.

St Peters Parsonage, Cooks River, Sydney. Courtesy of the Mitchell Library, State Library of New South Wales, PXA 1239.

King family portrait; includes Reverend and Mrs George King, centre front row, and Georgina, third from left back row. Courtesy of the Mitchell Library, State Library of New South Wales.

Miss Georgina King with family members; the boy is very probably her beloved nephew, Esca Humphrey. Courtesy of the Mitchell Library, State Library of New South Wales, PXA 153/27.

Reverend William Branwhite Clarke, 1878? Courtesy of the National Library of Australia, pic-an9351872;6, from *Sydney Mail*.

Dr George Bennett. Portrait. Courtesy of the National Library of Australia, pic-vn3791179, from G.M. Mathews collection of portraits of ornithologists.

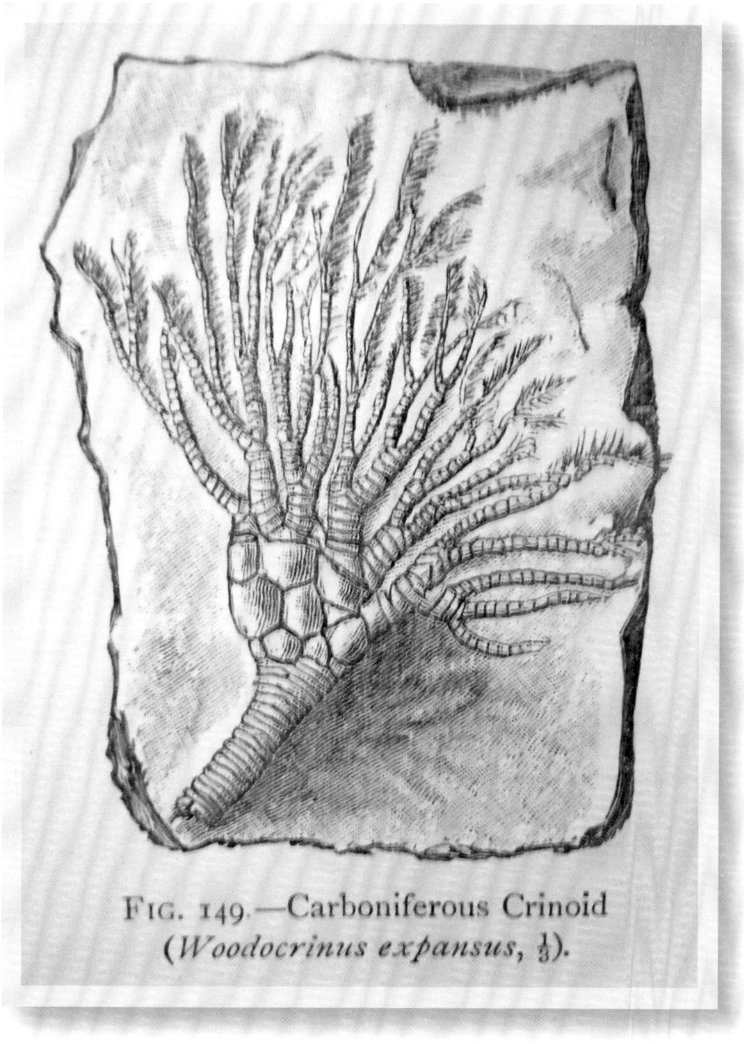

Devonian Carboniferous crinoid. From Geikie, A., 1899, *Class-Book of Geology*, London: Macmillan (illustration, p. 278).

The Zig Zag Railway, Blue Mountains.
Original lithograph in the authors' collection.

The Great Arch, Jenolan Caves.
Original lithograph in the authors' collection.

Sir Edgeworth David, ca 1916. Courtesy of the National Library of Australia, pic-an24376652, portrait by Judith Fletcher.

Springfield House, at Byng home of the Webb family.
Courtesy of Dr John Hawke and Mrs Alison Hawke.

Cooerwull House at Bowenfels, home of Andrew and Christina Brown.
Courtesy of Mr Tim Trevor-Jones and Mrs Elizabeth Trevor-Jones.

THE

MINERAL WEALTH

OF

NEW SOUTH WALES

AND

OTHER LANDS AND COUNTRIES

BY

GEORGINA KING, F.R.A.S.A.

Sydney:

WILLIAM BROOKS & CO., LTD., Printers

17 Castlereagh Street.

Front Cover of Georgina's pamphlet

The Mineral Wealth of New South Wales and Other Lands and Countries.

Courtesy of the National Library of Australia.

Aug. 27, 1921

MRS. DAISY M. BATES,
Who is in charge of the Native Camp, Ooldea, East-West Railway. The second instalment of "On the Great Plain's Edge," by Mrs. Bates, appears in this issue. (Dease photo.)

Mrs Daisy M. Bates, 1921.
Courtesy of the National Library of Australia, papers of Daisy Bates, Folio 88, MS 365-88-466.

Professor Sir Frederick McCoy, 1859.
Courtesy of the National Library of Australia, pic-an9727387;7, portrait by Hamel & Co.

Fossil samples 1 (*top*) and 2 (*below*) sent by Georgina to Sir Frederick McCoy at the University of Melbourne, 1896. Courtesy of Museum Victoria, P182375 & P206528.

Baron Ferdinand Jakob Heinrich von Mueller, ca 1879.
Courtesy of the National Library of Australia, pic-an23514205,
portrait by James F. Armstrong.

silver'.[13] It was an unfortunate choice of phrase given its association with deep betrayal, yet King had only his charges' welfare at heart. The suggestion that he send his pupils to Rottnest Island (which had been in use as a prison for delinquent Aborigines since 1838) filled the parson with horror. If that happened, he told his superiors, '*we shall not readily be intrusted with the guardianship of their little ones again*'.[14]

Decades passed and King's contribution in the missionary field was forgotten by all but those closest to him. Then, in 1910, George King's sacrifices and those of his wife were recalled by Mrs Daisy Bates, whose attitudes towards the native peoples of Western Australia more or less coincided with his own. Over the hundred or so years since then, Mrs Bates has been depicted variously as 'strait-laced do-gooder, pioneer anthropologist, true friend of the Aborigines, or eccentric recluse'.[15] In other words, she remains an enigma. While Parson King's career in Australia was founded on a sense of self-importance and a fair degree of bluster, Daisy's derived from a mesh of misleading information, not to say downright lies. Far from being 'county Irish' as she claimed, and sustained by the Protestant values inculcated by her privileged background, she came from a Catholic family and was forced to work for her living. She knowingly entered into a bigamous marriage with Jack Bates, having turned her back on a brief marriage with Harry 'The Breaker' Morant.[16] Her behaviour 'defied convention, her attitudes remained conventional' and her clothing dress 'never deviated from the strictest dictates of Edwardian fashion'. There were greater contradictions:

> *She devoted her life to Aboriginal people, often went hungry to give them food and cared for them most tenderly in sickness, but at the same time, she regarded them as somewhat unclean, even polluting, and always avoided skin contact by wearing gloves.*[17]

The friendship that developed between the mendacious Daisy and George King's daughter, who from childhood was punished for her uncomfortably strict adherence to the truth, is not as surprising as it seems. Georgina admired Bates's efforts to ease the passing of a supposedly dying race, while, for her part, Daisy initially exploited Georgina's pride in her parents' achievements but came to love her as a loyal friend.

In February 1910, Mrs Bates's article on the Kings for the *Western Mail* was finished.[18] 'I very much wished to write twice as much as I did write re your dear father & mother's work amongst the natives of the West', Daisy told Georgina, 'but the inexecrable editor limited me to a column & I could only exceed his orders by half a column'.[19] (Nonetheless, there *was* a section on Georgina and her scientific achievements, by way of thanks.) By now, Mrs Bates had good cause to feel grateful:

> *I hear you have given up all social life to my work. I am as happy as Larry over the sacrifice . . . How delightful to think you will one day pay a visit to the West! & you have chosen a most happy time. September & October are ideal months.'*

Daisy's passage through life was rarely smooth. Like Georgina, her aspirations to gain recognition from the male scholars who ran the show in her day were more often than not doomed to disappointment. Her hopes for the post of Chief Protector of Aborigines in the Northern Territory were dashed when Professor Baldwin Spencer of Melbourne was appointed in her stead. Her participation in the Oxford and Cambridge universities' expedition to Western Australia's north-west as assistant ethnologist[20] proved less a success than a professional disaster. From the moment she joined them, it was clear to other members of the party that Mrs Bates and Professor Alfred R. Brown, the leader, were totally incompatible and unlikely to get on. Daisy concentrated more on welfare than on science (she also had leadership aspirations), while Brown was a self-opinionated show-off. 'He was too dramatic a personality . . . He often made wild statements, he was brilliantly informed on all subjects'[21] – regardless of whether he knew anything about them or not.

> *He was quick to see that Mrs Bates was the possessor of a priceless store of knowledge . . . not in a condition that Brown considered easily available for the ends of science . . . The contents of her mind, in his estimation, were somewhat similar to the contents of a well-stored sewing basket, after half a dozen kittens had been playing there undisturbed for a few days. At first he optimistically thought he might disentangle some of that rich medley, but in this he proved mistaken. She was made for his exasperation, as he for hers.*[22]

Daisy's magnum opus, *The Native Tribes of Western Australia*, was well on the way to completion. In an action that matches Georgina for naiveté, she let Brown borrow a copy of the manuscript to read. The group split up on several occasions and when Brown left for England in 1912, he took part if not all of Daisy's work with him. He returned the manuscript but was later accused of reproducing sections as his own. The similar experiences – Georgina's with David et al. and Daisy's with Brown – brought the two mettlesome old ladies closer together, but their proposed meeting did not take place until 1914, and in Melbourne, not in Perth. In the meantime they continued to correspond, and kept conversant with each other's research through letters and the columns of *Science of Man*. And all the while, under his wife's patient guidance, Professor David's public career advanced steadily onward and upward.

In 1906 the professor was chosen as New South Wales's official representative at the tenth International Geological Conference in Mexico City. Thanks in part to a fruitful collaboration with Richard D. Oldham of the Indian Geological Survey, David was fast becoming an authority on the 'Past Ice Ages', featuring in three of his four conference papers. En route he visited the Deccan in India to collect evidence of glacial action, and then attended the British Association for the Advancement of Science meeting in York. Outwardly, at least, he was far different from the young man whose tentative offerings on glaciation were rebuffed by the geologists of London in 1887. His two papers for York, 'Our Diamonds in Nature in New South Wales' (a subject, incidentally, that Georgina had been studying for years[23]) and 'Our coal-measures of New South Wales', were safely parochial and very 'well received'.[24]

Privately, however, the professor was not doing quite as well. As he made for Melbourne by train on 6 May 1906 at the start of his marathon journey, he dashed off a note to Cara. He had, he told her, left his 'secretary' (presumably an early version of the Filofax) at the university, in his room. Perhaps, he suggested, she should check and see if there was anything of a business nature that needed to be dealt with.[25] Caroline David to all appearances accepted the lot of a public figure's wife. In an earlier age, Isabel Burton, wife of the oriental scholar and explorer, Sir Richard Francis Burton, was expected to 'pay, pack and follow' in the great man's wake. Cara David stayed put in Sydney but (like Mrs Burton) she tidied up the unpaid bills her husband had a happy knack of overlooking.

In 1907 David fulfilled his final obligation to the Geological Survey of New South Wales when his paper 'The Geology of the Hunter River Coal Measures, New South Wales. General Geology and the Development of the Greta Coal Measures' was published.[26] Part one of an intended two-part work, it had been on the backburner since 1891, but then – as his daughter explained in her 1937 biography, *Professor David* – he was always 'a slow but very thorough worker'.[27] Free at last of his commitment to his former employer, David celebrated by going off to Mount Kosciusko in the Snowy Mountains with a couple of colleagues in September, and learning how to ski.

David's subsequent career was marked with several happy accidents that served to enhance his standing, and the acquisition of this new skill may have been another. He had visited the area twice in the summer of 1906 – to a geologist with a declared interest in glaciations, the Australian Alps with their glacial lakes, glaciated rock-pavements and moraines were a constant source of interest – but on this occasion one suspects an additional motive. It was about this time that Lieutenant Ernest Shackleton, a junior member of Robert Falcon Scott's National Antarctic Expedition of 1901–1903, began to plan his own assault on the Great White South. Renowned for the grand failure of his second expedition, Shackleton began recruiting for his first towards the end of 1907. Perhaps (one speculates) an expert in past ice ages saw a chance to escape from the frigid confines of a present and sexless marriage – if only for a while.

With public interest in the expedition growing, family legend puts it rather differently.

> *The Professor, needless to say, was one of the most interested [in the project]. The romance of the idea, apart from the scientific interest of exploring in unknown regions, appealed strongly to him, and when Lieutenant Shackleton invited him to accompany the expedition, remain for one summer and return with the* Nimrod, *he joyfully accepted.*[28]

David's departure on the British Antarctic Expedition of 1907–1909 has shades of his Mexican trip the previous year. When he was safely on the boat to New Zealand he wrote a letter home to his wife, in which loving words and slavish protestations of devotion prepared the way for an unpleasant revelation.[29] Rather than worry Cara at the last moment and spoil the poignancy of departure (he said), he had waited until now to explain the shockingly high bill for 'those meteorological kites'. With that off his chest, the professor felt able to advise his wife how to cope – given the unexpectedly depleted state of the family finances – and once in Antarctica he proceeded to have the time of his life. He led the first ascent of Mount Erebus, an active volcano of 13,000 feet (the danger of eruption as nothing compared with Cara David's wrath) and overstayed his leave by well over a year.[30]

In March 1909 Professor David was back in Sydney. Georgina's account of the hero's return, while succinct, differs in detail from the tributes paid him by posterity. According to Miss King, Mrs David's intervention saved her husband from disgrace: 'Professor David went to the Antarctic. The authorities at the University were not well pleased at his absence without leave, and there was talk of making short work of his services. Mrs. David quietly retired to a Mental Home on the North Shore Line[31], and the Chancellor of the University was approached about her losing her reason over the matter, so he was pardoned. Sir Normand Maclaurin was the Chancellor at the time.'[32]

As part of the official welcome home, David was pronounced the Mueller Medallist of the Australasian Association for the Advancement of Science. He was elected president of the Royal Society of New South Wales. In 1910, the year he was consulted over the proposed site of the nation's new capital, 'The Palace' appointed him a Commander of the Most Chivalrous Order of Saint Michael and Saint George.

It was all extremely galling for Georgina, the only woman (apart from his long suffering wife) to know the professor's imperfections. Words like '(c)ourage, courtesy, enthusiasm, devotion to duty, unselfishness, modesty, generosity, and a host more qualities equally admirable'[33] must have made her want to vomit forth her own perceptions of the man's shortcomings. Instead, she countered in the only way she knew. 'By the request of friends', she prepared to republish her pamphlet, including the *Sydney Morning Herald* review of the 1906 edition. She added a new article, 'Earthquakes: The Glacial Periods' which the *Herald* had published on 23 January 1909, as well as a short account of 'the struggles I have had with the three geologists, Professor Liversidge, Professor David and Mr. E. F. Pittman . . . in making my discoveries known to the world'.[34]

By the time the pamphlet went on sale in February 1911, of the three men Georgina accused of scientific theft Archibald Liversidge was back in London (he retired from the Chemistry

Department in 1907) and Edward Pittman was plodding along in his usual unremarkable way. The third, T.W.E. David, was in England, about to receive an honorary degree of DSc from Oxford and soaking up admiration like a sponge.[35]

Over in the West, meanwhile, life for Daisy Bates was full of the usual ups and downs. The years spent pioneering new fieldwork methods, her observations and the experiences that made up the subject matter of 'The Native Tribes of Western Australia', all the years of hard work and determination had come to nothing. Her participation in the joint Oxford and Cambridge expedition had caused a fatal delay. Employed by a government of one political persuasion, its electoral defeat in 1911 left her without a sponsor. The new Labor government of John 'Happy Jack' Scaddan refused to publish her completed manuscript, returned it to her, and terminated her employment.

Journalism became her sole means of earning a living, and in Sydney T.W. Heney at the *Sydney Morning Herald*, no longer interested in Georgina's offerings, accepted those of Mrs Bates (a seasoned hack who knew how to give the public what it wanted). In 1913 Dr Alan Carroll, the impetus behind the Royal Anthropological Society of Australasia, died, and *Science of Man* likewise turned up its toes. For Georgina both events were catastrophic, but not so for Mrs Bates, who, unlike the older woman, was moving nearer to acceptance by her peers. That year, thanks to the intervention of the Reverend John Mathew,[36] Daisy was asked to contribute a paper to the AAAS in Melbourne. Georgina, for whom no such invitation was forthcoming, and who had so successfully brought Daisy's work to the notice of the *Sydney Morning Herald*, continued to campaign on behalf of her friend.

Since November 1912 Daisy had been Honorary Protector of Aborigines at Eucla, a town that had developed around the telegraph station 15 miles or so from the South Australian border on the Great Australian Bight. She wished to become a (paid) Protector of Aborigines along the proposed Trans-Australian Railway line from Kalgoorlie to Port Augusta, to be constructed 65 miles to the north. There, she would keep an eye on the fettlers as well as her native friends. Generous with her time as usual, Georgina wrote numerous letters to everyone with influence she knew or knew of, including Professor Baldwin Spencer, and even mistakenly travelled to Melbourne to lobby the Federal Minister for External Affairs (it was a state, not a federal matter). Despite writing a succession of long, importunate and discursive letters (Georgina was at no time in her life an exponent of the theory that 'less is more'), she wore no one down to the point of surrender.

In November 1913 Mrs Bates moved to the railway line anyway, 'deep in the bush and close to a storage tank', with about forty Aborigines camped nearby.[37] By the end of the year she was at 'Jeegala Creek, a lonely water-hole sixteen miles out of Eucla and seven miles from the South Australian border', where, she assured Miss King, 'No queen is safer in her place than I in my unfastened tent'.[38] It was a far remove from Georgina's lifestyle – she was in the Blue Mountains at Leura – or from David's, as he made a hurried trip back to England on scientific matters. While he busied himself with arrangements for the visit of the British Association to Australia the following year, Daisy was serving up a 'dinner of damper, tea and pudding for fifty-three of her Aboriginal friends'.[39] 'What pleasure I should have in clasping your friendly hand! Perhaps kindly fates will make that possible one day', she once wrote to Georgina, when the prospect seemed most unlikely.[40] But as 1914 dawned, the tide turned again for Daisy Bates: she received an invitation to take part in the British Association Congress orchestrated by Edgeworth David. 'In itself it was an acknowledgement of status in the scientific world. Daisy saw it as a Heaven-sent opportunity to press for the post of Protector.'[41] And, of course, it meant that she would at last meet Georgina King, that dear friend who had so many excellent connections.

CHAPTER TWENTY-ONE

Alas! Poor Yorick. I knew him . . .

The years 1888–1913, when the Association for the Advancement of Australasian Science was under the leadership of Archibald Liversidge and his immediate successors, formed the 'heroic phase' of Australian science. Between the centennial and the outbreak of the First World War in 1914, the British Association for the Advancement of Science, upon which the AAAS was based, bound 'the energies of colonial nationalism' to 'the spirit of the imperial federation', as one commentator has put it.[1] Meetings of both associations were an annual event; in the case of the revered senior body they dated back to 1831.

So when in 1914 the BAAS accepted an invitation to hold its annual meeting in Australia (the only time it has done so), boundless care, energy and enthusiasm were devoted to the preparations by its grateful Antipodean hosts. The purpose of such a gathering was threefold: to promote the exchange of ideas; to give Australia a chance to see famous minds in action; and to offer those minds a rare chance to see Australia (at considerable expense to the Australian taxpayer, it must be said).[2] By the time a group comprising 'more than 300 British, American, European, and other foreign and Dominion scientists'[3] reached Adelaide in August 1914, the party mood was tarnished. When they reached Melbourne the eight German participants in what was intended as a carefree intellectual junket were distinctly out of place – their arrival overshadowed by news of Germany's invasion of Belgium and the outbreak of war.

In an atmosphere of uncompromising jingoism (flag-bearing patriots had earlier invaded the streets of Melbourne, and

Echuca's topers refused to sup German beer), the Melbourne meetings went ahead. For this, full credit must be given to Professor David, yet despite his best efforts, the Melbourne meeting was marred by both overt and underlying tensions.[4]

While the Germans were being saved from public ire and swaddled in reassurance by Edgeworth David ('All men of science are brothers', he insisted[5]), those two battling scientific sisters, Daisy Bates and Georgina King, met for the very first time. Daisy's advent was an achievement in itself. Travelling from Eucla by camel buggy, she crossed 240 miles of the southern Nullarbor Plain to reach Fowler's Bay, and then proceeded by steamer to Adelaide and on by train to Melbourne – where she was interviewed 'with the same deference that had been accorded her in Adelaide'.[6]

Melbourne was also memorable for renewed skirmishing between Mrs Bates and her old enemy, A.R. Brown, who was now professor of anthropology at the University of Cape Town, South Africa. Brown was yet to turn a plain and common surname into the more distinguished double-barrelled 'Radcliffe-Brown', but guns and sniping were still very much the order of the day. When Brown indulged in his 'unfortunate habit of using the writings of others without either giving them due credit or even (if they were alive) asking their permission'[7], Daisy stood up and accused him of downright plagiarism. 'I don't think Brown will ever forget the incident', she noted grimly.[8] The experience brought Daisy and her chief supporter (whom she called 'one of God's good women') even closer.[9]

In Sydney, where Daisy stayed as Georgina's guest, they attended the Anthropology Section along with Rose Scott and Georgina's favourite nephew, Esca Morris Humphery, now an established doctor of medicine. As far as anthropology was concerned, there was an emphasis on primitive weapons (with the accent on the Australian Aboriginal) and matters relating to prehistoric man. On Friday, 21 August, they watched together from the gallery as Professor Edgeworth David, who had 'boned up' on anthropology as Walter Baldwin Spencer's guest in Melbourne,[10] produced 'the most dramatic incident of the anthropological section's meetings in Australia' in unveiling what has become known as 'The Talgai Skull'.[11]

The Talgai cranium is an ugly-looking brute of a thing; it is heavily encrusted with minerals, and has, 'for an Australian', remarkably prominent eyebrow regions. One side of it is crushed. One of the canines, or eyeteeth, protrudes 'like a great tusk'. More importantly, its appearance before some of the world's most esteemed scientists in Sydney provided a perfect counterpoint to recent discoveries made in Europe, England even, meriting phrases such as 'the most important moment in Australian anthropology' and 'dramatic and epoch-making' in newspaper reportage at the time. To understand its true impact on the attendance at Professor David's lecture, however, we must follow the development of geology as a science.

While both Georgina King and Edgeworth David had their part to play in the so-called 'heroic phase' of Australian science, the 'heroic age' of geology occurred well before either of them was born. And before that, in 1654, David's forebear Archbishop Ussher had established the chronology of the Bible by putting the date of Man's creation as the morning of 23 October 4004 BC – at 9 o'clock precisely.[12]

This notable achievement was to hobble the advance of science for over one hundred years. As serious students of geological phenomena struggled to change the perception of Ussher's Biblical 'truths', many ingenious theories abounded, accommodating both the sacred and profane. One such was Abraham Werner's 'Neptunism',[13] a catastrophic process of sudden and violent upheavals that almost exclusively involved the sea and great floods. The theory that new lands were created when old ones eroded was not only handy, but acceptable to the Church as well. After each flood, the last of which was Noah's 'as recorded by Moses' – and dated by Ussher as occurring in 2501 BC – a conscientious Creator would restock the land as the Holy Spirit moved Him. The creation of new species in such a manner also satisfied the naturalists.[14]

James Hutton, a Scot from Edinburgh, challenged this cosy state of affairs in 1785. A student of his native igneous granite, Hutton was a man born before his time. His published *Theory of the Earth* detailed the notion of *gradual* and *continuous* transformation – the change occurring uniformly over an infinity of time and as a result of great pressure and heat.[15] Then, as now, in the sheltered groves of Academe, where theories, once rooted, endure like mighty forest oaks, there was marked resistance to radical change. When Hutton's opponents ridiculed him openly, and applied the term 'Vulcanism' to his ideas, the public followed suit. And who could blame them? Thanks to a mathematically minded Irish cleric, society was conditioned to believe that the earth had existed for a period of 6000 years all up. The notion of *unlimited* time, with 'no vestige of a beginning and no prospect of an end',[16] was unimaginable. *For Ever and Ever, Amen* was all very well in the *Book of Common Prayer* but as part of the everyday it was another matter. Nor were the clergy best pleased to see 'Man' beginning to question God's system . . .

Thanks to the efforts of William 'Strata' Smith, eventually geology was put on a firm scientific footing. It became a leisurely and enjoyable pastime for all classes (as well as an arena for academics squabbling over the respective merits of water versus fire). Speculation gave way to fieldwork. 'The Father of English Geology', as Smith became known, explored England on foot unaided and alone, and in 1815 produced his 'Geological Map of England'. In support of the map and the *Memoir to the Map* he published with it, he produced two books (in 1816 and 1817) suggesting that rocks could be dated from the fossils they contained. By the 1820s Smith's method of collecting valid geological data became the principle upon which geology was based. He had put paid to the Neptunist–Vulcanist debate once and for all.[17]

Yet geology involved more than the examination of rocks and strata: it was at the cutting edge of the great debate about life on Earth and the relationship between God and Man. The clash between science and religion was inevitable – from now on science would strike at two deeply held beliefs. Firstly, that the Biblical texts were literal, and secondly, that human beings (referred to as 'Man') were a unique species vested with an immortal soul that absolutely distinguished them from all other species.[18] Furthermore, during a period of considerable social upheaval (this was the time of the Industrial Revolution), geologists appeared to attack the very foundations of an orderly society – by diminishing God's role as the fount of all knowledge.[19]

William Buckland, reader in geology at Oxford and later Dean of Westminster, 'sought to reconcile the discoveries of the geologists with the text of *Genesis*, particularly the description of the Flood'.[20] William Conybeare and William Phillips in their *Outlines of the Geology of England and Wales* (1822) 'allowed for the Flood and various other catastrophes and Divine interventions' in a canny compromise that saw their work run to several editions.[21] They were all on a hiding to nothing. Questions about the antiquity of the earth, the structure of its formations, and the significance of fossils were paving the way for the biggest shock of all: in 1844 the *Vestiges of the Natural History of Creation* was published anonymously in Edinburgh and that nasty little brute known as 'Evolution' was out of the bag, and taking its first faltering steps towards the light.

At the time, finding fossil animal bones was nothing new. Nor was finding primitive stone implements. They were collected, noted and stored. In Britain, the disconcerting idea that extinct species of animals might have co-existed with humans began to gain ground.[22] Kent's Cavern in Devon, England, first yielded its secrets in 1825, when flint tools were found in close association with the bones of extinct animals (although the Church was not happy about the juxtaposition). At the far extreme of Empire in 1835, Hugh Falconer, MD, superintendent of the botanical gardens at Saharanpur, India, and an enthusiastic palaeontologist, found the remains of *Colossochelys Atlas* – 'a gigantic extinct tortoise, some twelve feet long, eight feet broad and six feet high'.[23] He would also find the fossil bones of *Ramapithecus*, a primitive ape. Primaeval man, meantime, was turning up in Europe. In 1856 a significant collection of bones, including a skullcap, were discovered in the Neander Valley near Düsseldorf in Germany, and found their way to Professor Hermann Schaafhausen of Bonn, an early believer in evolution. Other finds from other sites showed distinct similarities.

We of the twenty-first century have lost our sense of wonder as the chronology of man is regularly extended further and further back into the past. 'Another face in our family tree', proclaimed the prestigious scientific journal *Nature* in March 2001, presaging a decade of further dramatic discoveries. 'The evolutionary history of humans is complex and unresolved. It now looks set to be thrown into further confusion by the discovery of another species and genus, dated to 3.5 million years ago.' The discoveries have continued ever since. In comparison, the Neander skullcap – with its prominent eyebrow ridges and belonging to a line of early humans that apparently became extinct – at a mere 50,000 years of age seems as nothing. Yet it was immeasurably important. Not that scientists at the time saw the grim relic for what it was – or if they did, they kept their own counsel. (Man, after all, was a handsome fellow created in God's own image.) 'This much was sure', comments the author of a book on the much later Piltdown discoveries in Southern England. 'When a fossil man was found at last nobody recognised him.'[24]

Professor Schaafhausen was circumspect when he published the Neanderthal remains in 1857. Apart from a declaration that here was a genuine fossil that lived in 'a period when the latest animals of the diluvium [i.e. 'Noah's Flood'] still existed',[25] he made no bolder claims. The analysis carried out on the limbs, ribs, etc., by Professor F. Mayer of Berlin reveals something of the quality of the subsequent debate:

> *A protuberance on the left elbow, said by Schaafhausen to be the scar of an old injury, was none other than a symptom of advanced rickets. The protruding eyebrow ridges confirmed this diagnosis. The owner was in fact a Mongolian Cossack on his way through Prussia in 1814 in pursuit of Napoleon's fleeing army. The pain of the disease had furrowed the forehead of the horseman, for such he was, as only a professional equestrian would have such bowed legs. The Cossack, said Mayer, had crawled into the Neanderthal cave and succumbed in agony. Mayer did not explain how the stricken man had managed to climb up sixty feet of vertical rock to the cavern nor did he even mention this fact.*[26]

The French Académie des Sciences toed the orthodox line and ignored the discovery altogether. There was one mention in the *Westminster Review* and another in the *Gazette*, but it was not noticed where one might have expected, i.e., by the Royal and Geological societies and the British Association for the Advancement of Science. Rather, a hunt for flint implements consumed the worthy members, but none of them made the link to Neanderthal Man. When the British Association met in 1860 at Oxford 'Apes and Angels' abounded, but – despite the inferences that humans evolved from one, if not the other – Neanderthal Man was a notable absentee.

Three years after the vicious Oxford debate of 1860, the man from the Neander Valley received his apotheosis. At the British Association meeting at Newcastle, Professor William King of Queen's College, Galway, proposed to make a separate species – *Homo neanderthalensis*. The first to create a new species of the fossil man, King also damned him: he looked like a chimpanzee, hence he must have shared the brutishness of the chimpanzee – a conclusion reflecting 'an undercurrent of belief about the moral status of the Neanderthals' that has remained with us ever since.[27] By the time the Association met at Nottingham in 1866, Darwinism was gaining ground. It ceased to be a 'tentative scientific theory and became a philosophy, almost a religion'.[28] Despite men like Charles Lyell finding 'man's unbroken descent from the brutes' too much to swallow,[29] Huxley's preference for the ape as grandsire was beginning to meet with almost universal assent. Once the battle between science and religion was over, everything fell into place.

The debate over the antiquity of *Homo neanderthalensis* continued for many years: 'The old arguments, indeed the old angers, were perpetuated until replaced by new ones, until the sheer weight of numbers of Neanderthal men made it impossible to reject them as isolated freaks.'[30] Now began the British Association's long connection with palaeontological research. Further exploration of Kent's Cavern (between March 1865 and June 1880) produced, among other finds, a human jawbone of indeterminate age – a poor return for the British Assocation's outlay of £1963. Meanwhile, the first Neanderthal lower jaw was discovered (toothless) at La Naulette, Belgium, in 1866. Cro-Magnon Man was found at Les Eyzies in southwest France two years later. There were five individuals including a child. In 1886 at Spy in Belgium two quite complete Neanderthals of obviously great antiquity were discovered, and from the anatomy of the legs arose the myth of the 'bent-kneed Neanderthals' walking just like apes.[31] In 1891 and 1892 in the Dutch East Indies, Eugène Dubois discovered fossils of a species he called *Homo erectus*. From it he created a new genus, *Pithecanthropus* – 'Ape-man'.[32] In 1907, from deep within a gravel pit at Mauer in Germany, a lower jaw of *Homo heidelbergensis* (Heidelberg Man) came to light. (This was subsequently dated as being possibly 500,000 years old and a potential ancestor of Neanderthal and *Homo sapiens* – modern man.[33])

And so it went on. The sole British contribution of any significance – and of perhaps no significance at all – was Hugh

Falconer's term: 'The Missing Link', coined by the doctor in 1864 and appropriated by Eugène Dubois for his Java ape-man. Meanwhile, the relationship between men and monkeys became a thing of folklore and music hall jokes, and British science, deprived of hominids of its own, looked on European finds with increasing envy.

The annual meeting of the British Association at Dundee in 1912 coincided with the 14th International Congress of Anthropology and Prehistoric Archaeology in Geneva. As an attraction for anthropologists the distinctly unglamorous Scottish city proved a very poor second, while the congress on the shores of Lac Léman sparkled like its waters. For French palaeontologists in particular, riding as they were on the crest of a very considerable wave, the gathering was 'as a Nuremburg rally for the Nazis', a chance to celebrate their supremacy over an ancient foe. French replaced English as the official language of the congress, and of the 200 papers, 195 were by French authors. In one, Professor Marcellin Boule of the Musée National d'Histoire Naturelle in Paris pointed out (with an irritating if well-founded Gallic smugness) that there were only twenty Neanderthals known to science, and none of them were British.[34] Lantern slides of splendid French Palaeolithic cave paintings in equally splendid colour followed (there were some Spanish ones as well), and in October *The Times* of London reported the discovery of clay figurines of a similar age at Ariège in southern France.[35]

Just as the year was drawing to a depressing close for British palaeontology, events took an unexpectedly promising turn. On 5 December 1912 the journal *Nature* noted that 'The remains of a human skull and mandible, considered to belong to the early Pleistocene period' had been discovered north of Lewes in Sussex. A week later it reported the event at greater length. On 18 December 1912 *Eoanthropus dawsoni*, 'Dawson's Dawn Man' – reconstructed (with some difficulty) by Arthur Smith Woodward of the British Museum – burst onto the scene at a meeting of the Geological Society at Burlington House, London.

The story of the find was inspirational, one that brought together many of the various elements working to establish the antiquity of Man. Charles Dawson was the archetypal amateur: a country solicitor of considerable private means. Arthur Smith Woodward was a palaeontologist at the British Museum (Natural History) and Dawson's friend. Other professionals, such as human anatomists and anthropologists, took an intense interest in a story that had been unfolding all year as follows. (The interest would become universal when the Dawn Man was revealed to be a hoax.)

On 14 February 1912 Dawson found a portion of human skull in a gravel bed at Piltdown, outside the small Sussex market town of Uckfield, and contacted his friend in London. The site, he noted, had considerable potential, and so it proved. In June he and Smith Woodward found another piece of the extremely thick, deep-chocolate-coloured skull, together with an elephant molar. (Just what elephants were doing in Sussex in prehistoric times was anybody's guess.) Over the summer more portions of the skull made their appearance, as did fossilised animal teeth and several 'eoliths' – the earliest of stone implements or 'stones of the dawn'. A broken lower jaw was found, remarkably ape-like in appearance and with two molars in situ showing a wear-pattern common to modern 'primitive' races (in which Australian Aborigines were included). 'Both were convinced that they had found the remains of [an] entirely new form of humanity – a creature who had once roamed across the High Plateau of Kent and Sussex at the dawn of the British Palaeolithic.'[36] Here was 'tangible, well-nigh incontrovertible proof of Man's ape-like ancestry'. Evidence, 'in a form long predicted, of a creature which could be regarded as a veritable confirmation of evolutionary theory'.[37] On this assessment Piltdown was even older than *Pithecanthropus* – Dubois' Java ape-man. England, not Asia, Germany or Belgium – and most certainly not France – had come up with 'The Missing Link'.

Palaeontology, anthropology and anatomy were all associated with the re-construction of Piltdown Man. Arthur Keith, keeper of the Hunterian Collection of the Royal College of Surgeons, lately president of the Anthropological Institute, a renowned human anatomist and a leader in his field, endorsed the fossil. So, too, did Grafton Elliot Smith, an authority on brain anatomy and human evolution and an expatriate Australian who would return to his native land for the British Assocation meeting. (Both men were among those later suspected as being the Piltdown hoaxer.) The Dawn Man of Sussex captured everyone's attention. 'I have been reading up everything I could get in connection with it', Daisy Bates confided to Georgina in 1913. 'It almost approaches the "Missing Link" don't you think? Scientists never dreamed that such remnants of prehistoric beings would be found in England',[38] yet at the meeting of the British Association in Australia in 1914, fraud was far from anyone's mind.[39] A mere fifty-five years after the *Origin*, genuine ape-like ancestors and their canine teeth were everywhere – or so it seemed. In little over half a century, geology had pushed back the period of man's existence on the earth many millennia beyond James Ussher's 6000 years.

Travelling, as it were, on the back of Piltdown Man, such British luminaries as Professors Rivers and Haddon from Cambridge and Professor W.J. Sollas of Oxford (the latter eclipsed by Edgeworth David on the coral atoll of Funafuti) arrived in Sydney in late August 1914. Dr Grafton Elliot Smith, who was described by the *Sydney Morning Herald* as 'one of the greatest Australians' and 'one of the world's foremost anatomists, and anthropologists',[40] had already milked the Piltdown scenario for all (or rather more) than it was worth, and went on to do the same for the Talgai Skull. All these men had theories on man's evolution, and all smiled on T.W.E. David as he brought off the coup of the year.[41]

His audience was not to know that in 1889 Professor David

had taken on Robert Etheridge's view that 'man had not inhabited Australia for a geologically significant period of time' and he had shown no interest in prehistoric man since then.[42] Until, that is, the lead-up to the Sydney meeting. Of course, writing up the successful Funafuti Expedition of 1897 kept him busy until 1904, and expertise in glaciation (enhanced by his *fugue* per *Nimrod* to Antarctica and back in 1907) took up his time in one way or another well into 1914. His dramatic *coup de théâtre* in Sydney, with the production of 'an aboriginal skull far more ancient that any so far found in Australia', one that 'carries the aboriginal race back into the pleistocene period, and cannot be less than 25,000 years old' must strike us as surprising. As must his incredible luck – in the same article the *Argus* reported (22 August 1914) that the skull 'came into scientific hands only a few days ago'. Curious, too, was the fact that Robert Etheridge, curator of the Australian Museum, an expert palaeontologist who had worked at the British Museum from 1874 to 1887, was not at his side as co-presenter. David's associate on this occasion was Professor James T. 'Jummy' Wilson, professor of anatomy at the university, whose research work had recently suffered considerably as a result of his administrative load.

Daisy Bates and Georgina King were present at the unveiling in Sydney. 'You have a wonderful memory', Daisy wrote to her friend a decade later.

> *As I read your dear letter the little 'gallery' we sat in to listen to Prof. David expound about the Talgai Skull came before me, & I saw Everard im Thurn reading his Presidential address – & David 'not quite sure' as to how his 'find' would be received & looking side-ways from under his penthouse eyebrows on the Oxford & Cambridge Professors – !*[43]

Georgina King would always hold that Piltdown was genuine and that Talgai was a fraud. She was wrong on both counts, but in some respects she was right. Piltdown deliberately combined a genuine fossil human skull with the jawbone of a modern orang-outan for the purpose of deception. The skull found in Queensland, while fitting in so conveniently with the Piltdown hypothesis and conveying the same 'archaic evolutionary traits',[44] *was* a genuine fossil, 'possibly of fair antiquity' and 'even Upper Pleistocene' – i.e., of the most recent geological age. The spectre of Piltdown apart, the only true frauds at the meeting were T.W.E. David and J.T. Wilson.

The two professors first met with the Talgai cranium, not in 1914 as was supposed, but at the Australian Museum in 1896, at a trustees' meeting held on 6 October. Among those also present were the curator, Robert Etheridge, and the secretary who kept minutes of this and subsequent meetings. There was discussion then and correspondence after as to whether to purchase the item for the museum. Since the fossil had not been found in situ but in the wash away of a creek, the trustees concluded that it did not 'possess what we call "geological history"'. While interested in the skull as a curiosity, in the end they did not press ahead.[45] Meanwhile, the rejected Talgai cranium underwent a type of evolution that would have fascinated the great Darwin himself. From having no proven geological significance in 1896 when David and Wilson first saw it, by August 1914 the skull proved 'that in Australia man attained to geological antiquity'.[46] It was a far cry from the views David had previously shared with Etheridge, and his conversion from sceptic to true believer verges on the positively Pauline. Picture him, theatrical as any Hamlet holding aloft the skull of Yorick, the late court jester. Unlike Shakespeare's gloomy prince, however, he could not bring himself to say, 'I knew him . . .', and one has to wonder why.

The Piltdown hoax remained undetected for forty years, and then in 1953 this most elaborate of hoaxes was exposed and hit the headlines in the press worldwide.[47] When the curious case of the Talgai Skull was discussed in a scientific journal, David's own duplicity was treated politely as an enigma. 'The Talgai cranium in its encrusted state looked like no other fossil cranium on record. If David and Wilson did see it in 1896, I am certain that they would have recognized it in 1914 . . .' so wrote N.W.G. Macintosh, Challis Professor of Anatomy, University of Sydney, in 1969. He continued:

> *Were they, in fact, not present [at the trustees' meeting], although the minutes say they were? If they did see it, why remain silent in 1914? One can only conclude by saying one gets used to mysteries with the Talgai cranium.*[48]

Dr Ian Langham, also of the University of Sydney, was prepared to go a little further in his conclusions of 1978. Emphasising the unmistakable appearance of the Talgai cranium, as had Professor Macintosh, he wrote: 'To men of David and Wilson's training and interests, the skull should have been absolutely unforgettable. Thus I conclude that in the way they unveiled it in 1914, David and Wilson were guilty, at the very least, of lack of candour.'[49]

In considering the questions raised by David's respected academic peers, we have the benefit of being acquainted with something of the professor's previous behaviour. The opportunity to be associated, even at second hand, with the glamorous Piltdown discoveries must have been irresistible. Such an urge is in keeping with what we know of the man (and Caroline, his wife). The publicity arising from the unveiling of the Talgai Skull was an event for which any Australian scientist still in thrall to Britain would have given (as it were) his very eyeteeth. Somewhat of a tyro (one suspects) as far as palaeontology was concerned, the professor succumbed to temptation, but was wise enough to limit the presentation to the briefest possible form. The resulting glow shed by the Dawn Man of Sussex undoubtedly warmed his ego. More importantly, it rounded off his persona as a complete professional, a scientific man of many parts, one who could speak with consummate ease on matters anthropological before some of the ablest exponents in the world.

This time, David's success in a milieu she considered very much her own was more than Georgina King could stomach. From August 1914 the kid gloves were unbuttoned and she began to show her claws.

CHAPTER TWENTY-TWO

Coalcliff: The Lie of the Land

Georgina's work on 'Our Aborigines' went back over a decade, as did her research into her personal evolutionary theory – that the so-called 'Missing Link' was a woman. Between its first appearance in December 1902 and 1912, Georgina's essay on 'The Appearance of Woman as a "Sport" in Nature, and the Evolution of Anthropoid Man' had re-emerged four times.[1] (The piece appeared in its final form in 1926 when the author was eighty-one, its popularity still undisputed.) Georgina was particularly interested in the earliest known examples of *Homo sapiens*, modern man, discovered in the 1860s onwards in the Vézère Valley of southwest France. She enthusiastically seized upon another proposition too, whereby a family of great tree apes or other such 'higher mammals' produced several 'sports' that became the ancestors of mankind. The botanical notion of 'sports' – mutations or deviations from a norm – disposed of Darwin's very much more gradual process of change, and embraced the notion of 'Evolution per saltum', that is to say, evolution 'with a jump' (for which the apes in question appear admirably suited). Georgina went one better than D.G. Bristow, whose particular theory this was. Rather daringly for the time, she compared the 'antero-posterior diameter of the pelvic basin of all animals – men included' and found it greater than the transverse. In woman, however, it was 'just the reverse'. Thus it was far easier, she maintained, for females to take an upright stance, and succeeding generations followed their mothers' example. Neanderthal Man, in fact, did not walk with bended knees (that was a misconception that came from T.H. Huxley), but neither Georgina nor any of the savants assembled at the British Association meeting in Australia knew that; nor in 1914 did anyone, of course, know that Piltdown Man was a fake. Or should that have been Piltdown *Woman*?

On 30 January 1913 the *Sun* in Sydney trumpeted a succession of headlines: 'A Missing-link', 'What the Sussex Skull Reveals', 'Women 200,000 Years Ago', 'New Light on Evolution'. The report that followed was a reprint of an item in the *Illustrated London News* that drew heavily upon the views of Arthur Smith Woodward of the South Kensington Natural History Museum. 'Through the dark forests of our land there roamed many hundred of thousand years ago, a strange hairy ape-like creature, a female member of a curious race, from which all animals shrank.' Although this fascinating example of 'a missing-link between the monkey and ourselves' was no less 'shuffling' in her gait than her male companions, Georgina felt her theory vindicated.

More courteous than many of his contemporaries, Smith Woodward – friend of the Dawn Man's actual discoverer, Charles Dawson – answered her letter on the subject and obligingly sent her photographs of the Piltdown skull, reconstructed as that of a woman. (These she later lodged with the Royal Australian Historical Society in Sydney.) So when she attended the British Association meetings with Mrs Bates in 1914 and talked with great men of science, such as Professors Rivers and Haddon from Cambridge and Walter Baldwin Spencer of Melbourne (all of whom were also actively interested in Australia's Aborigines), she felt a sense of belonging that she had never experienced before.

No wonder, then, that when David strode to centre stage in Sydney and proclaimed upon the antiquity of the first Australians, she felt the beginnings of a white-hot rage. Inspired by her father's work, had she not been saying the very same thing for years, in a paper read at the AAAS in 1900 and in several publications since?[2] David's interest in anthropology, on the other hand, was of very recent date, going back (let us say, for the sake of argument) to his trip to Britain in 1913, when he assisted David Rivett, the Australian organising secretary, in making arrangements for the British Association's visit the following year. While there, he cannot have failed to observe the scientific world awash with outpourings on the subject of Dawson's marvellous find. The Piltdown bones were considered as belonging to the early Ice Age (or Pleistocene), data apparently confirmed by the Talgai cranium with which it shared certain features – thus David's deliberate introduction of the fossil he had hitherto scorned was cynical in the extreme.

Far from making a chance discovery just before the Sydney meeting, with his 'Preliminary Notes' a hurried affair, Professor David had had something like a year to orchestrate the whole performance and track down the grotesque mineralised fossil. Once the congress was under way in August 1914, everything about the Anthropology Section's programme prepared the ground for his splendid *coup de théâtre*. And afterwards, the marauding leopard changed his spots and proclaimed the antiquity of the Aboriginals in Australia to anyone who cared to listen.

For Georgina, sitting in the gallery with Daisy Bates beside her, there was a ghastly sense of *déjà vu*. David's performance opened old wounds, for one thing, and revived that dreadful sense of dispossession. The man had barred her from geology; he had stolen her ideas and removed her work from the public domain; and here he was again, apparently set to excise her from another burgeoning branch of science. (But that was the beauty of an emerging field of study, as Daisy doubtless told her – anyone's theories were up for grabs, and the Davids of the world were no less unscrupulous than the Radcliffe-Browns.)

The meeting of the British Association in Sydney was pivotal for Georgina. It tipped the balance between her distrust and dislike of the Davids and her natural inclination for discretion. The complete Victorian lady in all respects other than her science, hitherto she had kept her feelings to herself, or discussed them in private with those she knew she could trust. From now on, things would be very different.

Robert Etheridge, curator of the Australian Museum, suspected the fortuitous element behind the 1914 'discovery' of the Talgai Skull to be a total fake and indicated as much to David in 1915,[3] but given Georgina's explosive temperament – admittedly damped down in her middle years, but ready now to burst forth into flame – he is unlikely to have shared his suspicions with Miss King, for all their friendship. When she decided to denounce David openly as a trickster, it was not for dishonesty in his scientific dealings but for fraud against the state.

Once the British Association meetings were over and the delegates on their way back to a conflict-stricken Europe, Georgina threw herself into the war effort in one of the few ways open to a woman of her years. She sent parcels and letters to the soldiers at the front. She took up her needles to knit for victory on behalf of the War Chest and the Red Cross and produced '195 pairs of very warm gloves, with gauntlets', along with 'Balaclava Caps'. She made 'one hundred and one Gollywogs for the Red Cross Toy Shop, and hundreds of Egg Cosies and other novelties' as well as 1385 'patriotic heart-shaped pincushions'.[4] And as she worked, she brooded. In the old days she would have bewailed her lot to Sir Frederick McCoy; her present friends proved even more supportive. Where McCoy always stood on the side of moderation (his stoush over coal with the Reverend Clarke excepted), women like Mrs Daisy Bates and Miss Rose Scott stood up for their rights in the world of men and welcomed the heat of battle. In late 1914, sixty-nine-year-old Miss King combined her sense of personal wrongs with one of patriotic zeal, put together a ragbag of facts (and possibly fictions), and waded into the fray. Her aim was to discredit Edgeworth David at the highest level.

The events in question went back many years, to September 1890 when Edgeworth David was acting geological surveyor-in-chief working in the Illawarra district of southern New South Wales. His boss, Charles Wilkinson, was overseas, attending the International Exhibition of Mining and Metallurgy in England, and David was left to complete the correlation of the northern, southern and western coalfields of New South Wales. Work on the Bulli coal measures took David from Coal Cliff (or Clifton) in the north to Ulladulla in the south, and in May the following year he was offered the Chair of Geology at the University of Sydney. The following month he proffered his resignation from the Department of Mines.

When Georgina charged the professor with fraud in October 1914, at a time of national crisis, her accusations centred on the Coal Cliff Mining Company and its exceptionally productive coal measures in the Illawarra. They came after she had read a (unidentified) newspaper article entitled 'State Coal. Resuming the Land',[5] reporting that the Minister for Mines, Mr J.H. Cann, intended to resume 200 acres in the Lithgow Valley area she knew so well. The coastal (Royal) National Park – where the seam was so far beneath the surface that 'it would not interfere with the use of the park as a pleasure resort' – was also in his sights. The park, founded in 1879, was the oldest national park in Australia. Part of it adjoined the rich freehold land of the Coal Cliff Mining Company.

Georgina's fixation with Coal Cliff resurfaced intermittently over the next twenty-five years and the basis of it is this: according to Georgina's sources, Edgeworth David had allowed prime mineral land belonging to the Crown to be disposed of under the guise of pastoral acres, at a vast saving to the new owner, who paid '£1. an acre – in all nine hundred acres, for nine hundred pounds'.[6] The 'new owner' was none other than Sir Alexander Stuart, colonial treasurer at the time.[7] In her usual manner she went straight to the top. She wrote to the Minister of Mines suggesting that 'while he was looking for coal mines, for the State, he should look into the matter of Coal Cliff . . . which Vickery now owns'.[8]

David's record as a government geologist was impressive, and for the previous quarter of a century Coal Cliff had been remarkable in Sydney circles only for the richness of the Vickery mine and the competence of David's work. All that changed with Georgina's correspondence to the Department of Mines. The same accusations resurfaced whenever David was awarded some honour or other – for example, at the Royal Society of New South Wales in May 1917.[9] ('I ask you Gentlemen, after reading this correspondence, if you think Major Professor David worthy of the Clarke Memorial Medal?') Following his knighthood at the end of 1920, Georgina again went on the attack, this time approaching the University Senate, and in 1922 when David was awarded funds through the generosity of Sir Hugh Dixson for his magnum opus *The Geology of the Commonwealth*, Miss King contacted the benefactor to voice her disgust: 'I am enclosing a copy of a correspondence I had with the Department of Mines about Professor David's transaction of Coal Cliff . . . you will see that Professor Sir Edgeworth David is not the man that should be instructed to write the Geology of the Commonwealth.'[10]

The letter she sent to Vice-Chancellor Sir Mungo MacCallum in June 1923 linked David's dishonesty with intellectual theft.[11] ('When he robbed the country for his Professorship by his transaction of Coal Cliff, it is no wonder he and his clique took all my discoveries.') The litany was reproduced for Professor Arthur C. Haddon, in Sydney for the Pan Pacific Conference that August, after the latter's public praise for Edgeworth David's many achievements.

And so on it went, year after year and into 1927, and gradually the specific claims became blurred within the general bulk of her discontent. And all the time she believed absolutely in what she was saying. So what should we make of her coal-inspired persecutions of a public hero?

First let us consider Sir Alexander Stuart, premier and colonial secretary of New South Wales from 1883 to 1885 (he was colonial treasurer in an earlier administration). A self-made man, he arrived in Sydney from New Zealand in October 1851 and spent a few months on the Victorian goldfields before returning to New Zealand. The following August he returned to Australia for good and found employment in the Bank of New South Wales. Proving himself administratively adept, he rose in banking circles. His mining interests appear to have dated from 1872.[12] When Stuart stood for parliament in 1874 he was elected the third member for East Sydney. In 1876 he became colonial treasurer in Sir John Robertson's third ministry.

Stuart's banking connections failed to bring him personal prosperity, but his varied business experience did teach him how to 'work the system'. In November 1879 he resigned from the Legislative Assembly to become New South Wales's agent-general in London (a position he was unable to take up). He used his last months in office to expedite the building of the 'Government Road from the Coal Cliff via Stanwell Park to the Blue Gum Forest on the Illawarra Road', an achievement we know as the South Coast Road.[13]

He was in debt to the tune of some £70,000 when he resigned in 1879. Coal Cliff with its six-foot-thick coal seam was considered one of the most important new collieries of New South Wales, yet was heavily mortgaged to merchant banker Thomas Walker. Stuart re-entered politics in 1880, this time representing Illawarra, and he took office as premier and colonial secretary from 5 January 1883. Thereafter, on the basis of his perceived lack of integrity he came under repeated attack in the House.

The member for Upper Hunter, John McElhone, was the main agitator in what proved a long, drawn-out debate. As the premier's former business partner, he presumably knew something of Stuart's modus operandi, and as a self-styled 'blowfly ... here to fossick out ill-smelling jobs and corruption',[14] McElhone set to work with a will.

Throughout 1883 Alexander Stuart and his new partner, the former premier John Robertson, came under great pressure concerning various aspects of their joint mining ventures. First there was the matter of the Illawarra Railway Line, intended to link Sydney with the southern Illawarra coalfields. The route as originally planned crossed one of Stuart's selections (number 21, comprising 320 acres). In 1883, however, the proposed route developed a surprising deviation that would have taken it through five of Stuart's selections amounting to 1110 acres, while passing close to another 1214 acres also in his name. On 16 October, Sydney Smith (the member for East Macquarie) rose to address the House. Smith had served in the Railways branch of the Department of Public Works for ten years, rising from the rank of porter to assistant traffic manager via positions as junior clerk and stationmaster, and while no means an expert, he spoke with a certain authority. It was indeed 'a strange thing', he observed, 'that the proposed new loop-line was not discovered prior to the Colonial Secretary taking the position of Acting Minister of Works'[15] – which Stuart did for two months from March 1883.

McElhone was less restrained. It was 'almost a moral certainty' (he asserted) that the land in question contained coal; 'that while acting as Secretary for Works and occupying the highest position any man in this country can occupy, [Stuart] used his position to suspend a contract let for carrying out works sanctioned by parliament'. His aim being 'to make a diversion by which the railway would go through 7 or 8 miles of his land and increase its value by a million sterling'.[16] There was worse to come. In 1884 (again said McElhone), Stuart had 'evaded the act . . . and obtained the deeds of 5,000 or 6,000 acres of land to which he has no more claim than I have'.[17]

The Act in question was the 1875 *Lands Acts Amendment Act*, which in reality amended very little. In New South Wales land was selected without prior survey, was paid for in instalments, and deeds were transferred subject to improvements being made.

McElhone accused Premier Stuart of failing to carry out the necessary improvements on his 'mining conditional purchases', (despite possessing a certificate from an inspector stating that he had done that very thing).[18]

The protagonists were experts in twisting words to suit their particular purpose and it all depended upon one's interpretation of the Act. The vicious attacks that McElhone began in 1883 continued throughout 1884. In October 1884 Stuart suffered a stroke, and although he resumed his duties in May 1885 he resigned his post in October. He died from typhoid in London in June 1886.

The Coal Cliff mine failed to reach anything like its full potential in Stuart's lifetime, and given his financial difficulties that is hardly surprising. Between 1878 and Stuart's death in 1886, things picked up but were dependent on banking loans. Other players entered the game. Judge John Hargrave, with whom Stuart had orchestrated the 'Government Road' initiative outlined on page 190, had been granting sections of his Stanwell Park property to his sons since 1878. Two years later the judge, who had a long history of mental instability, completely lost his marbles and was not responsible for his own actions, let alone anyone else's. In October 1883 Ralph and Lawrence Hargrave prepared to cash in on their assets. Ralph mortgaged some 617 acres for £18,531, or around £30 per acre, while the 220 acres given to Lawrence by his father in 1881 were sold for £6100, or about £27. 15s. per acre.[19] The sums involved are big enough to show that, whatever the rights or wrongs of his position, the late Alexander Stuart at £1 an acre had got himself a bargain.

Meanwhile, Coal Cliff's fortunes fluctuated wildly. On Stuart's death, control of the company passed to mortgagee Thomas Walker. Walker died three months later and his affairs passed into the hands of trustees. Coal production peaked in 1888 (with some 18,000 tons valued at £48,000) then was in decline until 1892. Ebenezer Vickery (the 'Vickery' mentioned in Georgina's accusations) acquired the company from the trustees of Thomas Walker in 1896. By 1907 Vickery's colliery was able to supply 200 tons of coal per day, and in the war years of 1914 to 1918 was capable of producing an average of some 190,000 tons a year.

The matter of Edgeworth David's involvement with the Coal Cliff scandal was fully investigated on behalf of Minister Cann by none other than Edward Fisher Pittman, now the under-secretary in the Department of Mines. Pittman and David had a great deal in common. Both men began their careers under C.S. Wilkinson, and when David arrived in New South Wales, in November 1882, Pittman was about to start a second stint as Wilkinson's assistant. Ten years later he helped David set up a School of Mines within the university, where he lectured part-time from 1893 to 1903. Thrown together by circumstance then choice, the close proximity of their homes in the Sydney suburb of Burwood helped strengthen their alliance. Not surprisingly, Pittman's investigation came out conclusively in favour of his former colleague.

There is nothing in the formal letters exchanged by Pittman and Miss King in October and November 1914 to indicate that his family and hers had also enjoyed a certain intimacy in the previous century. They too had been neighbours for a while and friends to a certain degree – something that changed with the ascendancy of the Davids ('You used to tell me so many things, but now you don't look for a high standard among you', she wrote.[20]). Once Pittman passed into the enemy camp (which was obvious by 1897) Georgina's feelings towards the public servant were inimical, to say the very least. By the time she made her first formal complaint concerning the matter of Coal Cliff, any contact between them was of a frostily formal nature.

On 2 November 1914 Pittman wrote to Miss King: 'I am directed by Mr. Secretary Cann to inform you that your statement above indicated has been investigated and found to be quite erroneous.'[21] And there, of course, the matter should have rested.

No details were forthcoming from E.F. Pittman, but the following facts speak out in favour of David's innocence:

1. He could not have passed land through the Lands Department for Stuart while the latter was colonial treasurer – Stuart held that office in 1876, David arrived in the colony at the end of 1882.

2. From 22 January 1883 when Stuart was acting Minister of Public Works, David was out of town, busy investigating the Vegetable Creek tin fields.

3. David did not begin work on the correlation of the New South Wales coal measures until 1886, the year following Stuart's resignation as premier and colonial secretary and the year of his death. At that point David was working in the Hunter Valley, nowhere near Coal Cliff.

To counter this, we might at a pinch build the following hypothetical case against him:

4. Stuart pulled a fast one while he was acting Minister for Public Works (in March 1883) and prevailed upon a civil servant to ratify the deeds appertaining to Coal Cliff – and that civil servant was an impressionable and inexperienced David back in the office from Vegetable Creek for a spell. This would fulfil the criterion that any direct dealing between the pair, on any matter whatsoever, would have had to have taken place between David's arrival on 27 November 1882, and Stuart's resignation as premier on 6 October 1885 – remembering that Stuart was out of action through illness between October 1884 and May 1885.

5. Let us divide Georgina's allegation (page 188 above) into two parts, covering two time frames: David, in

charge of the department *in 1890*, discovered that he – or someone else – had made a mistake *in 1883*. If this hypothetical person were David, then he would have broken his Vegetable Creek investigations at some time during 1883 and been 'nobbled' by Premier Stuart.

6. Provided 5. applies, then David's unlooked-for success in gaining the professorial chair takes on the complexion of a bribe. Georgina certainly believed this to be the case. Stuart by now was dead, but other beneficiaries may have acted in his stead.

With no hard evidence to support it, the case against David has to be dismissed. After all, there is nothing too exceptional about a local candidate with a wealth of local knowledge beating rivals from overseas – even in colonial times, when the cringe factor was at its most extreme. David had links with the university's Geology Department going back to the days of the late Professor W.J. Stephens, with whom he had acted as co-examiner in geology. Since Stephens's death in November 1890, David had worked on a temporary basis at the department, and had shown himself in possession of compelling lecturing skills. All this appears to have been enough to tip the balance in his favour. Thus, going counter to the university's selection committee back in the United Kingdom, which had recommended Dr William Sollas of Trinity College, Dublin – whose name, like David's, would be forever associated with Funafuti Atoll – David on his merits got his chair.

This may satisfy us, but it did not suit Georgina. She depicts Caroline David as not being content with pushing her reluctant husband into the public eye, but privately pulling wires behind the scenes with various unnamed puppets obligingly dancing to her tune. And there was more. Again, according to Georgina, undue influences were at work in the promotion of Edward Fisher Pittman:

> *Mr. C.S. Wilkinson was taken ill soon after [his return from England], and when he was on his death-bed – under morphine – Professor David went to him and asked him to send for Mr. Harrie Wood, the Under-Secretary for Mines, and ask for Mr. Pittman to be made the Government Geologist. That was to tie his tongue about Coal Cliff. Mr. Anderson should have been the Government Geologist, but he resigned and went to India and got a good appointment there.*[22]

Charles Smith Wilkinson died of carcinoma aged forty-eight at his Burwood home, three months after David's resignation from the Mines Department. If Georgina's account is to be believed, a difficult passing was made no easier by David's presence at his bedside, pleading Pittman's cause and taking advantage of the dying man's morphia-induced state of mind. What we are told of Wilkinson's final days goes against all we are told about Georgina's hapless quarry, in whom 'courage, courtesy, enthusiasm, devotion to duty, unselfishness, modesty, generosity, and a host more qualities equally admirable, all struggle[d] for first place',[23] but it *does* fit our image of David's wife. Was Mrs David the unseen catalyst who spurred on her 'Twed' to secure a power base from which better to influence his peers?

If the professor, innocent of all charges, was thoroughly the 'preux chevalier' as purported[24] and thus beyond reproach, was Caroline David, protecting her man like any feisty Suffolk fishwife, incapable of behaving like a lady?

CHAPTER TWENTY-THREE

Ginger for Pluck

With the return of her correspondence to the Mines Department – minus, it must be said, the initial accusatory letter – the matter of David and Coal Cliff should have been laid to rest in November 1914. But this failed to satisfy Georgina and, ageing, disillusioned and increasingly suspicious, she prepared to battle on alone. She told E.F. Pittman, 'I don't intend to be a martyr',[1] but she suffered all the same.

When she was a child, her elder brother Will and his friends called her 'Ginger for Pluck'. With fiery locks and a temper to match, the tiny battler hit out for truth and justice and was punished as a result. As a young woman, her father paid tribute to her fearlessness and honesty by dubbing her 'Zy', after the heroine of Bulwer Lytton's futuristic tale, *The Coming Race*. Equally larger than life and just as bound to any promise, in her youth and middle years Georgina had expected the same probity of others. Now an embittered old maid, she held true to her ideals and steadfastly refused to be interviewed by the Sydney popular press – adept then as now at sniffing out a story. It would, as she said, hurt the cause of science and go against everything she believed. Instead, she pursued her quarry in the way she knew best – through the words she wrote herself to some of the most distinguished figures in New South Wales.

Any journalist would commend Georgina's discretion in protecting her sources, and we can only speculate as to who they were. The first informant, 'a man in a high scientific position', who told her 'a few years ago' that 'Professor David was an honest man till his wife commenced to intrigue',[2] may have been Robert Etheridge, the friend who revealed the suppression of her pamphlet. Since then, his low opinion of the geologist had been reinforced by the Talgai affair. The second informant, a professor who 'told me Mrs. Edgeworth David managed cleverly about Coal Cliff, for it was the making of her husband',[3] is more difficult to 'finger'. Was it William Henry Warren, Dean of Science and later of Engineering, who had been so free with his advice to Georgina about her research and the foibles of his fellow men? Or Professor Anderson Stuart, Dean of Medicine, who was also in a good position to judge?

Thomas Peter Anderson Stuart (later Sir Anderson Stuart) was the university's founding professor of anatomy and physiology. A former demonstrator in physiology at Edinburgh University, he arrived in Sydney with his wife in March 1883 and came highly recommended (one of his testimonials was supplied by Joseph Lister). He had a close professional association with Edgeworth David, both at the university and over the ground-breaking Funafuti expedition of 1897. Stuart's tendency to make enemies was renowned, for he was a complex personality with no respect for incompetents (of whom he may have considered David a prime example).[4] Even so, his medical school proved far more successful than his marriage. During his widowerhood and until his remarriage (the first Mrs Stuart died tragically in 1886) he 'chummed' for a while with the bachelor Archibald Liversidge out at Darling Point and the pair struck up a lasting friendship.[5]

Anderson Stuart also got on well with Georgina King. They shared an interest in the Royal Alexandra Children's Hospital, and the brightly coloured gifts from the 'Gollywog lady' met with his total approbation.[6] It is not impossible that at some time during the domesticity he shared with Liversidge (from 1890 to 1894) he received certain confidences from the chemist who, like David, was involved in mining affairs. Moved by kindly feelings for the hard done by and compassionate spinster, did Anderson Stuart finally pass that information on? And was there anything in it, if he did?

Against the background of Georgina's repeated fulminations, the Davids moved ever onwards and up. The professor's war work on the Western Front in France (1916–1918) saw him thrice mentioned in dispatches and he was awarded the Distinguished Service Order. He returned to Australia in 1919 and was made a Knight of the British Empire the following year. Georgina's own progress was more of a sideways nature as she moved along the Bayswater Road in Darlinghurst in a constant change of lodgings. When her mind was not occupied with the problems of 'Iron' and its various uses in the modern world (the stability of the proposed Sydney Harbour Bridge was of particular concern), she continued to work for children's welfare or darted off in pursuit of yet another theory.

She started work on her memoirs. As she advised Edward Pittman in November 1914: 'I have been often asked to write my autobiography by my friends for I have many. Well now I shall write it, for I remember every word of what used to be told me, on good authority long ago.'[7] Secure in the knowledge that the predatory David was in the army and half a world away, she renewed her attempts to have papers read at the Royal Society of New South Wales and again was unsuccessful. In 1920, when she was seventy-five and increasingly afflicted by rheumatism, her campaign to expose the Davids' dishonesty received an unexpected fillip. Her niece Olive King, Kelso's daughter, returned from overseas and, rather than slowing down, matters gathered momentum.

Kelso's first wife, the unsympathetic Irene, had died in 1900, leaving two young daughters, Alice and Olive. Olive grew into an uncomfortably energetic and restless young woman whom her father – by now a businessman of substance, with fingers plunged into various profitable pies – obviously indulged. In 1910 Olive climbed Mexico's Mount Popocatapetl and at the outbreak of hostilities in 1914 was in Europe. She was twenty-nine, single, and rich. Far more liberated than Georgina, the product of an earlier generation, Olive bought an ambulance with her father's money and drove it to the Belgian front. Various adventures took her to the Greco-Serbian border where she joined the Serbian Army as a driver in 1916. In 1918, financed by a committee set up by her wealthy father in Sydney, the gutsy Olive opened seventeen canteens in Belgrade to administer much-needed practical relief to civilians and thought nothing of sleeping on top of the stores 'to fend off marauding thieves'.[8] Back home in 1920, enlisting in Aunt Georgie's private war must have seemed a doddle.

Olive's typewritten transcripts of Georgina's handwritten drafts added a certain cachet (and tidiness) to the old lady's efforts, but did not change the outcome. Miss King might not have intended to become 'a martyr', yet her injured feelings festered like a sore. With her niece's sympathetic presence providing the necessary impetus to keep her going, as well as the care lavished on her by her nephew Esca, now a general practitioner of medicine working in Sydney, Georgina prepared to go down fighting. As always, whenever the Davids were in the news she reacted, and from the time of the Pan Pacific Congress of 1923 she built up a picture, not of David's 'corrupt scientific clique' alone, but of a world where the press and academe were allied in a disgraceful coalition.[9] 'None of the Editors of the papers will ever allow a statement of Professor David's to be contradicted', she wrote to the *Sunday Times* at the end of 1924,[10] and certainly Georgina was *persona non grata* with the *Sydney Morning Herald*. The occasional letter might slip through the *cordon sanitaire* but generally speaking her articles were no longer welcome, or, indeed, any more relevant to the modern world than Georgina King herself – for all that bright intelligence fostered so assiduously by W.B. Clarke and Dr George Bennett.

Somehow (as can happen) it slipped out that Edgeworth David had his sights set on writing the definitive geology of the Commonwealth of Australia, and it became universal knowledge.

As a result the topic became indisputably his, as it were by right. To his students and acolytes it appeared an admirable choice. In February 1924 David resigned his chair and was given the title of Professor Emeritus by the Senate. He had mostly neglected anthropology since those glory days of 1914,[11] and from now on he would devote himself to the monumental task before him. But it proceeded no more quickly than his other work. Never one to write up his findings with a noticeable turn of speed, he completed his final commitment to the Department of Mines in 1907 – taking even longer than the seven years it took for his Funafuti work to be completed. Reports on various aspects of Antarctica preoccupied him from 1907 until 1914 and resurfaced on and off thereafter. When it came to 'The Geology', however, there was to be no conclusion in his lifetime. In 1927, writing from the British Museum to thank her for her most recent pamphlet on 'Evolution', Dr Arthur Smith Woodward told Georgina: 'Sir Edgeworth David finds the preparation of his new book a longer task than he expected, so he is still here.'[12] David, for his part, remained outwardly optimistic, as an interview he gave that year reveals:

> *'If I receive the last manuscripts from Australia by the middle of October, my book, "The Geology of Australia", will be ready for the printers in December,' said Professor Sir Edgeworth David, to the special representative of 'The Sun,' who found him in his house on Parliament Hill immersed in a mass of maps, diagrams, manuscripts and photographs . . .*
>
> *'My two years' work has been a labor of love, which I have immensely enjoyed,' Sir Edgeworth continued. 'I wish to pay the highest tribute to the generous assistance of British and Australian geologists, including a number of my old students, who are contributing chapters on special subjects. Without their help it would have been impossible to carry out this compendious work which is beyond the power of a single-handed effort. That map forms the basis of the whole work,' he added, indicating*

a big canvas spread on the floor, outlining in diverse colors the geological surface of Australia.[13]

Georgina had strongly opposed the grant to David (see Chapter 22) and as the great work stagnated, she was unable to refrain from gloating. The map, the first part of the magnum opus, duly saw the light of day in 1933, a year before David died, and met with universal acclaim, but the forerunner to the great 'Geology' never did see its companion volume in David's lifetime. And when it did appear in 1950, this 'landmark in the literature of Australian geology' was almost entirely the work of another – much more disciplined – scholar.[14]

'The classic scientific biography has been for the most part an exercise in hagiography', writes Margaret Wertheim in a major essay on flawed scientific genius that would surely have resonated well with Georgina King. (Isaac Newton, one of the 'Calculating Bastards' in question, was, for example, 'capable of staggering vindictiveness towards those he viewed as trespassers on his turf . . .') In such a biography (and 'let's face it, hagiography is boring', says Wertheim) 'some great man (and just about all such subjects were men) is lovingly depicted as a paragon of brilliance, hard-working application and sterling human character'.[15] The treatment meted out to David after his death fits such a description very well, but despite the best efforts of his eulogists, readers of this book – like its authors – may question David's place among science's true 'greats'.

Rather than a natural genius, David strikes us as a classic case of a certain kind of assiduous self-promoter; the public figure trapped in his own celebrity. Expected to shine on a regular basis, as an academic he was also under regular pressure to perform within his field. Accounts of his life show how David managed to survive such pressures while staying in the limelight. These accounts tend to side-step the issues of 'brilliance' and 'application' and dwell more on David's personality: the professor as human being; as father; as genial companion, and the like. They glorify his reactions to adventures rather than his intellectual feats. If we take as the model of genius 'a mind that is at once logical and intuitive' leading to 'great intellectual leaps', where 'strict method' is allied with 'a freedom to roam, to speculate',[16] then we come nearer to understanding why this less analytical approach to David's career has been favoured. A modern biography of Edgeworth David has recently been written by David Branagan, and the reader must decide whether the professor's contributions have been critically assessed, and whether what Wertheim terms 'revelations from the dark side of life and from the unorthodox fringes' have been rigorously examined.

This is what Georgina hoped would happen, even if she herself wisely chose not to publish an autobiography that is libellous in the extreme. As it was, the papers she lodged in the Mitchell Library, Sydney – a testament to one woman's belief in the wrongs she suffered at the hands of an unscrupulous set of Sydney scientists – were suppressed until after Edgeworth David's death, two years following her own.

'Recognition *will* come', Mrs Daisy Bates told Georgina. 'Posterity will deal rightly with us.'[17] To ensure her own recognition, Daisy readily went along with a proposal from the Commonwealth Government that she collate her own papers (at taxpayers' expense) and lodge them in the National Library of Australia. This she did in 1941 and she included letters and photographs that her friend Miss King, who was 'like a dear & beloved sister to whom I can open my heart',[18] had sent her. And there the numerous boxes that represent the archive of Daisy May Bates have rested ever since.

As the final act in our bid to reconstruct the life and trials of Miss Georgina King, we approached the 99 folios of Daisy's papers (MSS 365) with an understandable sense of expectation. We knew from the National Library of Australia catalogue that the letters written by Georgina were there as part of Folio 97. While the letters and copies of letters in the Mitchell Library are a selection made by Georgina to support her scientific work, those in the National Library were written from the heart to a trusted female friend; written to another woman who had also seen her work taken. Letters with a sense of immediacy that the King autobiography by its very nature must be said to lack.

We opened the relevant folder, only to find it empty.

The National Library holds its collections in trust for the people of Australia. It does not treat its treasures lightly. Nor does it make errors in listing and indexing those treasures when they are accepted into its care. In order to gain access to the National Library's manuscripts one must undergo a rigorous credibility check and, once approved, a scholar is trusted to read and return each item to its proper place. So what do we make of these missing letters written by Georgina King?

There are enough letters from Daisy to Georgina in the Mitchell Library to indicate what the contents of the lost items might have been. One response in particular touches on the matter of academic integrity, plagiarism, and self-seeking and unscrupulous behaviour. Edgeworth David is mentioned by name.[19] The conclusion may not necessarily be the correct one, but it is inevitable: at some point after 1941, when the papers were lodged in the National Library of Australia, a person or persons unknown protective of the professor's reputation, took steps to prevent Georgina from speaking to posterity as surely was her right. The abstraction of her letters – and, it should be pointed out, the catalogued photographs are also missing – can be seen as a cynical attempt to remove all evidence of a woman whose very decency, as well as her sex, put her at a disadvantage in the scientific world of nineteenth-century Australia.

'History abounds with cases of thwarted and truncated genius, men and women of extraordinary ability who, after lighting the landscape with flares of brilliance, have descended into disillusion, depression, psychosis and suicide', Wertheim also comments in her essay. Georgina, for all her gifts, does not qualify as a genius, any more than Edgeworth David. Nor – despite her increasing paranoia – did she totally self-destruct; rather she died peacefully in her bed in 1932 at the fine old age of eighty-seven. The autobiography she left us inevitably contains a great deal of repetition; she was eighty-five when the last pages were handed over to the Mitchell's librarian in 1930, and her collated papers are a cogent argument for the modern dictum 'Less is more'. She protested 'too much'; and in so protesting, detracted from a cause that the less sympathetic might dismiss as the ranting of a half-deranged and unfulfilled old woman.

By taking the King–Bates letters, the culprits have done their victim no disservice whatsoever. Instead, the empty folder argues more eloquently than any written word the case for Miss Georgina King.

Appendix

'The Palaeozoic Carboniferous Formations in New South Wales'[1] (published anonymously in the *Sydney Morning Herald*, July 1895)

Georgina's earliest version of this paper was first offered to the Royal Society of New South Wales in April 1892. A second version was produced after the Adelaide meeting of the AAAS in 1893. This was read and criticised by Professor Frederick McCoy in November 1893. Professor W.H. Warren had promised GK earlier that year that if McCoy passed it, he would get it accepted by the Royal Society. Hence (we suppose), he gave it to Archibald Liversidge for consideration—with the consequences we have described earlier within the main text. R.L. Jack criticised it for her in February 1895.

Eventually, Georgina's paper was published anonymously in the Sydney Morning Herald, *27 July 1895 and entitled 'The Palaeozoic Carboniferous Formations in New South Wales'. This is the version we have transcribed. (Georgina's original 1893 paper is in the McCoy correspondence in the Museum of Victoria, Melbourne.) The endnotes draw attention to other papers produced within the Royal Society of New South Wales while Georgina's work was circulating among its officials during the years 1892–1895.*

The text follows the 1893 version, other than as to paragraphs and details such as 'carboniferous' for Georgina's 'Carboniferous and other substitutions of lower case for upper case. We have made two breaks in the Sydney Morning Herald*'s text for clarity's sake.*

There are no land surfaces found in New South Wales with any terrestrial vegetation until the Palaeozoic carboniferous formations, which are equivalent to or contemporaneous with what in Europe is called the Devonian period, whereas in Europe terrestrial land surfaces may be known in Silurian and Devonian formations from the terrestrial cryptogamic vegetation which paved the way in advancing the evolution for a higher carboniferous flora in the European carboniferous formations. Any terrestrial vegetation, such as Lepidodendron, found in the Devonian formations in New South Wales, grew on the undulating portions of land or islands that had been upheaved during the time of the Palaeozoic carboniferous formations, and drifted into the adjacent "blue waters", where coral and the encrinites, &c., flourished and multiplied at the same time, and formed our carboniferous limestone beds.[2] The Palaeozoic coal flora in New South Wales was not developed as the coal flora of the European formations, which consisted of a larger and higher type of well-rooted vegetation and fruit-producing plants. The New South Wales Palaeozoic coal consists principally of the spores and stems of fibrous cryptogamic vegetation. These stems are sometimes found full of innumerable spores.

Glossopteris in Europe is exclusively a Mesozoic plant, but in New South Wales it is found in varied abundance distributed through all the productive Palaeozoic coal formations, and it is even found in shale above the upper coal measures of the Newcastle-Wallsend Company's mine at Wallsend, New South Wales.[3] The so-called kerosene shale is found heterogeneously associated with the New South Wales Palaeozoic coal formations, and it was discovered above all the coal seams at Wallsend, Newcastle. In our western district it often merges abruptly into the workable coal. The "kerosene shale" that was taken from Mount Kembla, Illawarra district, had three good workable coal seams below it.

No insects or impressions of insects have ever been found in our New South Wales Palaeozoic coal formations. They are often met with in great variety and numbers in the European coal beds, for the more advanced vegetation concomitant with insect life which formed the European coal did not exist in New South Wales during the Palaeozoic coal formations.

The European Devonian formations are principally composed of the fossil remains of marine animal life, including corals and encrinites; the latter curious and beautifully-coloured marine animals. Which sometimes had a gigantic jointed stem of from six to eight feet in length, and were located on or attached to rocks, and were accompanied by a cryptogamic flora.

Corals and encrinitic limestone beds are found on the same horizons as the New South Wales Palaeozoic coal formations, and the vast accumulations of the Mount Vincent (Maitland) district, which overlie the Greta coal seam, contain quantities of coral and encrinitic remains, as well as other marine fossils. In making these observations about our Palaeozoic carboniferous formations in New South Wales, being a full period in advance (in point of time) of the European carboniferous formations, the writer hopes to be useful in helping in the determining of the ages of our auriferous quartz reefs and metalliferous deposits, which will assist in the investigation of the occurrence of our mineral wealth.[4]

Great eruptive disturbances took place during the Palaeozoic carboniferous period in New South Wales, when basalt and thermal springs intruded their way through the fissures which occurred in the coal beds and contemporary formations, and deposited some of our gold-bearing reefs and other mineral wealth.

A band of carbonate of lime and quartz-crystals were found in a fault at the Newcastle-Wallsend Company's mine. Wallsend, New South Wales, about 200ft. below the surface, and a cavity was also found lined with crystals evidently deposited there in solution.

Basalt is also found in this mine intruding through the coal at a similar distance from the surface. An auriferous quartz specimen was picked up in a vineyard at Greta (Maitland district), which, a geologist said, had been transported there through the agency of ice from New England; but there evidently is a quartz reef in the neighbourhood belonging to the Palaeozoic carboniferous period, and this auriferous specimen was ejected during this Cretaceous-Tertiary period some considerable time after New South Wales was last upheaved, when the earth opened up in all directions, where there was volcanic activity, and ejected thermal springs, basalt, and all our alluvial wealth. The remains of a rich Tertiary vegetation are found buried beneath this intrusive matter in various places. The term Cretaceous-Tertiary is used advisedly for New South Wales, and Professor Ralph Tate, of South Australia, when speaking of the "Antiquity of Continental Australia", said that Eastern Australia had had land surfaces. "During the deposition of the carboniferous series, which is, however, in a large measure littoral"; and he added, "it may safely be asserted that Australia, certainly as far back as the deposition of the extensive marine cretaceous occupying the low level tracts of the interior, presented the aspect of a vast archipelago," and that "at the close of that epoch the various insular masses became welded together, so that the antiquity of Australia as a whole is only Post-cretaceous."[5]

[Authors' new paragraph] Our eucalypts and other indigenous vegetation are often seen with their roots resting on the Hawkesbury sandstone, &c, which are equivalent to the European cretaceous formations, the rich Tertiary soils being intrusive. There are coal formations with changed forms of vegetation in Eastern Australia during the Mesozoic or secondary period, from what had appeared during the Palaeozoic carboniferous period, and many unconformities which can be accounted for by repeated subterraneous outbursts, for by such means the gold, iron, &c., found in the Hawkesbury sandstone, &c., was ejected from our Palaeozoic formations, which had originated in matter that had sunk in lower formations, through subsidences. Upheavals of subsided metamorphic matter are

continually taking place in ocean beds, and we see the agitation they cause in water-spouts, &c., which are even now causing various unconformities, and supplying the waters of the sea with mineral wealth.

[Authors' new paragraph] A pretty specimen of auriferous quartz was also found just below the surface at Byng, and cubic crystals of iron pyrites of various sizes are found in intrusive granite, which crops up above the surface, and in various basalts, soapstone and serpentine, near Byng, in the neighbourhood of Mount Canoblas, western district. Veins of agate are also seen in this neighbourhood above the surface of the soil, which were deposited in boiling solutions.[6]

The writer found Glossopteris, &c., on one of the highest mountains at Bowenfels, belonging to the Palaeozoic carboniferous period, which had been ejected during this Cretaceous-Tertiary period. Subsidences and volcanic upheavals and ejections are always taking place in modified forms in the earth's crust, and encrinitic remains belonging to the Palaeozoic carboniferous period were found in a tin mine, with precious stones, tin, &c., in New England, and the tin-bearing deep leads undoubtedly belong to this Tertiary period, on account of the fossil remains of our extinct vegetation, which are found associated with the tin.

The distinguished geologist and palaeontologist, Sir Frederick McCoy, K.C.M.G., of Victoria, named one of the fossil Eucalypts of Victoria Pluti, as a dedication to Plutus, the god of riches, as it was found in beds associated with the rich Tertiary gold leads in Victoria. There is every evidence that the mineral wealth of Eastern Australia was produced in different ages. Sir Frederick McCoy and Mr. Robert L. Jack, F.G.S., the Government Geologist of Queensland, regard the Gympie goldfield (Queensland) as belonging to the Palaeozoic carboniferous period, and the latter says that his 'observation as to the presence of carbonaceous rocks charged with pyrites being an essential condition of the production of the gold, is as true as ever.'

New South Wales possesses a vast field for original research for the geologist and naturalist, for it is a precious fossil of antiquity, with rich intrusive igneous rocks. The present Cretaceous-Tertiary formations, with their jewelled matter, have not sunk beneath the sea since that period, and in the remnant of a rich and varied vegetation that appeared as the land rose out of the sea we, in our existing flora, have an illustration of the "survival of the fittest". Horny sponges, related to those found in the European Cretaceous formations, are often washed upon the Bulli beach (Illawarra district, southern coast), and on other beaches also, after stormy weather.

Acknowledgements

It has taken many years to achieve publication of this biography of Miss Georgina King, but despite the difficulties we have faced in bringing her story into the public domain, research at all times has been a pleasure. *Ginger for Pluck* concerns a most divisive event in Australian scientific history, and during the course of its creation we have consulted many archivists, librarians and historians. Without exception, they have been most generous with their assistance. Given the time that has elapsed since the book's inception, it is only natural that some people will have moved on to other employment or to retirement, and we gratefully acknowledge their help alongside the institution where they were working at the time of our research.

IN NEW SOUTH WALES: The librarians of the Mitchell Library of the State Library of New South Wales, with a special thanks to Kerrie Sullivan, Jennifer Broomhead, Robert Woodley and Cheya Cootes. We thank the Trustees of the Library most sincerely for permission to quote from the unpublished material so important to this book. The Powerhouse Museum (formerly the Technological Museum): Dr Kevin Fewster, Director; Helen Yoxall and Paul Wilson, Archivists, and their colleagues, who were exceptionally helpful both before and during our visit. We are grateful for permission to quote from the correspondence between J.H. Maiden, Curator in the 1890s, and Georgina King. At St Peter's Church, Cooks River: Rev. Tom Halls, Minister, and Rev. Angelo Porcu, Youth Minister; Mrs Laurel Horton, who kindly shared with us the History Committee's records of the Reverend George King. At the University of Sydney: Dr Ursula Bygott for her encouragement, and the librarians of the Fisher Library for providing access to the University Archives; also Dr David Branagan for his interest. At the New South Wales Department of Mineral Resources: Al Bashford, Senior Librarian, who generously shared his time and expertise. At the Royal Botanic Gardens, Sydney: Dr Tim Entwisle, Director, Plant Sciences, (now of Kew Gardens, England), and Dr Surrey Jacobs for information concerning the Zostera of New South Wales. At the Australian Museum: Jan Brazier, Manager, Archives & Records; Dr Ross Pogson. Mineralogy Manager. At the Anglican Diocese of Sydney: Dr Louise Trott, Diocesan Archivist. At the Royal Historical Society of Australia, Sydney: Ms Diana Hill. At the Royal Society of New South Wales, Sydney: Mrs M. Krysko and Ms Patricia Callaghan. At the Geographical Society of New South Wales, Sydney: Dr Don Biddle. At Orange: The librarians of Orange City Library, and John Hammond and Mrs Marie Hammond for introducing us to the story of the Tom family of Byng. We thank the following for bringing to life the period of Georgina's association with the Blue Mountains and the Lithgow area: John Low, Local Historian, City of Blue Mountains Library, Springwood; Jim Smith and Mrs Pamela Smith; John Bayliss, Lithgow Regional Library.

IN CANBERRA: Beverley Allen, Reader Services Librarian, and her colleagues at the library of the Australian Geological Survey Organisation, Symonston, ACT; and the staff of the General Collections and Greg Wilson, of the Manuscript Collection, at the National Library of Australia.

IN VICTORIA: At the Department of Natural Resources and Environment: Irene O'Neill. At the National Museum of Victoria, Melbourne, our sincere thanks to Elizabeth Thompson, Collections Manager, for tracking down and listing the specimens sent by Georgina King to Professor Sir Frederick McCoy, and for allowing us to take photographs; to Sandra Winchester and Frank Job, Librarians, and David Pickering, Library Services, for their help in the matter of the McCoy/King letters. We are extremely grateful to the Trustees of Museum Victoria for permission to quote from this important correspondence and to publish photographs. At the Royal Botanic Gardens our thanks to Dr J.H. Ross, Chief Botanist; to Sally Stewart for kindly providing us with an image of Georgina King; to Dr Monika Wells for her help and advice concerning the correspondence between Ferdinand Mueller and Georgina King; and to Jill Thurlow, Librarian, for her help in the matter of Mueller's Notes on *Boronia pinnata* and *B. floribunda*; our thanks, too, to Helen Cohn, Library Manager. At the University of Melbourne our thanks to Dr Gerry Kraft, Department of Botany, for his insights into the life of Jacob Agardh and nineteenth-century seaweed collectors; to Elizabeth Agostino and the staff of the Archives and Special Collections, the Baillieu Library; and especially to Dr R.W. Home of the Department of History and Philosophy of Science for his thoughtful critique of our manuscript in its early days. At the Borchardt Library, Latrobe University, Melbourne, Margot Hislop was most supportive of our work.

IN SOUTH AUSTRALIA: Susan Woodburn, of the Special Collections of the Barr Smith Library, the University of Adelaide, investigated the correspondence of Daisy M. Bates; also our thanks to Miss Edith Sinclair, who typed and classified Bates' manuscripts for the Commonwealth Government in the period 1936–1940 but did not deal with any correspondence.

IN WESTERN AUSTRALIA: Our thanks to Brian G. Solosy, Archivist, St. John's Church, Fremantle (for material relating to the early pastoral work of the Reverend George King), and B. Reece (editor of King's Western Australian letters, 1841–1848).

OVERSEAS: Our thanks to Catherine Wakeling, Archivist, The United Society for the Propagation of the Gospel, London; to Michael Houlihan, Chief Executive, National Museums and Galleries of Northern Ireland, Belfast; to Kate Pickard, Archivist, and the staff of the Royal Botanic Gardens at Kew, for their courteous welcome and the privilege of studying 'the Bentham/von Mueller correspondence' for the *Flora Australiensis* in the matter of *B. floribunda*.

While we were following in the footsteps of the inquisitive Miss King, Tim Trevor-Jones and Mrs Elizabeth Trevor-Jones allowed us to visit their property at Bowenfels where Georgina geologised so very happily. Dr John Hawke and Mrs Alison Hawke showed us great kindness at Byng, the small settlement set among the early goldfields of New South Wales where Georgina found much of interest to spur her on. We were also privileged to receive help from members of the King family in Australia and overseas, including Major Cecil Harding of Port Laoise, Ireland. Special thanks are due to Mrs E.P. (Pat) King, who passed on her family knowledge and provided a detailed family tree. Mrs Primrose Henderson of Belfast, Northern Ireland, sent information concerning the Irish connection and many family photographs. The late Whitney King invited us into his home in Melbourne, where he shared with us his early memories of the Sydney branch of his family and passed on the the Reverend King's unpublished 'Reminiscences'. He also gave us permission to quote from his great-aunt's unpublished materials and make use of them for this book. Sadly, Whitney died long before our work could reach fruition. We remember him for his courtesy, humour and encouragement of our endeavours. Of our friends and well-wishers, we particularly wish to thank Dr John Carter, and the late Brinley Hodges and Mrs Diana Hodges, whose hospitality in Canberra and Sydney was always greatly appreciated, enabling us, as it did, to search intensively for traces of Georgina King. Finally, at Wakefield

Press we thank everyone concerned with the publication of our book, especially Michael Bollen – without him, Georgina King's story would not have seen the light of day.

Notes

Chapter One – Bread upon the Waters

1 *Australian Dictionary of Biography*, vol. 5, p. 25: entry for KING, GEORGE (1813–1899); unpublished reminiscences by the Reverend George King, LLD, supplied by the late Mr Whitney King, pp. 9 and 12 ['Reminiscences']; Mitchell Library [ML] MSS 273/3: Georgina King, unpublished autobiography, vol. i, pp. 3–5 ['Autobiography'].

2 Jane Mathewson was born in 1813, the third daughter of Lavens Mathewson of Newtown Stewart and the widow of Alexander Stewart (died 1835). Rebecca May, the Kings' first child, was born 9 May 1841 (information supplied by Mrs E.P. King). The *Ganges*, 418 tons, commanded by Samuel C. Walker, left London's West India Dock for Swan River with the Reverend and Mrs King travelling in the cabin; the other emigrants were by and large labourers and shepherds. (*The Times*, London, 26 May 1841, p. 1; see also Erickson, R., 1988, *The Bicentennial Dictionary of Western Australians pre-1829–1888*, vol. iii, Nedlands: University of Western Australia Press, p. 1749.)

3 'Reminiscences', p. 12.

4 'Autobiography', p. 6.

5 'Reminiscences', p. 12.

6 ML MSS 5455 King Family: Papers of the the Reverend George King, 1836–1898, 1910: Correspondence 1840–1898, ['George King Papers']: box 4, item 3.

7 'George King Papers': box 1, item 1: letters 1 and 2 of 8 and 26 February 1841 respectively.

8 Frost, L. (ed.) (1984) 1995, *No Place for a Nervous Lady*, St Lucia: University of Queensland Press.

9 Bolton, G., Vose, H., Watson, A. (eds), 1991, *The Wollaston Journals*,

vol. 1 ['Wollaston, vol. 1'], Nedlands: University of Western Australia Press.

10 Ibid., p. 128.

11 Frost, op. cit., p. 43.

12 Ibid., p. 46.

13 By the end of 1842 Australind was flourishing: there were 365 inhabitants – or more than ten per cent of the total European population of Western Australia. It had overtaken Albany, which existed mainly as a service centre for passing whalers, and no one could have foreseen it was doomed to failure. Like its South Australian counterpart, the success of Western Australia depended on an influx of free emigrant workers providing cheap labour. When it came to uprooting themselves and moving half a world away, most participants preferred to go to the eastern states where the infrastructure needed for survival and advancement was already well in place. The Australind venture collapsed in 1843, although the Western Australian Company limped on till the 1880s.

14 'Wollaston, vol. 1', pp. 126–127.

15 'Reminiscences', p. 6.

16 'Wollaston, vol. 1', pp. 126–127.

17 Society for the Propagation of the Gospel, C/AUS/PER 1 [SPG C/AUS/PER 1]: Rev. George King to Rev. Ernest Hawkins, 28 October 1841. (St John's Church, Fremantle, archives: material supplied by B. Solosy.)

18 'Wollaston, vol. 1', pp. 128–29.

19 Ibid., p. xxix.

20 'Resourceful, enduring, sustained by his religious faith, he gradually acclimatised', say the editors of his journals. (Ibid., p. xxx.)

21 SPG C/AUS/PER 1: Rev. George King to Rev. Ernest Hawkins, 28 October 1841.

22 Ibid.

23 Ibid., 16 November 1841.

Chapter Two – Feed my Lambs

1 Bolton, G., Vose, H., Watson, A. (eds), 1991, *The Wollaston Journals*, vol. 1 ['Wollaston, vol. 1'], Nedlands: University of Western Australia Press., p. 181.

2 Ibid., p. 185.
3 Completed in September 1842, the first service was conducted on Sunday, 18 September 1842. (Ibid., p. 241.)
4 Bolton, G., Vose, H., Watson, A. (eds), 1992, *The Wollaston Journals*, vol. 2 ['Wollaston, vol. 2'], Nedlands, WA: University of Western Australia Press, pp. 85, 163–165.
5 Ibid., pp. 164–166.
6 Ibid., pp. 85, 163–165.
7 Bates, D.M., 'Church Pioneering in Western Australia: the First Anglican Church: the Late Dr. King's Work', *The Western Mail*, 4 June 1910, p. 41.
8 Reece, B. (ed.), 'The Letters of Rev. George King, Fremantle 1841–48', pp. 7–8. (Unpublished essay in the archives of St John's Church, Fremantle.)
9 Society for the Propagation of the Gospel [SPG]: copy of original in the archives of St John's Church, Fremantle, of the response of the Reverend George King to a Society questionnaire, dated 12 June 1846 ['King, 1846'] (supplied by B. Solosy).
10 Ibid.
11 Unpublished reminiscences of the Reverend George King, LLD, supplied by the late Mr Whitney King ['Reminiscences'], p. 13.
12 SPG C/AUS/PER 1: Rev. George King to Rev. Ernest Hawkins, 28 October 1841.
13 'George King Papers': box 1, letter 5, 31 December 1845.
14 'King, 1846'.
15 Ibid.
16 See 'Wollaston, vol. 1', pp. 125–126: entry for May–November 1841.
17 'Reminiscences', p. 15; 'George King Papers', box 1, letter 12. On 4 January he sailed for Adelaide per *Emma Sherrat*, cost of passage for the family being £40, then to Sydney per *Phantom* at a further cost of £35. (Ibid., box 2, item 6.)

Chapter Three – My Father's House

1 *Australian Encyclopaedia*, 1958, vol. 2, p. 363.
2 *Australian Dictionary of Biography [ADB]*, vol. 1, pp. 521–523: entries for HASSALL, ROWLAND (1768–1820) and HASSALL, THOMAS (1794–1868).

3 *ADB*, vol. 2, p. 424: entry for SCONCE, ROBERT KNOX (1813–1852).
4 Shaw, G.P., 1978, *Patriarch and Patriot: William Grant Broughton 1788–1853*, Melbourne: Melbourne University Press, p. 210.
5 *ADB*, vol. 2, p. 425: entry for SCONCE, ROBERT KNOX (1813–1852).
6 His eldest son, William, born in 1843, also had the name 'Selwyn'. The first and only bishop of New Zealand and Melanesia, George Augustus Selwyn (1809–1878) was consecrated in 1841.
7 Georgina King to T.W.E. David, 'Elga', 17 December 1917 (archives of the University of Sydney, file no. 8764: Georgina King).
8 Archives of the Diocese of Sydney: Bishop of Australia Registers ['Bishop of Australia Registers'] vol. 2, 1848–1855', p. 62.
9 Clune, F., 1961, *Saga of Sydney*, Sydney: Subscriber's edition, p. 197.
10 Unpublished reminiscences of the Reverend George King, LLD, supplied by the late Mr Whitney King ['Reminiscences'], p. 16.
11 Ibid., p. 16.
12 *ADB*, vol. 3, pp. 91–92: entry for BARKER, FREDERIC (1808–1882).
13 *ADB*, vol. 5, p. 25: entry for KING, GEORGE (1813–1899).
14 *The Judgment of the Bishop of Sydney in the case of the Rev. George King, M.A., Licensed Minister of St. Andrew's, Sydney, Delivered at the Diocesan Registry, March 5th, 1861. (With an Appendix), 1861, Sydney: Joseph Cook [Judgment]*, p. 17: King to Bishop, 24 July 1858.
15 Rev. H. Tincombe to James Macarthur, 19 December 1860, referring to comments by Geoffrey Eagar who at the time was the auditor of the University of Sydney and an associate of King (a founding Fellow of St Paul's College (Mitchell Library [ML] A2934, vol. 28, 955, Macarthur Papers: frames 507–15).
16 *Judgment*, pp. 17–18: King to Bishop, 14 August 1858.
17 *Judgment*, p. 18: 'Now after more than nine years service in a parish where I have experienced very great kindness and affection from my parishioners, I shall be content to sacrifice my own personal feelings in the matter, and devote my energies to another district rather than jeopardise the peace of the Church.'
18 *Judgment*, p. 19: Bishop to King, 19 August 1858.
19 This was the second such summons: King had already appeared before the chancellor of the diocese the day after the offence. This second appearance was put down for 'Thursday week the 28th day of

February instant [1861] at Eleven o'clock in the forenoon'. ('Bishop of Australia Registers', 3, pp. 156–157 'Citation'.) Ibid., p. 146. The chancellor was the Hon. Sir William Westbrook Burton.

20 Ibid., pp. 161–162: 'As, however, Mr. King appears to have acted in the belief that he was defending his rights as a parochial minister, and in uncertainty as to the Bishop's claim, and as the object of the judgment is not to inflict punishment, but to maintain the due authority of the Bishop, and to bring this matter to a satisfactory conclusion, I am willing to grant Mr. King another licence for the same Church . . . Provided never the less that nothing in this licence shall extend and be construed to extend to abridge our Episcopal authority and Office or of our successors in administering holy ceremonies and performing the function belonging to us.'

Chapter Four – The Beginning of Wisdom

1 'My Father was dining at Government House one night, when the conversation turned to people disappearing, and were never heard of after. My Father said he was told that the house he lived in belonged to a man named Jackson who had disappeared, and the agent still collected the rent, and when the Government heard of it, they took it over, and he was paying rent to the Government. Sir Charles Fitzroy, who my Father was dining with, said, "Send in an application for the house as a Parsonage, and I will see that you get it, for you should not be paying rent"' (Mitchell Library [ML] MSS 273/3: Georgina King, unpublished autobiography, vol. 1 Ibid., p.8a).

2 Ibid., p. 10.

3 [O]ur nurse, Margaret Glenn, used to buy brandy-snaps, and put them under the door, as they were so thin, and I could eat them with my dry bread', Ibid., p. 9.

4 Ibid., pp. 4–5.

5 Ibid., p. 9.

6 Jones, S. and Stackhouse, J., 1983, *Gentlemen Scientists: Natural History in N.S.W.*, Sydney: Historic Houses Trust of New South Wales, p. 4. The Botanic Gardens were established at Farm Cove, on the site of the government farm (the first in the colony). Public access was restricted until they were opened to the public in 1831.

7 Hoare, M., 1981, 'Botany and Society in Eastern Australia', in D.J.

Carr and S.G.M. Carr (eds), *People and Plants in Australia*, Sydney: Academic Press, p. 185.

8 Ford's *Sydney Commercial Directory, for the Year 1851*, Sydney: W. & F. Ford, facsimile reprint, 1978, Library of Australian History, North Sydney, p. xxii. Clarke was also on the committee of the Australian Society 'For the Encouragement of Arts, Science, Commerce, and Agriculture, in Australia' and was secretary of the Diocesan Board of Missions, for the Diocese of Sydney.

9 W.A. Rainbow, 'Brief History of the Australian Museum', *The Australian Museum Magazine*, vol. 1, 1922, pp. 167–168.

10 George Bennett's catalogue was published in 1837, as *A Catalogue of Specimens of Natural History and Miscellaneous Curiosities deposited in the Australian Museum*. (See Coppleson, V.M., 1955, 'The Life and Times of Dr. George Bennett', in *Bulletin of the Post-graduate Committee in Medicine*, University of Sydney, vol. 2, no. 9, December 1955, p. 215.)

11 In January 1840 he did much valuable work in the company of James Dwight Dana (1813–1895) of the United States Exploring Expedition. Dana's conclusions supported 'Clarke's opinion, contested at that time, that there was perfect conformity between the upper and underlying beds in the coal formations, and that all belonged lower than the coal deposits of India and Europe in the palaeozoic period' (*Australian Dictionary of Biography [ADB]*, vol. 1, p. 279: entry for DANA, JAMES DWIGHT).

12 During Bishop Broughton's last visit to England, a meeting of the colony's leading Anglicans was held in Sydney on 15 December 1852 at St James's Grammar School to propose the foundation of St Paul's College, at the University of Sydney. Chief Justice Sir Alfred Stephens presided. The meeting concluded that because of deficiencies in the university's constitution, it rested upon others to oversee the moral and religious welfare of the undergraduates. Among the first Fellows of St Paul's elected in 1853 were: Rev. R. Allwood, M.A.; Rev. W.B. Clarke, M.A.; Rev. George King, MA; Rev. William Stack, B.A.; Rev. Alfred Stephen, B.A.; Rev. W.H. Walsh, M.A. (George King Papers, ML MSS 5455, box 4: printed items, item 1: *By-Laws and Statutes of and relating to St. Paul's College within the University of Sydney with some account of its Foundation, Sydney*: Joseph Cook, n.d., p. 10).

13 J. Jervis, 'Rev. W.B. Clarke, M.A., F.R.S., F.G.S., F.R.G.S.', *Journal of the Royal Australian Historical Society*, vol. 30, part VI, 1944, pp. 348, 360.

14 See M. Organ, 'W.B. Clarke as Scientific Journalist', in *Historical Records of Australian Science*, vol. 9, no. 1, 1992, where Clarke's contributions and personality are put under the microscope less benignly than usual.

15 'Encrinites' or 'crinoids' – literally 'stone-lilies' – emerged in the Silurian period (which pre-dated the Devonian), then increased in number and variety. They belong to the Echinodermata. (See Geikie, Sir A., (1886), 2nd ed. 1890, *Class-Book of Geology*, London: Macmillan & Co., pp. 251, 372 for a description; also p. 278 for the illustration of a Carboniferous crinoid.)

16 Clarke's geological specimens and library were eventually sold to the New South Wales government for the princely sum of £7000. (Jose, A.W. and Carter, H.J. (eds), 1925, *The Illustrated Australian Encyclopaedia*, vol. 1, Sydney: Angus & Robertson, p. 272.) The collection was lost in the great fire that swept through the Garden Palace in 1882.

17 On 26 November 1835 in Sydney, Bennett married his first wife, Julia Cameron, daughter of the former commandant of Port Dalrymple, Van Diemen's Land, and his Portuguese wife. Another daughter married George Strickland Kingston and became the mother of George Cameron Kingston, a premier of South Australia.

18 Ford's *Sydney Commercial Directory for the Year 1851*. (See note 8 above for details.)

19 Coppleson, op. cit., p. 219.

20 Jane's work with birds and reptiles was sent home from Fremantle to the museum in Belfast, where Georgina was able to view it in the 1880s. 'Autobiography', pp. 6–7.

21 Bennett, G., 1860, *Gatherings of a Naturalist in Australasia; being observations principally upon the animal and vegetable productions of New South Wales, New Zealand, and some of the Austral islands*, London: John Van Voorst Milson's Point: Currawong Press, facsimile edition, 1982, p. 250. The illustrations are by George French Angas, with the exception of Helena Scott's painting of *Ceratopetalum gummifera* (Christmas Bush).

22 Ibid., p. 138.

23 'Autobiography', pp. 10–11.
24 Ibid., p. 24.

Chapter Five – The Dwellings of the Wilderness

1 During Bishop Broughton's last visit to England, a meeting of the colony's leading Anglicans was held in Sydney on 15 December 1852 at St James's Grammar School to propose the foundation of St Paul's College, at the University of Sydney. Chief Justice Sir Alfred Stephens presided. The meeting concluded that because of deficiencies in the University's constitution, it rested upon others to oversee the moral and religious welfare of the undergraduates. The college was established in 1854, the foundation stone laid in January 1856, and the building completed in 1859.
2 Mitchell Library [ML] MSS 273/3: Georgina King, unpublished autobiography, vol. 1 ['Autobiography'], pp. 25–26.
3 A residential school was set up at 152 Liverpool Street in 1860; by 1861 it moved to 368 Castlereagh Street. In 1868 it moved to Ormonde House in Paddington until, King's daughter tells us, '... the institution grew so much that my father got the government to give the land on the Newton Road where the Deaf and Dumb Institute now exists'. Ibid., pp. 25–26. The governor who granted the land in 1872 and then became the Institute's patron was Sir Hercules Robinson.
4 ML Q572.9901/K: 'The Diary of the Rev. George King, L.L.D.' He had been successful in setting up a school in Fremantle.
5 King to Bishop, 20 September 1859 (*The Judgment of the Bishop of Sydney in the Case of the Rev. George King, M.A., Licensed Minister of St. Andrew's, Sydney*, p. 29).
6 'Autobiography', pp. 10–11.
7 George King often called Georgina 'Zee', after the statuesque heroine of Bulwer Lytton's romance *The Coming Race*, published in 1871.
8 'Autobiography', p. 1.
9 Ibid., p. 11.
10 Ibid., p. 12.
11 Ibid., p. 11.
12 Ibid., p. 16. 'Lyndcote' was the earliest of Charles Edward Jeanneret's three houses on Hunter's Hill. In 1973 it was still

standing in Stanley Road. 'It is of charming appearance, with a garden of generous proportions and a low stone retaining wall upon which one can most conveniently lean while admiring its beauties. Though from the street it appears to be single-storeyed, from the Parramatta River aspect it stands three storeys high. It is built from stone quarried on the property. Jeanneret never lived at "Lyndcote"' (Emanuel, C. and Thompson, P., 1973, *Hunter's Hill Sketchbook*, Adelaide: Rigby, p. 52).

13 'Autobiography', p. 16.

14 Ibid., pp. 12–13.

15 Ibid., 12–13.

16 *Sydney Morning Herald*, Letters to the Editor, 22 July 1862, 23 July 1862, 25 July 1862, 1 August 1862 (two), being correspondence from H. Kerrison James, an Anglican official, and the Reverend George King on the subject of £25 paid annually to King from the Moore Farm estate until 1860.

17 The cathedral as described in 1861: 'The patience of many has been wearied out from the length of time it has been in building. Of late, however, it has gradually been verging towards completion, and we hope, for the honor of that Church that claims it, that it may soon be ready for use. The eastern window and elaborately carved work is very fine. The temporary church of St. Andrew is alongside' (*The Stranger's Guide to Sydney arranged in a Series of Walks*, 1861, Sydney: J.W. Waugh, p. 33). 1978 reprint (see Ford).

18 Clune, F., 1961, *Saga of Sydney*, Sydney: subscribers' edition, pp. 447–48.

19 *Australian Encyclopedia*, 1956 edition, vol. 8, p. 398.

20 Information supplied by Mrs Laurel Horton, St Peter's Parish History Committee.

Chapter Six – In Spirit and in Truth

1 Mitchell Library [ML] MSS 273/3: Georgina King, unpublished autobiography, vol. 1 ['Autobiography'], p. 22.

2 For an account of Spiritualism in the 1860s and 1870s, see Carter, J.M.T., 1999, *Painting the Islands Vermilion*, Melbourne: Melbourne University Press, Chapter Six: 'Spiritual Communications, etc', and by the same author, 2000, *Eyes to the Future: Sketches of Australia and her Neighbours in the 1870s*, Canberra: National Library of Australia,

Chapter Six: 'True Believers'.

3 Unpublished reminiscences by the Reverend George King, LLD, supplied by the late Mr Whitney King ['Reminiscences'], p. 2.
4 Ibid., pp. 2–3.
5 'Autobiography', p. 23.
6 *Chambers's Encyclopaedia*, vol. vii, p. 579 and vol. viii, p. 606.
7 'Autobiography', p. 22.
8 In 1826 Frederick Fisher, a ticket-of-leave man, disappeared without trace, and was later seen sitting on the slip-rails of a paddock pointing to where his remains were subsequently uncovered.
9 'Autobiography', p. 22.
10 Ibid., p. 74.
11 Ibid., p. 9.

Chapter Seven – Stages in the Odyssey of a Soul

1 Moyal, A., 1986, *A Bright and Savage Land*, Ringwood: Penguin, p. 140. Those against included Ferdinand Mueller, Frederick McCoy, and William Sharp Macleay (who confused Darwin's ideas with those of the Frenchman, Lamarck).
2 W.S. Macleay to Robert Lowe, Viscount Sherbrooke, May 1860, quoted ibid., p. 141.
3 *Chambers's Encyclopaedia*, vol. ix, p. 577.
4 Quoted in Harvey, Sir Paul (ed.), *The Oxford Companion to English Literature*, (3rd ed.), Oxford: The Clarendon Press, p. 139: entry for CARLYLE, THOMAS.
5 Blainey, G., 1957, *A Centenary History of the University of Melbourne*, Melbourne: Melbourne University, p. 47.
6 Mitchell Library [ML] MSS 273/3: Georgina King, unpublished autobiography, vol. 1 ['Autobiography'], pp. 24–25.
7 'Man, essentially a naked spirit, cannot live, and move abroad, and operate upon his fellows, unless he be arrayed in some investiture woven for the soul; hence arise languages, religions, polities, philosophies. God himself for our apprehension needs must wear His garments of time and space. The old Puritanism of Carlyle's ancestors had transformed itself into nineteenth-century transcendentalism' (Edward Dowden, introduction to *Sartor Resartus*, pp. ix–x).
8 Wynne Davies, M. (ed.), *Prentice Hall Guide to English Literature*, p. 387: entry for CARLYLE, THOMAS.

9 Georgina at the time was struggling on her own to understand Euclid. 'When I found in Herbert Spencer's "First Principles" "By the persistence of force we meet the persistence of some cause that transcends our knowledge and experience, and in asserting it, we assert non conditioned reality, without beginning and end." It was just what I wanted at the time. I puzzled so much over "A point is that which has no parts", "A line is length without breadth", when I first commenced to teach myself Euclid' ('Autobiography', p. 25).
10 Wynne Davies, op. cit.: entry for CARLYLE, THOMAS.
11 'My mother also took a niece and nephew to live with us who had lost their mother' ('Autobiography', p. 13).
12 Allen, J.A., 1994, *Rose Scott: Vision and Revision in Feminism*, Melbourne: Oxford University Press, p. 35.
13 'Autobiography', p. 13.
14 Ibid., pp. 24–25.
15 Ibid., pp. 13–14.
16 Ibid., p. 13.
17 Ibid., p. 2.
18 Dowden, op. cit., p. xii.
19 'Autobiography', p. 25.

Chapter Eight – Brotherly Love

1 'When my younger sister, Helena, was dying, she left me her two children, but the little baby girl died, and her boy, Esca Morris Humphery was the darling of my life for six years. I kept him on the Mountains as much as I could, and his Father built a Cottage for us at Springwood, and we had a happy time there' (Mitchell Library [ML] MSS 273/3: Georgina King, unpublished autobiography, vol. 1 ['Autobiography'].)
2 The track crossed Knapsack Gully on Lapstone Hill, by means of a viaduct 388 feet in length. Then the time-consuming zig-zag came into operation: first and third legs with engine in front, the second with the train in reverse. The journals kept, for example, by British travellers William Bethell and John Morison in the 1870s and held by the National Library of Australia give eyewitness accounts of the process. (See Carter, J.M.T., *Eyes to the Future*.)
3 Passengers could leave Redfern Station at 9 am and reach Bowenfels at 2.45 pm.

4 'Autobiography', p. 15.

5 Chief engineer John Whitton had never seen a zig-zag but had worked on railways, canals and bridges in Britain. From 1856 he was engineer-in-chief in charge of laying out and constructing railways in New South Wales. (*Australian Dictionary of Biography [ADB]*, vol. 6: entry for WHITTON, JOHN, 1820–1898.)

6 Stockton, J., 'Health and Education: Local Industries Built on Air', in Stanbury, P. and Bushell, L., 1985, *The Blue Mountains: Grand adventure for all*, Sydney: The Macleay Museum, University of Sydney, p. 82.

7 Governor Macquarie's Journal, quoted in Campbell, J.J. (ed.), 1937, *Historical Notes on the Earliest Days of Springwood and District*, Springwood: Jackson Stonewall (facsimile edition of 1986), p. 5.

8 *Historical Walking Tour of Springwood Township*, Springwood Historical Society; *Rural Cumberland Year Book for 1885*, Sydney: Fuller & Co., p. 173.

9 From 1867–1869.

10 Garran, A., ed., (1886) 1974, *Australia: the First Hundred Years being a facsimile of Volumes I and II of the Picturesque Atlas of Australasia*, Sydney: Ure Smith, p. 53.

11 'Autobiography', p. 13.

12 Franklin, M., 'Rose Scott', in D. Spender (ed.), *The Peaceful Army*, Ringwood, Vic.: Penguin Books, p. 100.

Chapter Nine – Coming of Age: AAAS, 1888

1 See for example 'The Country' by William Woolls, ca. 1834 (included in Kramer, L. (ed.), *My Country: Australian Poetry & Short Stories Two Hundred Years*, vol. 1, p. 23).

2 Bentham, G., 1863–1878, *Flora Australiensis: A Description of the Plants of the Australian Territory* (seven volumes), London: Lovell Reeve and Co., vol. 1, p. 10.

3 Joseph D. Hooker (1817–1911), director of the Royal Botanic Gardens at Kew, is a prime example. While on J.C. Ross's 1839 *Erebus* expedition to the Antarctic, Hooker collected in New Zealand, Tasmania and Port Jackson, and published three significant volumes as a result, under the general title of *The Botany of the Antarctic Voyage*.

4 Judge Barron Field (1786–1846), quoted in the *Australian Encyclopedia*, vol. 2, entry for 'Societies, Learned', p. 476.

5 'It is, therefore, possible that the Council may be compelled occasionally to deny to authors of valuable contributions that which their ambition or their merits may claim, the full publication of those contributions . . .' W.B. Clarke, inaugural address, 9 July 1867, in *Transactions of the Royal Society of New South Wales*, vol. 1, 1867, p. 9.

6 MacLeod, R. (ed.), 1988, *The Commonwealth of Science: ANZAAS and the Scientific Enterprise in Australasia 1888–1988*, Melbourne: Oxford University Press, pp. 21–22 and 26.

7 Mitchell Library [ML] MSS 273/3: Georgina King, unpublished autobiography, vol. 1 ['Autobiography'], p. 15.

8 *Australian Dictionary of Biography [ADB]*, vol. 5, pp. 93–94: entry for LIVERSIDGE, ARCHIBALD (1846–1927).

9 Ibid.

10 The *ADB* describes Bennett's life and achievements in its first volume, 1788–1850, although he lived until 1893.

11 See Liversidge, A. and Etheridge, R. (eds), 1889, *Report of the First Meeting of the Australasian Association for the Advancement of Science, August and September, 1888*, Sydney: AAAS, p. xix [*Report*].

12 Macleod, op. cit., p. 19.

13 'Ladies are eligible for Membership', *Report*, p. xiv.

14 Home, R.W. (ed.), 1988, *Australian Science in the Making*, Melbourne: Cambridge University Press, pp. 40–41.

15 Carlyle, T. (1836), 1899, *Sartor Resartus*, London: Ward Lock & Co., p. 152.

16 Ibid.

17 'Autobiography', vol. 1, p. 29.

18 'It was there I first met Dr. R.L. Jack, the government geologist of Queensland and we became friends', Georgina wrote in her autobiography almost forty years later. The word 'friendship' was perhaps another of her exaggerations.

19 'Origin of the Laterite in the New England District of New South Wales' and 'Cupriferous Tuffs of the Passage Beds Between the Triassic Hawkesbury Series and the Permo-Carboniferous Coal-Measures of New South Wales' (Liversidge and Etheridge,

op. cit., pp. 233–241 and 275–290 respectively), and a note: 'Micropetrographical Notes on some of the Hydrothermal Rocks of N.S. Wales' (ibid., pp. 290–291).

Chapter Ten – A Toast to the Ladies

1 Mitchell Library [ML] MSS 273/3: Georgina King, unpublished autobiography, vol. 1 ['Autobiography'], p. 6.

2 Captain James Mangles, R.N., a visitor to the Swan River in 1829–1831, was a cousin of Lady Stirling, the governor's wife.

3 Moyal, A., 1981, 'Collectors and Illustrators: Women botanists of the nineteenth century', in D.J. Carr and S.G.M. Carr (eds), *People and Plants in Australia*, Sydney: Academic Press, p. 336. Mangles was grateful enough to Mrs Molloy to send her botanical books and a *hortus siccus*, but in her lifetime no flower honoured her by name. In 1842, however, James Drummond wrote to W.J. Hooker at Kew requesting that a *boronia* 'that stood high as a man on horseback' be named after Mrs Molloy. The letter was published in the Kew Journal. In 1844 Bartling published a description of *Boronia elatior*, identical to *B. molloyae*.

4 Skene, J., 1997, 'The Power of Naming: Women Botanical Collectors and the Contested Spaces of 19th Century Botany', *Studies in Western Australian History*, 17, p. 4.

5 Dr John Lindley (1799–1865) first professor of botany at London University and secretary of the Horticultural Society, quoted, ibid., p. 5.

6 *Touchstone*, 2 October 1869, p. 3.

7 The algologist, W.H. Harvey (1811–1866), visited Australia in 1854 and reported back on Mueller's general amiability. (See Ducker, S.C. (ed.), 1988, *The Contented Botanist: Letters of W.H. Harvey about Australia*, Melbourne: Melbourne University Press, p. 413.) See *Shorter Oxford Dictionary*, vol. 1, p. 1123, for a definition in vogue since 1688.

8 See Hamersley, M.J., 1981, 'Botany and Society: Swan River Colony', in Carr, op. cit., for details of Mueller's female collectors in Western Australia.

9 Letter from Philip Webster of the Fremantle Horticultural Society to the Editor, 9 May 1870. (Quoted, ibid., p. 267.)

10 *West Australian*, 20 June 1885: letter signed 'Mueller'. (Ibid., p. 276.)

11 Mueller's sister, Clara Christine Marie (Mueller) Wehl (1833–1901), collected from Lake Bonney and Mount Gambier. His niece, Louisa Therese Wehl (1860–1952), collected in Clare, Appila-Yarowie, and at the top of the St Vincent Gulf area. At one time she lived in Gladstone. Another niece, Henrietta, became Mrs Sinclair and moved to Queensland.

12 Artist, 1867, *The Wild Flowers Around Me*, with 13 hand-coloured plates. (Carr, D.J., 1981, 'The contribution of women to Australian Botany', in Carr, op. cit., p. 325.

13 See Clarke, P., 1990, *Pioneer Writer: The life of Louisa Atkinson: novelist, journalist, naturalist*, Sydney: Allen and Unwin.

Chapter Eleven – A Place in the Sun

1 'My Brother is naturally kindhearted but is influenced by my sister – She said to me the other day that she knew Miss Turner who made so much money by writing popular stories, and why could I not make money that way – I went to my room and had a good laugh, for I thought to myself I suppose after all my papers on the "Carbon Group of Minerals" is a romance in science' (Archives of the Museum of Victoria [MOV], Sir Frederick McCoy 'Correspondence 1854–1899, K and L', Letters from Georgina King: G.K. to Sir Frederick McCoy, 25 February 1896). All G.K. letters to McCoy are headed Montesca, Beresford Road, Homebush, Sydney, unless otherwise stated.

2 Mitchell Library [ML] MSS 273/1/1b: C.S. Wilkinson to G.K., 11 July 1889; ML MSS 2117/27–30: E.F. Pittman to G.K., 23 May 1893; ML MSS 273/1/5: T.W.E. David to G.K., June 1890.

3 ML MSS 2117/13: H.C. Russell to G.K., 12 February 1891.

4 *Australian Dictionary of Biography [ADB]*, vol. 10, p. 382: entry for MAIDEN, JOSEPH HENRY (1859–1925).

5 Powerhouse Museum Archives [PMA]: MRS 13, Letters of thanks (second series), 1890–1921, vol. 1, pp. 103–104 and vol. 4, pp. 5–6. One of the sponges (E3015) was destroyed on 18 October 1911.

6 PMA: MRS 4, Letterbooks (first series), 1882–1921, vol. 10, p. 901: J.H. Maiden to G.K., 15 August 1894.

7 Ibid., vol. 16, p. 365: R. Baker to G.K., 6 November 1900: 'Dear

Miss King, I beg to thank you for your kindness in forwarding the box of native plants as they are very acceptable at this time of the year for our flower court.'

8 ML MSS 273/3/40a–40b.

9 MOV: G.K. to F. McCoy, 27 May 1895 and 18 March 1896.

10 ML MSS 2117/1/251–254: F. McCoy to G.K., 11 October 1897.

11 ML MSS 2117/1/255–262: Rev. W. Potter to G.K., 6 November 1897.

12 See for example Atkinson's article on 'The Kurrajong Waterfalls' published in the *Sydney Mail*, 18 August 1860, and on 'Botanical Ramblings' in the *Sydney Morning Herald*, 2 September 1862 – both written as 'A Voice from the Country'.

13 Lawson, E., 1995, *The Natural Art of Louisa Atkinson*, Sydney: State Library of New South Wales Press, p. 115.

14 The National Herbarium of Victoria [MEL] holds four letters on the subject dated 14 August 1894 (MEL 94. 08. 14); 28 August 1894 (MEL 94. 08. 28); 28 August 1894 (MEL 94. 08. 28); 16 October 1894 (MEL 94. 10. 16).

15 ML MSS 273/1/31b: F. McCoy to G.K., 26 November 1896.

16 Letter from Rev. W. Potter (see note 11).

17 MEL 250283. Georgina sent her first recorded botanical specimen to Mueller in July 1892; it was found growing in a Homebush garden, very likely Jane King's.

18 MEL 252815, 242156 and 726746 respectively.

19 MEL 285557 and 114411 respectively. She provided more than one specimen of each plant.

20 MOV: F. Mueller to G.K., 16 September 1896 (in McCoy correspondence).

21 Ibid.

22 Ibid., 24 September 1896.

23 Ibid., 28 September 1896.

24 *The Proceedings of the Linnean Society of New South Wales, Vol. XXI*, Sydney: 1896, pp. 503–504.

25 MOV: J.G. Luehmann to G.K., 16 January 1897 (in McCoy correspondence).

Chapter Twelve – Science and Societies

1 Field (1786–1846) was an 'exclusivist' (or anti-emancipist) judge of

the Supreme Court of Civil Judicature of NSW. (See *Australian Dictionary of Biography [ADB]*, vol. 1, p. 374.)

2 Hoare, M., 1981, 'Botany and Society in Eastern Australia', in D.J. Carr and S.G.M. Carr (eds), *People and Plants in Australia*, Sydney: Academic Press, p. 185.

3 Ibid., pp. 187 and 215.

4 'Marrying into prominent "squattocracy" families they [the Macleays] become part of the legislators', lawyers', judges' and political network by which the colony – at least before responsible government in the late 1850s – was governed and organised. It was a socially and politically powerful establishment' (ibid., p. 201).

5 Mrs Robert Lowe quoted in Bligh, B., 1980, *Cherish the Earth: The Story of Gardening in Australia*, Sydney: David Ell Press, p. 55.

6 Since 1849 the museum had been installed in its permanent home opposite Hyde Park. The Act of Incorporation of 1855 gave the trustees absolute autonomy in the running of its affairs.

7 Inaugural Address to the Royal Society of New South Wales by the Vice-President, W.B. Clarke, *Transactions*, vol. 1, 1867, p. 27.

8 Archives of the Museum of Victoria, Sir Frederick McCoy 'Correspondence 1854–1899, K and L', Letters from Georgina King [MOV]: G.K. to F. McCoy, 25 October 1893.

9 Powerhouse Museum Archives [PMA]: MRS 4, Letterbooks (first series) 1882–1921, vol. 10, p. 774: J.H. Maiden to G.K., 21 June 1894.

10 PMA: MRS 202, Inwards correspondence, 1881–1952, 1893/607: G.K. to J.H. Maiden, 22 August 1893.

11 Mitchell Library [ML] MSS 273/3: Georgina King, unpublished autobiography, vol. 1 ['Autobiography'].

12 PMA: MRS 202, 1893/607: G.K. to J.H. Maiden, 22 August 1893.

13 *Proceedings of the Linnean Society of New South Wales, 1894*, vol. 9 (Series 2nd), pp. 375–383 – reprint held at ML MSS 2117/3/4.

Chapter Thirteen – Gold Standards

1 *Australian Dictionary of Biography [ADB]*, vol. 3, p. 421: entry for CLARKE, WILLIAM BRANWHITE (1798–1878).

2 Ibid., p. 422.

3 The choice fell on Samuel Stutchbury, and, while official praise for Stutchbury was fulsome, an editorial in the *Sydney Morning Herald*

(written by none other than Clarke) smacks of sour grapes: '. . . a naturalist of some eminence, Curator of a Museum in England, is to come out; but it is very unlikely that that gentleman will feel himself ready to undertake a geological survey though highly useful as an observer and collector' (quoted in Mozley, A., 1965, 'The foundations of the geological survey of New South Wales, *Journal and Proceedings, Royal Society of New South Wales*, 98, p. 91.)

4 Mitchell Library [ML] MSS 273/3: Georgina King, unpublished autobiography, vol. 1 ['Autobiography'], p. 14.

5 Ibid., pp. 47–48. Albert Helms, MA, PhD (Berlin) replaced Liversidge as 'Demonstrator in Practical Chemistry' in 1880.

6 Mellor, D.P., 'Founders of Australian Chemistry: Archibald Liversidge', *Proceedings of the Royal Australian Chemical Institution*, August, 1957, p. 416.

7 Ibid.

8 ML MSS 273/2/220–24: G.K. to Judge Backhouse, 21 September 1929 (copy).

9 Ibid.

10 Weatherstern, P.W. (ed.), n.d., *W. Folster's Articles: The Writings of William (Bill) Folster*, Orange: Paul Weatherstern, p. 88.

11 Kay, D.J., 1991, *Exploring the Golden West: Central Western New South Wales (A Heritage Field Guide)*, Kenhurst: Kangaroo Press, p. 102: entry for GUYONG.

12 Weatherstern, P.W., op. cit., p. 96.

13 'Autobiography', p. 41.

14 Ibid., pp. 41–42.

15 ML MSS 273/2/220–24: G.K. to Judge Backhouse, 21 September 1929 [Copy].

16 'Autobiography', pp. 41 – 42

17 See Preface to *The Mineral Wealth of New South Wales*, 1906 edition.

18 'Autobiography', p. 43.

19 *Journal and Proceedings of the Royal Society of New South Wales*, vol. 28, 1894, pp. 185–188. That year Liversidge rehashed a paper read at the Royal Society on 2 December 1891 for *The Chemical News and Journal of Physical Science* of 6 April 1894, pp. 162–163. In this (p. 162) he refers to 'the serpentine from Gundagai and Lucknow', areas well known to Georgina.

20 In 1861 Clarke was awarded £3000 for his part in the discovery of gold – although he had to fight for his money.
21 ML MSS 2117/1/63–64: H.C. Russell to G.K., 11 August 1893.
22 ML MSS 2117/1/65–66: H.C. Russell to G.K., 7 September 1893.
23 Powerhouse Museum Archives [PMA]: MRS 202, Inwards correspondence, 1881–1952, 1893/607: G.K. to J.H. Maiden, 22 August 1893. [spell out first in chapter's endnotes?]
24 PMA: MRS 4, Letterbooks (first series) 1882–1921, vol. 10, p. 152: J.H. Maiden to G.K., 14 November 1893: 'Dear Madam, In reply to your letter of the 22nd. August last, I beg to inform you that the black soil from Springfield, Byng, does not appear to contain bituminous matter, it is a ferruginous clay, containing some organic matter which probably has a swampy origin. The cubic forms of iron in the Soapstone are pseudomorphs (limonite after iron pyrites), when broken the pyrites is seen in its unaltered form of pseudo morph.

The rock from the top of the hills in the same locality is most probably a form of Epidote in quartz.

Yours t[r]uly, J.H. Maiden, CURATOR'
25 'On the Origin of Moss Gold', *Journal and Proceedings of the Royal Society of New South Wales*, vol. 27, 1893, pp. 287–298; 'On the Condition of Gold in Quartz and Calcite Veins', ibid., pp. 299–303; 'On the Origin of Gold Nuggets', ibid., pp. 303–343; 'On the Crystallization of Gold in Hexagonal Forms', ibid., pp. 343–346; 'Gold Moiré-Metallique', ibid., pp. 346–347. There was also an exhibit by Liversidge: 'A Combination laboratory, Lamp, Retort & Filter Stand', ibid., pp. 347–348.

Chapter Fourteen: – The Long Arm of Coincidence

1 Eventually published as 'The Palaeozoic-Carboniferous Formations of New South Wales' in 1895 in the *Sydney Morning Herald* and *The Sydney Mail* on 27 July and 3 August respectively.
2 The system includes the Coal Measures, Millstone Grit and Mountain Limestone.
3 See Valance, T.G., 1981, 'The fuss about coal: Troubled relations between palaeobotany and geology', in D.J. Carr and S.G.M. Carr (eds), *Plants and Man in Australia*, Sydney: Academic Press, pp. 136–175.

4 Mitchell Library [ML] MSS 2117/1–5: H.C. Russell to G.K., 9 August 1888.
5 ML MSS 273/1/1b: C.S. Wilkinson to G.K., 11 July 1889.
6 ML MSS 2117/23–26: C.A. Leibius to G.K., 20 May 1892.
7 ML MSS 2117/33–34: H.C. Russell to G.K., 14 October 1892.
8 ML MSS 2117/1/35–36: H.C. Russell to G.K., 11 February 1893.
9 ML MSS 2117/1/47 – 48: H.C. Russell to G.K., 13 March 1893.
10 ML MSS 273/3: Georgina King, unpublished autobiography, vol. 1 ['Autobiography'], p. 38.
11 Whether these skills were acquired in an orphanage, where she was trained as a governess, or whether she became a protégée of the Outram family, celebrated for their service to the British crown in India (the version Daisy herself promoted), is uncertain. See Bartlett, A., 1997, *Daisy Bates: Keeper of Totems*, Melbourne: Reed Library, p. 3; White, I. (ed.), 1985, *The Native Tribes of Western Australia*, Canberra: National Library of Australia, p. 3; and Hall, R., 'Conniving Miss Daisy', *The Weekend Australian*, 9–10 May 1998, p. 27.
12 'Her education appears to have been completed in a finishing school in Belgium', writes Elizabeth Salter, 'but of this she speaks not at all.' Salter, E., 1971, *Daisy Bates: the Great White Queen of the Never Never*, Sydney: Angus and Robertson, p. 9.
13 Allen, J., 1994, *Rose Scott: Vision and Revisionism in Feminism*, Melbourne: Oxford University Press, p. 65.
14 *ADB*, vol. 11, p. 242: entry for PITTMAN, EDWARD FISHER (1849–1932).
15 Mellor, D.P., 'Founders of Australian Chemistry: Archibald Liversidge', *Proceedings of the Royal Australian Chemical Institution*, August, 1957, p. 416.
16 *Productus* is a brachiopod found in Permo-carboniferous strata along with Palaeozoic plants such as Glossopteris and Vertebraria. See Geikie, A., 1899, *Class-book of Geology*, London: Macmillan & Co., p. 280, fig. 153a and p. 287, fig. 160a.
17 David, T.W.E., 1887, 'Geology of the Vegetable Creek Tin-mining Field, New England District', *Memoirs of the Geological Survey, N.S.W.*, no. 1.
18 Ibid., p. 54.

19 Ibid.
20 *Journal and Proceedings of the Royal Society of New South Wales, 1893*, vol. 27, pp. 18–19.
21 *Proceedings of the Linnean Society of New South Wales*, series 2, ix, pt. 2, pp. 249–257.
22 *Records of the Geological Survey of New South Wales*, iii, pp. 194–201.
23 *Proceedings of the Linnean Society of New South Wales*, series 2, viii, pt. 1, pp. 121–125.
24 'Autobiography', pp. 48–49.
25 Ibid., p. 38.
26 Ibid., p. 47.

Chapter Fifteen – The Changing of the Guard

1 Mitchell Library [ML] MSS 2117/1/183–185: William Wyatt Gill to G.K., 3 August 1896.
2 Archives of the Museum of Victoria, Sir Frederick McCoy 'Correspondence' 1854–1899, K and L'. Letters from Georgina King [MOV]: G.K. to McCoy, 25 November 1895.
3 Vallance, T.G., 1981, 'The fuss about coal: Troubled relations between palaeobotany and geology', in D.J. Carr and S.G.M. Carr (eds), *Plants and Man in Australia*, Sydney: Academic Press.
4 Branagan, D.F., 1972, *The Geology and Landscape of New South Wales*, Milton, QLD: Jacaranda Press, p. 28.
5 *Australian Dictionary of Biography [ADB]*, vol. 3 p. 421: entry for CLARKE, WILLIAM BRANWHITE (1798–1878).
6 Blainey, G., 1957, *A Centenary History of the University of Melbourne*, Melbourne: Melbourne University Press, p. 19.
7 MOV: G.K. to McCoy, 25 November 1894.
8 ML MSS 273/3: Georgina King, unpublished autobiography, vol. 1 ['Autobiography'], pp. 21–22. Mrs Bennett subsequently offered her husband's invaluable library to the university for £2000, an offer that was declined.
9 MOV: G.K. to McCoy, 25 November 1894.
10 Ibid.: 'I am sending you back my paper which please keep as a remembrance of your kindness to me. Should you think it, at any time, worthy of any of *your Societies* and useful to science please give it to one of them. I have added your note to the first page.'

11 Ibid., G.K. to McCoy, 2 January 1896.

12 Blainey, op. cit., p. 37.

13 'My Brother-in-law, Mr. Humphery, says it is very kind of you to write to me as you do, and he hopes I will preserve your letters which are so gracious' (MOV: G.K. to McCoy, 1 September 1895).

14 Vallance, op. cit., p. 158.

15 ML MSS 2117/163–165: McCoy to G.K., 8 July 1896.

16 MOV: G.K. to McCoy, 27 May 1895.

17 Scott, E., 1936, *A History of the University of Melbourne*, Melbourne: Melbourne University Press, p. 34.

18 MOV: G.K. to McCoy, 5 April 1896.

19 The natural history collections were financed by the Victorian government and housed in the Philosophical Institute (later the Royal Society) of Victoria. McCoy 'high-jacked' them in August 1856 and – in defiance of public opinion – installed them in rooms allotted at the university. And there they remained until his death.

Chapter Sixteen – Rocks and Rock Hounds

1 King, G., 1895, *The Palaeozoic Carboniferous Formations in New South Wales and the Occurrence of our Mineral Wealth*, Sydney: Angus and Robertson, p. 6.

2 '[I]n June, 1889, Professor David, then in the Department of Mines, read a paper at the Linnean Society, "Notes on the Origin of Kerosene Shale," in which he said another geologist "believed that the so-called kerosene shale occurred in the lower productive coal measures, otherwise known as the Greta series of permo-carboniferous age, and this fact first recognised by him, may prove a valuable help in the correlation of the different coalfields of New South Wales." I knew that this was wrong, for the Greta series has never been found in our Western district, where I knew such large deposits existed' (King, G., (1896) 1911, *The Mineral Wealth of New South Wales and Other Lands and Countries*, Sydney: William Brooks, Preface to the Third Edition, p. 9).

3 Mitchell Library [ML] MSS 273/3: Georgina King, unpublished autobiography, vol. 1 ['Autobiography'], pp. 153–154.

4 Cooerwull Public School Centenary 1867–1967: *Souvenir Booklet*, p. 5.

5 Department of Environment and Planning, 1987: *Survey of Historical Sites Lithgow Area*, Sydney: Department of Environment and Planning. (Report on the survey prepared for the Heritage Council of NSW by The University of Sydney, 1981.) Chapter 4: 'Special Study: The Andrew Brown Sites.'

6 Gell had studied under the Gothic revivalist, A.W.N. Pugin. In Lithgow he designed the buildings on what is still called 'the Pottery Estate'. These included new brick kilns and homes for the employees, the most flamboyant of which was his 'Gothic gem' of a home at 24 Lithgow Street. (See Lithgow Regional Library's file on GELL, EDWARD, in particular Lupp, G., 'Edward Gell, Architect: a biography, vol. ii, 1871–1899', pp. 76–77. [Lithgow Regional Library, 75/5122].)

7 Paridaens, I., 'Hartley Vale', in A.S. Luchetti, I. Paridaens and A. Cargill, 1979, *The Oil Shale Industry: Experience in the Western Coalfields of New South Wales*, Lithgow: Lithgow District Historical Society, pp. 31 and 33.

8 'Mother is better again so I am going to the Hartley Vale Kerosene Shale mine tomorrow, to return the next day, as my sister is going away for a change on Monday with her family and should Mother be ill again she will be able to come to her this week.' (Archives of the Museum of Victoria, Sir Frederick McCoy 'Correspondence' 1854–1899, K and L'. Letters from Georgina King [MOV]: G.K. to McCoy, 2 January 1896.)

9 On 20 March 1896 the National Museum registered the following items brought by G.K. from Sydney: '1 specimen of "Vertebraria australis" found in "Kerosene shale" at "Hartley Colliery, Blue Mountains" (P10304); 1 specimen of "Vertebraria australis" (Auth. & Date McCoy) of the Permian Period from "Hartley Colliery, Blue Mountains" (P182347); 1 specimen of "Rhizome or root stem" of "Rheinschia (Rienitsia?] australis" from the Permian/ Carboniferous Period found at "Hartley Vale Kerosene Shale Mines" (P182332).' In all, there are over 200 specimens collected by Georgina in the palaeobotany collection.

10 MOV: G.K. to McCoy, 6 May 1896.

11 During the Permo-Carboniferous period of 260 or so million years ago. (See White, M., 1986, *The Greening of Gondwana*, Frenchs Forest, NSW: Reed Books, pp. 99–102 and following.)

12 'Autobiography', vol. 3, p. 20.

13 MOV: G.K. to McCoy, 16 November 1896.

14 Ibid.

15 A tiny township, just over the Dividing Range in gold country. It was a busy place in 1896 with its own railway station.

16 'My people are beginning to realize there must be something in my science when so great and distinguished a man as yourself is so good and kind to me – but none of them know anything of science and it was the scientific men here who spoke against my work, who misled them' (MOV: G.K. to McCoy, 22 March 1896).

17 MOV: G.K. to McCoy, 8 July 1895.

18 ML MSS 2117/1/141–144. McCoy to G.K., 26 May 1896.

19 King, G., 1896 [1906 reprint], *The Mineral Wealth of New South Wales*, Sydney: Angus and Robertson, preface to republished edition, p. 5.

20 As Georgina told McCoy: 'I was angry with his injustice to me for so long, so the fault was not all on his side – then he would not acknowledge I had been useful to science, so as Carlyle said "We were 'are' all Islands shouting lies to each other across seas of misunderstanding".' (MOV: G.K. to McCoy, 2 January 1896.)

21 ML MSS 2117/1/141–2: McCoy to G.K., 26 May 1896.

Chapter Seventeen – De Profundis

1 Ralston, B., 1990, *Jenolan: The Golden Ages of Caving*, Winmalee, NSW: Three Sisters Publications, p. 9.

2 Cook, S., 1889, *A Journey into Australian Wonderland*, London: Eyre and Spottiswoode.

3 Ibid.

4 Garran, A. (ed.), 1888, *The Picturesque Atlas of Australasia*, (1976 facsimile edition), Sydney: Paul Hamlyn, pp. 151, 153.

5 Smith, J., 1984, *From Katoomba to Jenolan Caves: The Six Foot Track 1884–1984*, Katoomba, NSW: Second Back Row Press, p. 12.

6 Ibid. p. 12.

7 Ibid., p. 46, quoting John Le Gay Brereton (1871–1896).

8 Horne, J., 1994, *Jenolan Caves: When the tourists came*, Crows Nest, NSW: Kingsclear Books, p. 12.

9 Archives of the Museum of Victoria, Sir Frederick McCoy 'Correspondence' 1854–1899, K and L'. Letters from Georgina King [MOV]: G.K. to McCoy, 30 March 1896.

10 The limestone rocks of the Jenolan area were deposited in a shallow sea during the Siluro-Devonian Period (as C.S. Wilkinson wrote in the *Railway Guide of New South Wales* of 1886) and were 'a living mass of coral, stone lilies and molluscs' (quoted in Smith, op. cit., p. 40). We also acknowledge the notes on the 'Geology and Geomorphology of Jenolan Caves' by R.A.L. Osborne of the Department of Geology & Geophysics of the University of Sydney, and the help of the Jenolan rangers during our visit in February 2001.

11 Mitchell Library [ML] MSS 273/2/220–24: G.K. to Judge Backhouse, 21 September 1929.

12 'I broke up my home at Homebush in 1900, and after a trip to the mountains and Hobart came to live in Sydney. A scientific man asked me for one of my pamphlets, but I told him that they were stored with my books and insured but he could get one at Angus and Robertson's. He said, "We have tried to get it there but have never succeeded. Try to get to the bottom of it. There is a new partner there, Mr. Thompson. Go to him." I did so and found that my pamphlet: The Mineral Wealth of New South Wales had never been on their books.' (Mitchell Library [ML] MSS 273/3: Georgina King, unpublished autobiography, vol. 1 ['Autobiography'], pp. 51–52.)

13 MOV: G.K. to McCoy, 2 January 1896.

14 David, T.W.E., 'Sill Structure and Fossils in Eruptive Rocks in New South Wales', *Journal and Proceedings of the Royal Society of New South Wales*, xxx, pp. 285–290.

15 Ibid., pp. 287 and 285 respectively.

16 Ibid., p. 285.

17 Pittman, E.F., 'Note on the Geology of the Hill End Gold-field', *Records of the Geological Survey of New South Wales*, vol. 6, April 1899, part 2, Sydney: Department of Mines, p. 82.

18 Powerhouse Museum Archives [PMA]: MRS 202, inwards correspondence, 1881–1952, 1894 /421: G.K. to J.H. Maiden, 21 May 1894.

Chapter Eighteen – Mrs Professor David's Husband and his Wife

1 National Library of Australia [NLA] MS 8890 David Family Papers, series 2, folder 27a: Letters about Caroline David, 1980–1986: Item 4: Anne Godfrey-Smith to Noeline Kyle, n.d. The 1993 *Australian Dictionary of Biography [ADB]* entry for DAVID, CAROLINE MARTHA (1856–1951) says that she was orphaned and brought up by her grandmother. (See vol. 13, p. 575.)

2 The Edgeworths of Edgeworthstown, County Longford, in southern Ireland, boasted among their ranks the 'Abbé Edgeworth' who attended Louis XVI at the foot of the guillotine in Paris in 1793, and the novelist Miss Maria Edgeworth (1767–1849) whose books were 'too didactic'; the plots 'poor', 'the *dramatis personae* sometimes too wooden' yet 'which still deserve[d] to be read'. Patrick, D. and Geddie, W. (eds), 1923, *The Illustrated Chambers's Encyclopedia: A dictionary of universal knowledge*, London: W. & R. Chambers, vol. 4, p. 200.

3 NLA MS 8890, series 2, folder 30: biography of C. Mallett by Joyce Collins entitled 'Caroline Martha Mallett'.

4 Ibid., referring to Whitelands Admission Register for 1875.

5 Ibid., p. 6.

6 Ibid., p. 8.

7 In 1878 David gained first class honours in classics at 'Moderations' (the first public examinations) but failed to read for finals: '[He] had overrun his strength, and a rude interruption came to his University work when his doctor ordered complete rest.' ('H.J.C.' [Herbert James Carter], 'Tannatt William Edgeworth David. 1858–1934', Memorial Series no. 6, from the *Proceedings of the Linnean Society of New South Wales*, vol. lxi, parts 5–6, 1936, p. 342.)

8 He attended Professor Joseph Prestwich's course on geology and became his lifelong friend. (See Carey, S.W., 1990, *Sir Edgeworth David Memorial Oration*, Parkville: The Australasian Institute of Mining and Metallurgy, p. 2.) During the years 1880–1882 he was influenced by a geologist cousin, William Ussher, to study glaciation in his native Wales. His first scientific paper, 'Evidence of Glacial Action in the neighbourhood of Cardiff', was published in 1881 by the Cardiff Naturalists' Society.

9 *ADB*, vol. 13, pp. 575–576: entry for DAVID, CAROLINE MARTHA (1856–1951).

10 David, M.E., 1937, *Professor David: The life of Sir Edgeworth David, K.B.E., D.S.O., F.R.S., M.A., D.Sc., LL.D.*, London: Edward Arnold, p. 25.

11 In December 1882 he was at Yass collecting fossils for an exhibition in Amsterdam; in June and July 1883 to August 1884 he was surveying the New England tin fields with C.S. Wilkinson, his chief; in 1885 the two surveyors were working in the Newcastle area studying the Narabeen shales.

12 Quoted in Branagan, D.F., 2005, *T W Edgeworth David: A Life*, Canberra: National Library of Australia, p. 36.

13 Quoted in David, M.E., op.cit., p. 27.

14 'H.J.C.', op. cit., p. 343.

15 Ibid.

16 Desmond, A. and Moore, J., 1992, *Darwin*, London: Penguin Books, p. 168.

17 Ibid.

18 An Australian contribution to logistics was deemed essential and it was to Thomas Peter Anderson Stuart, the founder of the Medical School at Sydney, that the Royal Society turned for advice.

19 She spent much of her life trying different religions – and could not accept Darwinism. (See NLA MS 8890, series 2, folder 25.)

20 Edgeworth David, Mrs, 1899, *Funafuti: Or three months on a coral island: an unscientific account of a scientific expedition*, London: John Murray; Melbourne: Melville, Mullen & Slade, pp. 292–293.

21 On 7 September 1898 the drill reached 973 feet, and the core was sent to Sydney. On 11 October 1898 a depth of 1114 feet was reached and operations ceased. (No more diamonds for the drill.)

22 David did not publish his results until 1904, but personal benefits came right away. In 1899 he was awarded the Bigsby Medal of the Geological Society (London) for his work on Funafuti; fellowship of the Royal Society (London) followed in 1900.

23 See, for example, David, Mrs Edgeworth, op.cit., pp. 293, 295, 296, 300, 301 where Mrs David refers to the 'leader of the expedition', but then she refers to him as her husband in a touching story about a storm which weathered on a raft in the middle of the atoll: *I must*

run across the island in spite of the dense darkness, wind and rain, just to look at another woman; but at that moment a man stooped under the eaves of my hut, and stood there, hatless, bootless, dripping, and smiling! It was my husband. The relief was too much; and then he looked so droll, dressed only in a very thin and much worn suit of pyjamas, which stuck to him like a skin, his hair in flat rat-tails round his face, and water running in streams from nose, ears, fingers, and feet – I was bound to sit down and laugh before I could get him dry clothes and his food. (Ibid., p. 302.)

Chapter Nineteen – The Law of Averages

1 Allen, J.A., 1994, *Rose Scott: Vision and revision in feminism*, Oxford: Oxford University Press, p. 83.

2 *Report of the Women's Literary Society*: Sydney, August 1894, p. 6 (held in the National Library of Australia).

3 Allen, op. cit., p. 127.

4 Hooper, F., 1964, *The Story of the Women's Club: The First Fifty Years*, Sydney: The Women's Club, p. 7.

5 Mrs John See, one senior vice-president, would become Lady See in January 1901 when her husband became premier of NSW. Lady Lyne, wife of Sir William Lyne, premier of NSW since September 1899 and from January 1901 first federal minister for home affairs, was the other.

6 Hooper, op. cit., p. 7.

7 Allen, op. cit., p. 65.

8 Ibid.

9 Mitchell Library [ML] MSS 273/3: Georgina King, unpublished autobiography, vol. 1 ['Autobiography'], p. 9.

10 David, T.W.E., 'On the Evidence of Glacial Action in the Carboniferous and Hawkesbury Series, New South Wales', *Quarterly Journal of the Geological Society*, xliii, pp. 190–196. When the paper was read on David's behalf, members expressed their disagreement and regretted that the author was not present to defend his views.

11 'Modified Forces and our Mineral Wealth' written as 'Truth' and published in the *Sydney Morning Herald*, 6 June 1896.

12 Articles published to date in *Science of Man* were 'Woman as a Sport in Nature and Evolution of Anthropoid Man', December 1902;

'The Unconscious Intelligence of the Universe commonly called Instinct', January 1903; 'Archeological Research', April 1903; and 'The Aborigines of Australia and Tasmania', May 1903.

13 'Autobiography', pp. 55–56.

14 ML MSS 273/1/41: G.K. to Robert Etheridge, 22 May 1902: 'Dear Mr. Etheridge, On 8th of this month I wrote to Prof. David saying that I withdrew the offer I made him of permission to make what use of my paper, "The Earth's Throes with regard to Mineral & Alluvial Wealth and the Glacial Periods", as at the time I offered it to him, I had not found out that my pamphlet, "The Mineral Wealth of New South Wales", had been suppressed. Yours sincerely, etc.'

15 This was later published as part of the official record in 1903 (*Record of the Jubilee Celebrations of the University of Sydney. September 30th 1902*, Sydney: William Brooks and Co., p. 106).

16 'Autobiography', p. 89.

17 Ibid., p. 100.

18 Ibid., pp. 100–101.

19 Ibid., p. 102.

20 Ibid., p. 103.

21 Ibid., p. 103.

Chapter Twenty – 1903–1913: Miss King and the Queen of the Desert

1 'The Origin of the Jenolan, &c., Caves', 1 September 1903; 'The Earth's Throes: Intrusive Mineral Wealth and the Glacial Periods', 20 February 1904; 'Our Iron Deposits and Mineral Wealth', 21 December 1904; 'Earthquakes: The Glacial Periods', 23 January 1909; and 'Peoples and their Customs', 25 August 1913.

2 Mitchell Library [ML] MSS 273/3: Georgina King, unpublished autobiography, vol. 1 ['Autobiography'], p. 69.

3 *Australian Dictionary of Biography [ADB]*, vol. 9, p. 259: entry for HENEY, THOMAS WILLIAM (1862–1928).

4 'Dear Miss King, I return the Science paper. It is rather old for any practical purpose today. Your article is still in my hands, but the opportunity of using a strictly scientific paper, is limited,' Heney wrote, 10 October 1912 (ML MSS 273/1/137).

A year later he was even firmer: 'Dear Miss King, I do not propose to publish your paper on "Terrestrial Magnetism", and beg to return it herewith.' (ML MSS 273/1/139)

5 Hooper, F.E., 1964, *The Story of the Women's Club: The First Fifty Years*, Sydney: The Women's Club, p. 13.

6 Mulvaney, D.J., 'Australasian Anthropology and ANZAAS "Strictly Scientific and Critical"', in R. MacLeod (ed.), 1988, *The Commonwealth of Science: ANZAAS and the Scientific Enterprise in Australasia, 1888–1988*, Melbourne: Oxford University, pp. 199 and 202. (NB: The author erroneously refers throughout to the society's journal as *The Science of Man*.)

7 Ibid., p. 202.

8 *Science of Man*, vol. 9, no. 10, 1 October 1907, p. 156.

9 King, G., 'The Discovery of the "Missing Link": The Appearance of Women as a "Sport" in Nature, and The Evolution of Anthropoid Man', *Science of Man*, vol. 5, no. 11, 27 December 1902, p. 186.

10 Frost, L. (ed.), (1984) 1995, *No Place for a Nervous Lady*, St. Lucia: University of Queensland Press, pp. 44–45: 'Journal of Louisa Clifton': entry for 20 March 1841.

11 Reece, B. (ed.), 'The Letters of Rev. George King, Fremantle 1841–1848' ['Reece'], p. 6.

12 Ibid., p. 5.

13 Unpublished reminiscences supplied by the late Mr Whitney King ['Reminiscences'], pp. 13–14.

14 'Reece', p. 7.

15 Davison, G., Hirst, J., Macintyre, S., 1998, *The Oxford Companion to Australian History*, Melbourne: Oxford University Press Australia, p. 63: entry for BATES, DAISY MAY.

16 Ibid.

17 White, I. (ed.), 1985, *Daisy Bates: the Native Tribes of Western Australia*, Canberra: The National Library, p. 22.

18 *The Western Mail*, 4 June 1910.

19 ML MSS 1492: Daisy Bates, Correspondence 1910–1942: Bates to G.K., 24 February 1910.

20 1 March 1910: *Science of Man*, vol. 11, no. 11, 1 March 1910, p. 216, reports 'Interesting Correspondence' from Mrs. Daisy Bates, dated 5 February 1910.

21 White, op. cit., p. 8, quoting G. Watson's 1946 *But to What Purpose: the Autobiography of a Contemporary*, London: The Cresset Press, pp. 83–89.

22 White, op. cit., p. 8, quoting G. Watson (op. cit.), pp. 105–106.

23 ML MSS 273/3/122–123, T.W.E. David to G.K., June 1890: 'I have particularly studied your essay on the "Origin of diamonds and precious stones", and there is much in it that I would like to discuss with you.'

24 National Library of Australia (NLA) MS 8890 David Family Papers, series 1, folder 3: David to Mrs David, 28 August 1906. Both papers were published in the *Report of the British Association for the Advancement of Science*, York, 1906 (1907), as 'The Occurrence of Diamonds in the Matrix at Oakey Creek, near Inverell, New South Wales' (pp. 562–563), and 'Notes on the Permo-Carboniferous Coalfields of Australasia' (p. 576).

25 NLA MS 8890 David Family Papers, series 1, folder 3: David to Mrs David, 23 May 1906.

26 *Memoir of the Geological Survey of New South Wales*, Geology no. 4, Sydney: Department of Mines.

27 David, M.E., 1937, *Professor David: The Life of Sir Edgeworth David, K.B.E, D.S.O., F.R.S., M.A., D.Sc., LL.D.*, London: Edward Arnold, p. 42.

28 Ibid., pp. 117–118.

29 NLA MS 8890 David Family Papers, series 1, folder 3: T.W.E. David to Mrs David, 21 December 1907.

30 Ibid., 1 January 1908.

31 'As Madge later wrote to her father – perhaps hoping to instil a morsel of guilt in him ... she "had never seen anyone in such terrible grief as Mother was" the day she received the news. In fact, Cara may actually have become temporarily mentally disturbed – according to family memory, going missing for a few days in the mountains. She possibly commenced going to sanatoriums at this time, and her health seems to have suffered for a considerable period.' (Branagan, D.F., 2005, *T.W. Edgeworth David: A Life*, Canberra: National Library of Australia, p. 158.)

32 'Autobiography', pp. 54–55.

33 Woolnough, W.G., *Lone Hand*, 1 June 1909: 'Professor David: an appreciation', p. 204.

34 King, G., 1911, *The Mineral Wealth of New South Wales*, Sydney: William Brooks, p. 8.

35 See, for example, 'Professor David: an appreciation', (note 33, above), pp. 201–205, where W.G. Woolnough (a former student and beneficiary of David's patronage) fulsomely praises his mentor in a sometimes inaccurate account of his career to date. David, for instance, did not graduate 'with high honors in classics' (p. 202), and, interestingly, David – for all his supposed modesty – did not correct the error. The piece reads more like an obituary than a tribute to the living.

36 John Mathew was interested in Aboriginal ethnography throughout his life in Australia (he emigrated from Scotland as a lad of 15 in 1864). He too had difficulties with established ethnographers – in his case, Baldwin Spencer, A.W. Howitt and Lorimer Fison. (*Australian Dictionary of Biography [ADB]*, vol. 10, pp. 440–441.)

37 ML MSS 1492 Daisy Bates, Correspondence 1910–1942: Bates to G.K., 23 November 1913.

38 Quoted in Salter, E., 1971, *Daisy Bates: the Great White Queen of the Never Never*, Sydney: Angus and Robertson, p. 159.

39 Ibid., p. 169.

40 ML MSS 1492 Daisy Bates, Correspondence 1910–1942: Bates to G.K., 17 November 1913.

41 Salter, op. cit., p. 170.

Chapter Twenty-one – Alas! Poor Yorick. I knew him . . .

1 MacLeod, R. (ed.), 1988, *The Commonwealth of Science*, Melbourne: Oxford University Press, p. 8.

2 The Commonwealth of Australia provided £15,000. (Ibid., p. 57.)

3 Ibid., p. 57.

4 *Argus*, 15 August 1914.

5 See *Proceedings of the Linnean Society of New South Wales*, vol. xli, parts 5–6, 1936, p. 345.

6 Salter, E., 1971, *Daisy Bates: The Great White Queen of the Never Never*, Sydney: Angus and Robertson, p. 176.

7 See Bates, D.M. (edited by Isobel White), 1985, *The Native Tribes of Western Australia*, Canberra: National Library of Australia, p. 31, note 4.

8 Salter, op. cit., p. 176.

9 Mitchell Library [ML] MSS 1492 Daisy Bates, Correspondence 1910–1942: Bates to G.K., 11 September 1914.

10 Mulvaney, D.J., 'Blood from Stones and Bones: Aboriginal Australians and Australian Prehistory', *Search*, vol. 10, no. 6, June 1979, pp. 214–218.

11 *Medical Journal of Australia*, vol. 1, no. 13, 26 September 1914, p. 308.

12 Ussher, J., 1654, *Annales Veteris et Novi Testamenti* (two volumes). The English translation appeared in 1658.

13 Abraham Gottlob Werner (1750–1817) was appointed professor of mineralogy at the School of Mines at Freyberg, Saxony, in 1775. For a fuller explanation of his and other theories see Basalla, G., Coleman, W. and Kargon, R.H. (eds), 1970, *Victorian Science: A self-portrait from the presidential addresses of the British Association for the Advancement of Science*, New York: Doubleday and Co, pp. 372–377.

14 Bolam, J.P., 'Sir Charles Lyell, 1797–1875', in R.C. Olby (ed.), 1967, *Early Nineteenth Century European Scientists*, Oxford: Pergamon Press, p. 122.

15 John Playfair, a disciple of Hutton, was expansive about the concept of uniformitarianism: 'neither among the records of the earth nor in the planetary motions can any trace be discovered of the beginning or of the end of the present order of things; that no symptom of infancy or of old age has been allowed to appear on the face of Nature, nor any sign by which either the past or the future duration of the universe can be estimated.' (Sir A. Geikie, 1893, 'Geological Change', in H. Shapley, S. Rapport and H. Wright (eds), 1943, *A Treasury of Science*, New York: Literary Classics, p. 389.)

16 Knight, D.M. (1972), 1989, *Natural Science Books in English, 1600–1900*, London: Portman Books, p. 169.

17 The map was of great importance because the 'Wernerian method of identification, being purely mineralogical, did not provide a sufficiently fine key to distinguish strata within broad mineral types'. (Bolam, op. cit., p. 123.)

18 Gillispie, C.C., 1959, *Genesis and Geology: A study of the relations of scientific thought, natural theology, and social opinion in Great Britain, 1790–1850*, New York: Harper Torchbooks, p. 223.

19 Ibid., p. 227.
20 Knight, op. cit., p. 176.
21 Ibid., p. 175.
22 In France, on the other hand, the Académie des Sciences clung to orthodoxy.
23 Millar, R., 1972, *The Piltdown Men*, London: Victor Gollancz, p. 23.
24 Ibid., p. 29.
25 Schaafhausen quoted in ibid., p. 31.
26 Ibid., p. 32.
27 Tattersall, I., 1999, *The Last Neanderthal: The Rise, Success, and Mysterious Extinction of our Closest Human Relatives*, New York: Westview Press, p. 79.
28 Desmond, A. and Moore, J., 1992, *Darwin*, London: Penguin Books, p. 281.
29 Ibid., p. 515.
30 Millar, op. cit., p. 67.
31 Tattersall, op. cit., p. 86.
32 Since the 1950s, Java man has been included in our genus, *Homo*. The skullcap found by Dubois has been dated as 700,000 years old.
33 Tattersall, op. cit., p. 71.
34 Boule apparently overlooked the discovery in 1874, at Pontnewydd, Wales, of probable Neanderthal fragments. These would be the most northerly occurrence of the species – and one of the oldest.
35 Millar, op. cit., pp. 110, 111.
36 Spencer, F., 1990, *Piltdown: A Scientific Forgery*, London: Natural History Museum; Oxford: Oxford University Press, p. 34.
37 Weiner, J.S., (1955) 1980, *The Piltdown Forgery*, New York: Dover Publications, p. 1.
38 ML MSS 1492 Daisy Bates, Correspondence 1910–1942, Bates to G.K., 28 August 1913.
39 By 1915 belief in a 'pre-Pleistocene human ancestor [that] had combined a humanlike braincase with an apelike jaw and face carried the day, in England at least'. (Tattersall, op. cit., p. 93.)
40 3 July 1914.
41 On Friday 21 August, section president, Sir Everard im Thurn, C.B., KCMG, opened the Anthropology Section with 'A Study of Primitive Character.' As the second of two following presentations

came a 'Preliminary Communication on an Australian Cranium of probable Pleistocene Age' by Professor David and James T. Wilson, Challis Professor of Anatomy. (The two men were associated in other ventures, see *Australian Dictionary of Biography [ADB]*, vol. 12.)

42 He had published two papers on Aboriginals with Etheridge in 1889: 'Report on the Discovery of Human Remains in the Sand and Pumice beds at Long Bay', and 'On the Examination of an Aboriginal Rock Shelter and Kitchen Midden at North Harbour, Port Jackson'.

43 See ML DOC 2245/5: letter from D. Bates to G.K., August–November 1925.

44 Mulvaney, op. cit., p. 214.

45 Macintosh, N.G.W., 1969, 'The Talgai Cranium: The value of archives', *Australian Natural History*, 1969, vol. 16, no. 6, 194.

46 *Report of the Eighty-Fourth Meeting of the British Association for the Advancement of Science, Australia: 1914, July 28–August 31*, 1915, London: John Murray, p. 531.

47 '[I]t is now clear that the distinguished palaeontologists and archaeologists who took part in the excavations at Piltdown were the victims of a most elaborate and carefully prepared hoax. Let it be said, however, in exoneration of those who have assumed the Piltdown fragments to belong to a single individual, or who, having examined the original specimens, either regarded the mandible and canine as those of a fossil ape or else assumed (tacitly or explicitly) that the problem was not capable of solution on the available evidence, that the faking of the mandible and canine is so extraordinarily skilful, and the perpetration of the hoax appears to have been so entirely unscrupulous and inexplicable, as to find no parallel in the history of palaeontological discovery' (Weiner, 1953, p. 53).

48 Macintosh, op. cit., p. 195.

49 Langham, I., 'Talgai and Piltdown: the common context', *The Artefact*, 1978, http://140.232.1.5/~piltdown/map_prim_suspects/SMITH, p. 16. With the exception of Mulvaney, op. cit., none of the biographical notices for David examined by the present authors makes mention of the intense interest sparked by David's coup, which in the present context is 'at the very least' perplexing. D.F. Branagan comments that by 1914 Wilson and David 'had pretty

much forgotten it' (Branagan, D.F., 2005, *T.W. Edgeworth David: A Life*, Canberra: National Library of Australia, p. 250).

Chapter Twenty-two – Coalcliff: The Lie of the Land

1 Georgina King's 'The Appearance of Woman as a "Sport" in Nature, and the Evolution of Anthropoid Man' appeared in *Science of Man* in 1902, 1906, 1908 and 1912. It was privately printed in 1906 as a separate essay, and again in 1926 as part of G.K.'s pamphlet *Evolution*.

2 'I was led to look for chipped implements in following up my father's investigations about our aborigines. He wrote in 1868, "That they were not one unmixed race, which could be seen from certain physical peculiarities, as well as from language and habits, and that he had studied the character of the primary aborigines of the bush in their native state in Western Australia, and that a few of them were seen in South Australia, and the remnant of two or three tribes in New South Wales." . . . There is no doubt, but that the primitive aborigines of Australia belonged to the early Stone age, and came here before the shrinking of the earth's crust, during the Tertiary age of eruption, when Tasmania was a part of Australia, and there were shallow seas.' (Third edition of *The Mineral Wealth of New South Wales*, p. 12.)

3 Macintosh, N.G.W., 1969, 'The Talgai Cranium: The value of archives', *Australian Natural History*, 1969, vol. 16, no. 6, p. 194.

4 Mitchell Library [ML] MSS 273/3: Georgina King, unpublished autobiography, vol. 1 ['Autobiography'], p. 106.

5 ML MSS 273/1/141a (no origin, undated).

6 ML MSS 273/1/141b: note to replace a G.K. letter of 16 October 1914 to Hon. J.H. Cann regrettably lost by the Department of Mines.

7 'Autobiography', p. 37.

8 ML MSS 273/1/141b. In her copy she adds: 'Coal Cliff was worth a million'.

9 ML MSS 273/1/195–203, and 209–217.

10 ML MSS 273/2/7: G.K. to Sir Hugh Dixson, 6 September 1922 (copy).

11 ML MSS 273/2/27: G.K. to MacCullum, 30 June 1923.

12 In 1872 he and a partner obtained a lease for mining purposes over 80 acres of land at Blathery Creek, County of Gordon. (National Library of Australia [NLA] MS 4667 Woolnough, W.G., Papers, 1894–1958: Mineral Lease no. 3217 granted 10 May 1872 to Alexander Stuart, City of Sydney, merchant, and Horace Woolnough, City of Sydney.)

13 NLA MS 3582: Petition enclosed in letter to Alexander Stuart from John Fletcher Hargrave, 30 June 1879. As well as Stuart and Fletcher, signatories were 'Residents, Free Selectors, Miners and other persons interested in the construction of the Government Road', including Thomas Hale, 'General Manager, Coal Cliff Colliery' and miners from Coal Cliff, North Bulli and Clifton.

14 *New South Wales Parliamentary Debates for 1883*, volume x, 9 October–12 December 1883, p. 537.

15 Ibid., p. 59.

16 Ibid., p. 78.

17 *New South Wales Parliamentary Debates for 1884*, volume xii, 4 March–6 May 1884, p. 2267. (The map published in the Mines Department's *Annual Report* for 1890 reveals that, at 5569+ acres, the Coal Cliff acreage was not only considerable, it was far greater than that of any other company operating in the area – and all of it was freehold.)

18 'I repeat if the Colonial Secretary and his partner, Sir John Robertson, have this certificate for improvements they have obtained it by fraud and gross corruption. That is plain English, and it cannot be mistaken. I challenge the Colonial Secretary to take anybody over that land and to allow them to see if what I say is not true – that it is not improved to the extent of 1s. an acre – that not a ton of coal has been taken out of it.' Ibid., volume x, 9 October–12 December 1883, p. 530.

19 The actual amount mortgaged by Ralph Hargrave was 617 acres 2 roods 32 perches. (See Land Title Office, Old System Vendors Index 279, numbers 38 and 39. Lawrence Hargrave's transaction is recorded at numbers 40 and 41.)

20 ML MSS 273/1/147 (original): G.K. to Pittman, 5 Nov. 1914. (ML MSS 273/1/171 is her copy.)

21 ML MSS 273/1/145: G.K to Pittman, 5 November 1914. (ML MSS 273/1/169 is G.K.'s copy of the original.)

22 'Autobiography', pp. 36–37.

23 Woolnough, W.G., *The Lone Hand*, 1 June 1909, p. 202.

24 Davidson, Sir Walter, governor of New South Wales, address to the 1923 Pan Pacific Conference: 'our preux chevalier, Professor (and Lieutenant-Colonel) Sir Edgeworth David – the pioneer on Funafuti, and explorer of Antarctica, a sapper and miner on the battlefront, and scientific discoverer of the Maitland coal-fields' (in Lightfoot, G. (ed.), 1924, *Proceedings of the Pan-Pacific Science Congress (Australia)*, volume 1, Melbourne: H.J. Green, p. 31.)

Chapter Twenty-three – Ginger for Pluck

1 Mitchell Library [ML] MSS 273/1/147: G.K. to E.F. Pittman, 14 November 1914.

2 Ibid.

3 Ibid.

4 See Epps, W., 1922, *Anderson Stuart, M.D.: Physiologist, Teacher, Builder, Organizer, Citizen*, Sydney: Angus and Robertson, p. 2: 'Rarely indeed did he make a mistake as to the capacity or characteristics of his colleagues, or in choosing a man – or a woman – for any particular position or duty. Hence he was always well served and his schemes did not often miscarry from wrong selection of his agents.

As the chairmen of a meeting, large or small, he had the faculty of getting business done in a remarkably short time, however important the matter for discussion might be. This was due to the fact that he knew every detail of the matter brought forward, could always show a greater knowledge of the subject than most of his colleagues or opponents, and had an incisive way of expressing his opinions and a dominating influence over men. Perhaps, sometimes, this characteristic was too manifest for his own popularity, and a little more *suaviter in modo* would have left his victory more complete.'

5 Ibid., p. 51: 'We had two Goa boys, the one as cook and the other as house-servant. The cooking was excellent. After my marriage Liversidge paid me a sort of compliment by not taking anyone else, and living by himself until he left the State to reside near London.'

6 ML MSS 273/3: Georgina King, unpublished autobiography, vol. 1

['Autobiography'], pp. 73–74: 'For many years I have been making Gollywogs for the children of the Royal Alexandra Hospital for Children, and the authorities call them the new anaesthetic, as they quiet a child sooner than anything else after an operation. I make them from new stockings, and dress them in floral sateen and other bright colours, and children love them. Perhaps it is the primitive in their nature. When it was arranged that the British Association was to visit Australia, it was said that the medical section would take up anaesthetics. I met Sir Anderson Stuart soon after and I told him that I would send him two Gollywogs for the section, as they were called the new anaesthetic at the Children's Hospital. He said "do and won't they be jealous".'

7 ML MSS 273/1/147.

8 *Australian Dictionary of Biography [ADB]*, vol. 9, pp. 597–598, entry for KING, OLIVE MAY, (1885–1958).

9 Such (she stated) was the case of C.B. Fletcher, editor of the *Sydney Morning Herald*. Fletcher's book, *The Problems of the Pacific*, was praised by David at the Congress as 'the most fascinating book he has ever read'. Fletcher for his part 'knows well that Professor David is the most dishonest man in the community [yet] he has eulogised him on every occasion.' (See 'Autobiography', vol. 2, Chapter 11.)

10 ML MSS 273/4/60: G.K. to C.G. Corbett, 15 December 1924.

11 One exception was the R.M. Johnston memorial lecture in Hobart in 1923, when he touched on the Palaeolithic and Neolithic ages in Australia – those very 'Two Stone Ages' that Georgina had been proclaiming for many years.

12 'Autobiography', vol. 2, p. 18.

13 ML MSS 273/2/203: news clipping from the *Sunday Sun*, 1 August 1927, with a note added by G.K.

14 David is credited with the authorship of *The Geology of the Commonwealth of Australia* which finally appeared in 1950 and was largely the work of a former student, W.R. Browne (Edgeworth David, Sir T.W. and Browne, W.R., 1950, *The Geology of the Commonwealth of Australia*, London: Edward Arnold). All Browne had to work on were 'bundles of rough notes; of some chapters there was practically nothing', as the *ADB*'s entry for BROWNE, WILLIAM ROWAN (1884–1975) puts it (vol. 13, p. 280).

15 Wertheim, M., 'Calculating Bastards', *The Australian's Review of Books*, December 1998, p. 7.

16 Campbell, F., review of *The Man who Deciphered Linear B: The Story of Michael Ventris*, by Andrew Robinson, Thames & Hudson. (*The Weekend Australian*, 29–30 June 2002, 'Books Extra', p. 6.)

17 ML MSS 273/2: D.M. Bates to G.K., 'Native Camp, Ooldea', 16 June 1927.

18 ML DOC 2245/5: D.M. Bates to G.K., August to November 1925, section dated 10 August 1925.

19 ML DOC 2245/6: D.M. Bates to G.K., August to November 1925, section dated 21 October 1925.

Appendix

1 The original title was 'Some Remarks on the Palaeozoic Carboniferous Formations in New South Wales, and the Occurrence of our Mineral Wealth'.

2 In 1893 David and Pittman co-authored two papers: 'On the Occurrence of *Lepidodendron australe* in the Devonian Rocks of New South Wales', *Records of the Geological Survey of New South Wales*, iii, pp. 194–201, and 'Note on the Occurrence of Lepidodendron in Upper Devonian Rocks at Mount Lambie, near Rydal, N.S.W.', *Proceedings of the Linnean Society of New South Wales*, series 2, viii, pt. 1, pp. 121–125.

3 In 1894 David published a 'Note on Stratigraphical Distribution of Glossopteris in New South Wales', *Proceedings of the Linnean Society of New South Wales*, series 2, ix, pt. 2, pp. 249–257.

4 David, the 'expert' on the Greta coal measures, appears to have reacted to this paragraph, to the extent of suppressing the publication of his 1892 Hobart AAAS paper.

5 'Inaugural Address', Australasian Association for the Advancement of Science (AAAS), Adelaide, September 1893.

6 See Chapter 13 for Archibald Liversidge's interest in the same minerals.

Select Bibliography

Some sources which have been used only to a lesser extent have been mentioned in the notes, and not here. The lists are arranged as follows:

General reference
Contemporary sources: manuscript, microfiche and microfilm; newspapers and journals; books and pamphlets
Later works: books, articles and published lectures

General reference

Australian Dictionary of Biography [ADB]
Australian Encyclopaedia, 1958
The Illustrated Chambers's Encyclopedia: A dictionary of universal knowledge, 1923
The Illustrated Australian Encyclopaedia, 1923
The Oxford Companion to Australian History

Contemporary sources

Manuscript, microfiche, and microfilm

Bates, Daisy M. 'Correspondence 1910–1942', Mitchell Library (ML), State Library of New South Wales

Bates, Daisy M. 'Papers', National Library of Australia, Canberra (NLA)

'Bishop of Australia Registers', Diocesan Archives, Anglican Diocese of Sydney

'David Family Papers', National Library of Australia

King, Georgina. 'Papers' and 'Autobiography', Mitchell Library, State Library of New South Wales

King, the Reverend George. 'Letters, Fremantle, 1841–48', Society for the Progagation of the Gospel, Records in the Library of Rhodes

House, Oxford, UK (microfilmed as part of the Australian Joint Copying Project)
King, the Reverend George. 'Papers, 1836–1898, 1910', Mitchell Library, State Library of New South Wales
King, the Reverend George. 'Reminiscences', in private hands
McCoy, Sir Frederick. 'Correspondence', Museum of Victoria (MOV)
Museum of Victoria, 'Palaeobotanical collections and catalogues'
National Herbarium, Melbourne, 'Catalogues and correspondence'
Powerhouse Museum, Sydney, 'Letterbooks'
Society for the Propagation of the Gospel: Correspondence
University of Sydney Archives: Senate Correspondence

Newspapers and journals

Sydney Mail
Sydney Morning Herald
West Australian
Western Mail

Reports, journals and proceedings

Annual Reports of the New South Wales Department of Mines
Journal and Proceedings of the Royal Society of New South Wales
Memoirs of the Geological Survey of New South Wales
Proceedings of the Linnean Society of New South Wales
Records of the Geological Survey of New South Wales
Report of the First Meeting of the Australasian Association for the Advancement of Science, August and September 1888
Science of Man

Articles, books and pamphlets

Bennett, G., 1860, *Gatherings of a Naturalist in Australasia; being observations principally upon the animal and vegetable productions of New South Wales, New Zealand, and some of the Austral islands*, Milson's Point: Currawong Press (facsimile edition, 1982).
Bentham, G., 1863–1878, *Flora Australiensis: A Description of the Plants of the Australian Territory*, London: Lovell Reeve and Co, seven volumes.
Carlyle, T., (1836) 1899, *Sartor Resartus*, London: Ward Lock.

Coxen, C., 1894, 'Obituary notice of Dr. George Bennett'. *Proceedings of the Royal Society of Queensland*, 10, pp. 37–38.

David, C. [Mrs Edgeworth], 1899, *Funafuti: Or three months on a coral island: an unscientific account of à scientific expedition*, London: John Murray; Melbourne: Melville, Mullen & Slade.

David, T.W.E., 1887, 'Geology of the Vegetable Creek Tin-mining Field, New England District', *Memoirs of the Geological Survey of N.S.W.*, no. 1.

David, T.W.E., 1896, 'Sill structure and Fossils in Eruptive Rocks in New South Wales', *Journal of the Royal Society of New South Wales*, 30, pp. 285–290.

Geikie, Sir A., (1886) 1890, *Class-Book of Geology (2nd ed.)*, London: Macmillan.

King, G., 1895, *The Palaeozoic Carboniferous Formations in New South Wales and the Occurrence of our Mineral Wealth*, Sydney: Angus & Robertson.

King, G., 1896 [republished and enlarged 1906, 1911], *The Mineral Wealth of New South Wales and other lands and Countries*, Sydney: Angus and Robertson.

King, G., 1926, *Evolution: The discovery of the missing link*, Sydney: William Brookes.

Later works

Books

Allen, J.A., 1994, *Rose Scott: Vision and Revision in Feminism*, Melbourne: Oxford University Press.

Bartlett, A., 1997, *Daisy Bates: Keeper of Totems*, Melbourne: Reed Library.

Beasley, B. and Béchervaise, J., 1977, *University of Melbourne Sketchbook*, Adelaide: Rigby.

Blainey, G., 1957, *A Centenary History of the University of Melbourne*, Melbourne: Melbourne University.

Bolton, G., Vose, H. and Watson, A. (eds), 1991, *The Wollaston Journals*, vol. 1. Nedlands, WA: University of Western Australia Press.

Bolton, G., Vose, H. and Watson, A. (eds), 1992, *The Wollaston Journals*, vol. 2. Nedlands, WA: University of Western Australia Press.

Branagan, D.F., 1972, *The Geology and Landscape of New South Wales*, Milton, Qld: Jacaranda Press.

Branagan, D.F. (ed.), 1973, *Rocks – Fossils – Profs: Geological Sciences in the University of Sydney 1866–1973*, Sydney: Science Press.

Branagan, D.F., 2005, *T.W. Edgeworth David: A Life*, Canberra: National Library of Australia.

Carr, D.J. and Carr, S.G.M. (eds), 1981, *People and Plants in Australia*, Sydney: Academic Press.

Carr, D.J. and Carr, S.G.M. (eds), 1981, *Plants and Man in Australia*, Sydney: Academic Press.

Clarke, P., 1990, *Pioneer Writer: The life of Louisa Atkinson: novelist, journalist, naturalist*, Sydney: Allen and Unwin.

Clune, F. 1961. *Saga of Sydney*. Sydney: Subscriber's edition.

David, M.E., 1937, *Professor David: The life of Sir Edgeworth David, K.B.E., D.S.O., F.R.S., M.A., D.Sc., LL.D*, London: Edward Arnold.

David, T.W.E. and Browne, W.R., 1950, *The Geology of the Commonwealth of Australia*. London: Edward Arnold.

Department of Environment and Planning, 1987, *Survey of Historical Sites Lithgow Area*. Sydney: Department of Environment and Planning.

Desmond, A., 1984, *Archetypes and Ancestors: Palaeontology in Victorian London 1850–1875*, Chicago: The University of Chicago Press.

Donald, J.K., 1991, *Exploring the Golden West: Central Western New South Wales (A Heritage Field Guide)*, Kenhurst: Kangaroo Press.

Epps, W., 1922, *Anderson Stuart, M.D.: Physiologist, Teacher, Builder, Organizer, Citizen*, Sydney: Angus and Robertson.

Erikson, R., 1988, *The Bicentennial Dictionary of Western Australians pre 1829–1888*, vol. iii, Nedlands: University of Western Australia Press.

Frost, L. (ed.) (1984), 1995, *No Place for a Nervous Lady*, St Lucia: University of Queensland Press.

Gillispie, C.C., 1959, *Genesis and Geology: A study of the relations of scientific thought, natural theology, and social opinion in Great Britain, 1790–1850*, New York: Harper Torchbooks.

Himmelfarb, G. (1959), 1968, *Darwin and the Darwinian Revolution*, New York: W.W. Norton.

Home, R.W. (ed.), 1988, *Australian Science in the Making*, Melbourne: Cambridge University Press.

Hooper, F.E., 1964, *The Story of the Women's Club: The First Fifty Years*, Sydney: The Women's Club.

Horne, J., 1994, *Jenolan Caves: When the tourists came*, Crows Nest, NSW: Kingsclear Books.

Jones, S. and Stackhouse, J., 1983, *Gentlemen Scientists: Natural History in N.S.W.*, Sydney: Historic Houses Trust of New South Wales.

Knight, D.M. (1972), 1989, *Natural Science Books in English, 1600–1900*, London: Portman Books.

Lawson, E., 1995, *The Natural Art of Louisa Atkinson*, Sydney: State Library of New South Wales Press.

Luchetti, A.S., Paridaens, I. and Cargill, A., 1979, *The Oil Shale Industry: Experience in the Western Coalfields of New South Wales*, Lithgow: Lithgow District Historical Society.

MacLeod, R. (ed.), 1988, *The Commonwealth of Science: ANZAAS and the Scientific Enterprise in Australasia 1888–1988*, Melbourne: Oxford University Press.

Millar, R., 1972, *The Piltdown Men*, London: Victor Gollancz.

Moyal, A., 1976, *Scientists in Nineteenth Century Australia: A documentary history*, Stanmore: Cassell.

Moyal, A., 1986, *A Bright and Savage Land*, Ringwood, Vic: Penguin.

Olby, R.C. (ed.)., 1967, *Early Nineteenth Century European Scientists*, Oxford: Pergamon Press.

Ord, M. (ed.), 1988, *Historical Drawings of Moths and Butterflies by Helena and Harriet Scott*, Ash Island Series, vol. I. Rosewell, NSW: Craftsman House.

Ord, M. (ed.), 1988, *Historical Drawings of Native Flowers by Helena and Harriet Scott*, Ash Island Series, vol. II. Rosewell, NSW: Craftsman House.

Ralston, B. (1990), 1993, *Jenolan: The Golden Ages of Caving*, Winmalee, NSW: Three Sisters Productions.

Salter, E., 1971, *Daisy Bates. The Great White Queen of the Never Never*, Sydney: Angus and Robertson.

Scott, E., 1936, *A History of the University of Melbourne*, Melbourne: Melbourne University Press.

Shaw, G.P., 1978, *Patriarch and Patriot: William Grant Broughton 1788–1853*, Melbourne: Melbourne Univeristy Press.

Smith, J., 1984, *From Katoomba to Jenolan Caves: The Six Foot Track 1884–1984*, Katoomba, NSW: Second Back Row Press.

Spencer, F., 1990, *Piltdown: A Scientific Forgery*, London: Natural

History Museum; Oxford: Oxford University Press.

Stanbury, P. (ed.), 1975, *100 Years of Australian Scientific Explorations*, Sydney: Holt, Rinehart and Winston.

Tattersall, I., 1999, *The Last Neanderthal: The Rise, Success, and Mysterious Extinction of our Closest Human Relatives*, New York: Westview Press.

Weatherstern, P.W. (ed.), n.d., *W. Folster's Articles: The Writings of William (Bill) Folster*, Orange: Paul Weatherstern.

Weiner, J.S. (1955), 1980, *The Piltdown Forgery*, New York: Dover Publications.

White, I. (ed.), 1985, *The Native Tribes of Western Australia*, Canberra: National Library of Australia.

White, M., 1986, *The Greening of Gondwana*, Frenchs Forest, NSW: Reed Books.

Willis, M., 1949, *By Their Fruits: A life of Ferdinand von Mueller botanist and explorer*, Sydney: Angus and Robertson.

Windschuttle, E., 1988, *Taste and Science: The Macleay Women*, Glebe, NSW: Historic Houses Trust of New South Wales.

Articles and published lectures

Andrews, E.C., 1942, 'The heroic period of geological work in Australia', *Journal of the Royal Society of NSW*, LXXVI, pp. 96–128.

Branagan, D.F., 1982, 'Georgina King: geological prophet or lost?', *The University of Sydney Archives Record*, 9, no. 2, pp. 6–8.

Bygott, U., 1982, 'Georgina King—amateur geologist and anthropologist: 1845–1932', *The University of Sydney Archives Record*, 9, no. 2, pp. 11–18.

Carter, J.M.T., 'Portrait of a Lady: Caroline Martha David', *National Library of Australia News*, September 2002, pp. 11–13.

Carter, J.M.T., 'For the Sake of All Women', *National Library of Australia News*, January 2003, pp. 19–20. (Reprinted in *The Australian Geologist*, newsletter no. 128, 30 September 2003.)

Carter, J.M.T., 'Wanderings and Gatherings: Travels of a surgeon--naturalist', *National Library of Australia News*, December 2003, pp. 3–6.

Coppleson, V.M., 'The Life and Times of Dr. George Bennett', *Bulletin of the Post-graduate Committee in Medicine*, University of Sydney, vol. ii, no. 9, December 1955.

Gilbert, L.A., 1970, 'Plants, politics and personalities in nineteenth-century New South Wales', *Journal of the Royal Australian Historical Society*, 56, pp. 15–35.

Gilbert, L.A., 1982, 'Plants and Parsons in Nineteenth-Century New South Wales', *Historical Records of Australian Science*, 53, pp. 17–32.

Jervis, J., 1944, 'Rev. W. B. Clarke, M.A., F.R.S., F.G.S., F.R.G.S. "The Father of Australian Geology"', *Journal and Proceedings of the Royal Australian Historical Society*, 30, part vi, pp. 345–457.

Langham, I., 'Talgai and Piltdown: The common context', *The Artefact*, 1978, http://140.232.1.5/~piltdown/map_prim_suspects/SMITH.

Macintosh, N.G.W., 1969, 'The Talgai Cranium: The value of archives', *Australian Natural History*, vol. 16, no. 6, 194.

Mulvaney, D.J., 'Blood from Stones and Bones: Aboriginal Australians and Australian Prehistory', *Search*, vol. 10, no . 6, June 1979.

Organ, M., 'W.B. Clarke as Scientific Journalist', *Historical Records of Australian Science*, vol. 9, no. 1, 1992.

Rainbow, W.A., 'Brief History of the Australian Museum', *The Australian Museum Magazine*, vol. 1, 1922.

Reece, B. (ed.), 'The Letters of Rev. George King, Fremantle 1841–48', Archives of St John's Church, Fremantle. (Unpublished.)

Skene, J., 'The Power of Naming: Women Botanical Collectors and the Contested Spaces of 19th Century Botany', *Studies in Western Australian History*, 17, 1997.

Index

D

E

F

G

H

I

J

K

L

M

N

O